MW00388137

Fascinating People
and
Astounding Events
from
American History

Fascinating People
and
Astounding Events
from
American History

RONALD D. SMITH
WILLIAM L. RICHTER

ABC-CLIO

Santa Barbara, California
Denver, Colorado
Oxford, England

Library of Congress Cataloging-in-Publication Data

Smith, Ronald D., 1935–
    Fascinating people and astounding events from American History/ by
Ronald D. Smith and William L. Richter.
    Includes index.
    1. United States—History—Anecdotes.   I. Richter, William L.
    (William Lee), 1942– .   II. Title.
    E178.6.S634   1993   973—dc20   93-23532

ISBN 0-87436-693-3

99 98 97 96 95 94 93   10 9 8 7 6 5 4 3 2 1

ABC-CLIO, Inc.
130 Cremona Drive, P.O. Box 1911
Santa Barbara, California 93116-1911

This book is printed on acid-free paper ⊖.
Manufactured in the United States of America

to

Kael, Avery, and O'Bryan Smith

and

C. Dennis and Jean Richter Whitehead

Contents

Chapter VI: The Reconstruction, 107

Chapter VII: The American Empire, 115

Preface

This volume of anecdotes and brief essays is composed of resource materials for students and teachers of American history, as well as the general reader. The authors chose the particular topics with a specific formula in mind. First, all selections relate information that is in itself genuinely interesting quite apart from any pedagogical intent. The selections highlight a wide range of historical events and processes and invite browsing by the student or general reader for the sheer interest in and enjoyment of American history. Such a purpose, well served, justifies the study and love of history without need for functional or utilitarian rationale, rendering it to an equally shared level of appreciation with poetry, music, dance, fiction, or film.

Second, and perhaps more practical in intent, is the desire to arm history teachers with easily and quickly accessible materials that can be used to make subjects and classes more interesting and exciting, as well as introduce some of the important and significant developments in American history in a fashion that ensnares the student in a web of learning of which the anecdote is but a few enticing strands. It is the anecdotal content, however, that will attract the students' interest if properly presented, and hence all will be more interested in the full scope of a unit, say, that handles the conditions of several decades that led to an explosion called the Civil War.

The authors understand that instructional approaches, lesson plans, and techniques vary nationwide, and that is one reason for such a wide and diverse collection. Following is a list of some sample questions intended to offer help along the line of approach and use of the materials.

- Why is Christopher Columbus facing a reputation problem as we pass the 500th anniversary of his famous voyage?
- Why is there a brand of motor oil named "Quaker State?"
- Could one be prosecuted today for committing the actions for which a witch was burned in 1692?
- Did whites take scalps?
- Could the United States have had a royal family?
- Did early Americans write graffiti on walls?
- Why was it more profitable to turn corn into whiskey than ship bulk kernels to market?
- What kind of men were the Founding Fathers? Why all the derogatory stories about Thomas Jefferson?
- Were political campaigns in the Age of Jackson more interesting or fun than those today?
- How did early Americans rationalize slaveholding?
- Apart from strictly religious hymns, what tune would be familiar to nearly all Americans in 1862?
- What is the evidence that "civil" wars can be especially uncivil?
- Just how important was a simple non-mechanical invention called "barbed wire"?
- Did a "Steel Drivin' Man" named John Henry ever exist?
- Why did someone say "raise less corn and more hell" in 1890s Kansas?
- When did Americans come to have a candy bar named "Baby Ruth?"
- At the base of the Statue of Liberty are the famous words, "give us your tired, your poor, your huddled masses yearning to breathe free," but did U.S. immigration policy reflect those sentiments?

- Have women in general always used cosmetics or beauty aids?

- Why was an organization founded with the initials NAACP?

- In broad historical terms, just how "big" was World War II?

- Police departments usually have a "commissioner," but why does major league baseball need one?

- What is "Liberty Cabbage"?

- Why have American historians chosen the term "roaring" when describing the decade of the 1920s?

- Can you offer some evidence of conditions produced by World War II that caused the United States to surpass Sweden as the highest per-capita coffee consuming nation in the world?

- Understanding that the United States was not bombed or invaded, in what ways were people at home personally affected by problems produced by a world at war from 1939 to 1945?

- Compared to the rest of the world, how much better did Americans live in terms of material comfort during the post-World War era?

- Did rhythm and blues capture the white world, or did the white world degrade the purity of a good thing?

- With the Cold War in mind, might one employ the "domino" theory, so popular in explaining the presence of U.S. troops in Southeast Asia, to explain the end of Soviet domination in Eastern Europe epitomized by the fall of the Berlin Wall? Enumerate the successive falling pieces.

- In what ways might it be argued that the U.S. move toward the Strategic Defense Initiative, a program popularly known as "Star Wars," contributed to the end of the Cold War? What roles were played in this by Ronald Reagan and Mikhail Gorbachev?

Such questions, the more provocative the better, can be an effective tool to challenge and entice student interest, almost like a trivia game where much awaited answers can be embellished to carry out the full learning message intended. Beyond the select questions provided above, some models for technique and implementation of resource materials may prove useful to the teacher. We offer the following examples for integration of materials by the teacher.

- Although the general theme may be the wide variety of characters associated with our forceful separation from England and the building of a new constitutional republic on the western side of the Atlantic, it can prove effective to commence with rapid-fire data from the actions and antics of several well-known personages and leave overall purpose to summation. Thus we relate the blatantly illegal smuggling practices of John Hancock, offer brief glimpses of personages at the Constitutional Convention, examine charges levied against Thomas Jefferson by his enemies, and look at the notorious activities of Aaron Burr. But ultimately one arrives at the accomplishments that secured a stable political system for several decades to come.

- Our relations with the British were plagued by incidents and friction for years following the Revolutionary War. One might start with the anti-John Jay graffiti on a New York wall, continue with Andrew Jackson at the Battle of New Orleans and the pickling of General Pakenham's body, concluding with the Peace of Ghent and British willingness to compromise on issues then (status quo ante bellum) and later (Aroostook War, Webster-Ashburton Treaty). Then the real questions of friction become more easily understandable and the subsequent peace settlement and future problems relevant.

- Americans live in a nation in which health foods and liquor are both multi-billion dollar businesses. A story of the whys of Sylvester Graham's cracker and the thrust of the nineteenth-century temperance movement, along with the origins of the word *teetotaler*, might remind students of the old French saying, "the more things change the more they remain the same.

- The personal feelings of Americans about slavery, its continuance and especially its expansion, became acute and heated in the two decades before the Civil War. To relate this point to students with the greatest clarity and impact we need to illustrate on the one hand the fear of slave revolt, show the justification for slavery's very existence, and portray the violence that accompanied this viewpoint as exemplified by the caning of Senator Charles Sumner on the Senate floor. On the other hand we might show John Brown's forceful opposition to slavery, which resulted in raids, murder, his execution, and the song that immortalized him to an entire generation, and Harriet Beecher Stowe's novel, which pictured slavery in such an inhuman way that the problem could not be ignored. The bitter and brutal aspects of a "brothers' war," the world's worst during the nineteenth century, should prove easy to portray with attending examples.

- There are two key developments in American history that involve the importance of government in objective and neutral hands: civil service reform and pure food and drug regulations. Both can be frightfully dull if approached from a general topic format. But if tackled from a different angle, the results can leave a beneficial and sometimes indelible stamp on student learning. In the case of civil service, the teacher can describe the benefits for big city machine operatives, like Chester A. Arthur of New York, created by the spoils system—controlling appointments to government jobs. Then one might ask just how did Arthur sell out his cronies and support the Pendleton Act? How do we select government employees now and is "affirmative action" a new feature in this process? Are the results seen in better government, or did back-room politics do a better job? In the case of unadulterated food and drugs, the teacher can read directly from Upton Sinclair's *The Jungle,* recount President Teddy Roosevelt's reaction, and finally consider the reports of federal inspection agents. All of this can lead to a discussion and understanding of government in the role of independent umpire and the wide variety of products and practices that are regulated today. It can also relate nicely to the more modern issue of environmental pollution.

- World War II is often referred to by the veterans who fought it as the "Big One." Those men and women today are generally sixty-eight or older, while others who remember the domestic conditions created by it can be as young as fifty-five. Textbook and study materials can provide information on the scope, planning, problems, treaties, and other aspects of the war. But it is also useful for students to understand the sacrifices necessary to win the "Big One." Can they envision a grocery or department store with 80 percent of their favorite items missing from the shelves for four years? Does every family they know have a brother, sister, father, or cousin who has left for four years or more, many never to return? Which songs were popular that carried a special message for the lonely either at the front or at home? Such questions offer a different entrée to World War II classroom coverage.

- Election campaigns, regular events in all American lives, offer teachers a fine opportunity to relate anecdotes of previous campaigns for comparison and contrast in the light of information services during earlier eras of our history. Since we now live in an age where we are supplied information on a candidate's childhood breakfast habits, or a candidate's grades in law school twenty-five years ago, to say nothing of more intimate desires, much can be done with earlier campaigns to encourage student interest in current political developments. Thus one can show a strong presidency as evidenced by Harry Truman's forthrightness or Dwight Eisenhower's placement of troops at Little Rock, both involving crucial and weighty issues in our lives. And certainly all students will comprehend an age of electronic snooping with Watergate developments and all that followed, and find relevance to the campaign debacle of Gary Hart as well as problems faced in 1992 by Bill Clinton. All of which were preceded by the James G. Blaine gaffe of "rum, Romanism, and Rebellion," Henry Clay's "Corrupt Bargain," or, even more relevant today as the Viet Nam War generation approaches political control, Daniel Webster's hesitant support for the War of 1812, which hurt his presidential aspirations decades later.

- Nostalgia has become conspicuously popular in recent years, particularly as we view the phenomenon exhibited in films, styles, and especially music revues, remembrances, and re-creations. So, not only does the student familiar with Natalie Cole need to know how important her father Nat "King" Cole was to Americans, but they need to be able to sort out other important influences in popular music which are of significant power to grant name and terminology to trends.

- Any serious observer of history and international affairs over 50 years of age today would concede that one of the most monumental developments of world impact in their lifetime was the collapse of the Berlin Wall and the attending events that preceded, enjoined, or continue to result from that milestone. It represents both problems and challenges to the history teacher, for there must be a shift in the treatment of ideas and events from the mid-twentieth century to the present. Explaining the Cold War, the Soviet Bloc, NATO, and the Cuban Missile Crisis become all the more difficult to handle, to say nothing of the role of Nikita Khrushchev, the Berlin Airlift, or the space race. Teachers must be prepared to relate a variety of incidents and anecdotes—from Richard Nixon's "kitchen debate" to the confrontation of Ronald Reagan and Mikhail Gorbachev in Iceland—in offering a sequence of the postwar developments of the break-up of the Soviet Union and the emergence of Boris Yeltsin.

Acknowledgments

No work is solely the product of the authors, so we would like to thank the many people who have helped us — or rather, endured our constant pestering about each new fact we discovered, and our endless tales of American history trivia and research problems. John Akers is due our thanks for the rough typing, and Professor Retha Warnicke and the members of the Department of History of Arizona State University at Tempe supported the project from the beginning. In Tucson, Professors Roger Nichols, head of the Department of History at the University of Arizona, and Harwood Hinton, now retired, rendered their constant encouragement. We would like to express our appreciation to Ed Busch, Air Force WW II, China–Burma Theater for the information he provided. Others who provided much needed moral backing when the going got rough include Bruce Dinges of the Arizona Historical Society; Robert Hershoff, Charles Peters, and Andrew Makutch of the University of Arizona Library; and Gerald T. Bradley and Gerald M. Dzara, good friends and students of history. We would also like to extend a special thanks to Professor Paul G. Hubbard, our colleague and mentor, for his extraordinary friendship over the years. Finally we appreciate the encouragement of our wives, Barbara J. Smith, who gracefully lost her kitchen table to the writing effort, and Lynne C. Richter, who now admits that she would rather talk about horses than history—anytime. That to these people belongs whatever merit this volume possesses, we gratefully acknowledge.

Fascinating People
and
Astounding Events
from
American History

CHAPTER I

Exploration and the Colonial Era

Christopher Columbus—From Great Voyager to Dead White Male Scoundrel

As pointed out recently by intellectual historian and essayist Garry Wills, perhaps no other figure in the history of the Americas has taken quite the historiographical beating as Christopher Columbus. Traditional accounts, epitomized by Washington Irving's noted nineteenth-century biography, made Columbus into a sort of ideal British American, a Genoese navigator who was a secular free-thinking hero rather than the Inquisition-supporting Catholic mystic he truly was, a neutral Italian sailor rather than an overt anti-British Spanish agent. Irving's account was modernized by Samuel Eliot Morison, who portrayed Columbus as a shrewd Yankee yachtsman, sailing by innate skills and mysteriously keeping his secrets of navigation and world geography to himself—a true genius who accidentally bumped into a new world he found on successive journeys by clever dead reckoning.

This traditionalist viewpoint was aptly revealed to the American public in 1892, the 400th anniversary of Columbus's first westward journey, at the great Chicago World Columbian Exposition (a sort of World's Fair). Backed by the civic notions and great wealth of the Gilded Age, Chicago's grain, railroad, and livestock millionaires funded a celebration that Henry

Adams described as "the first expression of American thought as a unity." Building a great white city, which Garry Wills compares to Theodore Roosevelt's Great White Fleet of the coming American imperialism, the 1892 Columbian Exposition exuded the attributes that also made the Great Navigator famous—courage, determination, persistence, optimism and confidence. These were the values portrayed in Roosevelt's four-volume *magnum opus, The Winning of the West,* and Rudyard Kipling's British Empire poetry—the "victory of sturdier blood" over "lesser breeds without the law." In a phrase, the traditionalist viewpoint of Columbus was much like the theme that sent Columbus himself on his New World voyages: Gold, God, Glory.

How things have changed in a hundred years. The preparations for the 1992 celebration of the quincentenary of Columbus's landfall at Whatling's Island in the lower Bahamas have been a cacophony of confusion and uncertainty, accompanied by a search for so-called political correctness. The mayor of Chicago in the 1980s was not Carter Harrison, elected by the white, middle-class, on-the-make, aggressive, white hero-worshipping, extremely self-confident nineteenth-century American. Instead it was Harold Washington, Chicago's first African-American city leader, who had been elected by a constituency of poor blacks denigrating white heroes and criticizing such qualities as those that had launched the Exposition in that city a century earlier. Modern funding was not privately provided but drawn from the coffers of government, which largess, critics pointed out, could have been better spent on social problems of inner-city blight rather than on throwing a large lakefront party honoring a Dead White Male (DWM, or Dweem, in current jargon).

Perceptions of Columbus himself had so changed in the ensuing 100 years as to question his place in history, not only in the United States, but in country after country around the world—even in Mexico, Spain, and the Caribbean. Rather than an admired hero, Columbus is now viewed by many as a cruel exploiter—the original American slave driver who brought a holocaust of unprecedented proportions to the New World. He began a process whereby eight million Native Americans (no longer called Indians, as the Genoese sailor had incorrectly named them) died, mostly of strange, exotic diseases they could not withstand, and were replaced by millions of enslaved Africans who were alleged to be genetically acclimated and disease-proof, and whose descendants now populate much of the Caribbean basin. Native American leaders and now many others call attention to the fact that the winning of the West was the losing of the West by its original inhabitants—a theme that created much domestic controversy in the United States when it was touted in a 1990 Smithsonian Institution art exhibit, and one that recently has been revived in a 6-part cable television special on the Discovery Channel. The idea that the quincentenary could be called or even thought of as a jubilee was deemed a contradiction in terms.

In addition, critics continue, Columbus was not much of a geographer or an innovator. His notions of the spherical shape of the world were not new, as Irving had once maintained; they were commonly held by educated men of his day. The real issue was the size of the globe, and in this Columbus was patently wrong. He might have been in real trouble from his mutinous crew had he not blundered into a land mass only one-third of the actual distance to his Asian destination of Cipango or Japan. He was wrong in many intellectual points he had tried to urge on his scholarly critics, and so much a Christian mystic (no wonder Queen Isabella, no slouch at Christian mysticism herself, backed his voyages) as to assert that he had found the biblical Garden of Eden during his third expedition.

The celebration of the 400th anniversary of Columbus's initial voyage redefined the nation in its day, essayist Wills maintains, and the 500th will do no less for ours. The unity of a century ago is absent today, a factor mostly to blame on multiculturalism and on the resentment toward DWMs, who represent only the colonial, exploitive elements of American history. This really should be no surprise. Most of the world is nonwhite. The United States has had its traditional chauvinism increased in the latter part of the twentieth century by the emphasis on the superpower conflict. This has caused us to neglect the emergence of a reinvigorated Third World whose anticolonialism has made the face of the earth into a different place than the one celebrated in Chicago a century past or the one Christopher Columbus handed down to our ancestors half a millennium ago. Reinterpretation is what history is all about.

The Wampum That Bought Manhattan Island

Surely one of the most enduring popular myths in American history is that the Dutch governor of New Netherlands, Peter Minuit, bought Manhattan Island from the Canarsee Indians in 1626 for $24 in cheap trade goods and beads—the bargain of many centuries. Peter Francis, Jr., however, in his acclaimed paper "The Beads That Did Not Buy Manhattan Island," points out that this simply was not true.

Francis, cofounder of the Society of Bead Researchers and director of the Center for Bead Research, decries the fact that "a lot of nonsense has been published—and continues to be published" on the subject of beads, the wampum so prominent in modern movies and fiction. Wampum, a tubular bead of white, purple, or black color and about a quarter of an inch long, was the most important bead in American history, says Francis. Wars were fought over it and peace was made with it, but it never was a form of Native American money. Whites on the frontier may have used it as a money substitute, but "when you have a society that didn't have any currency" like the varied Native American nations, "beads didn't suddenly become currency," Francis concludes.

Wampum instead had a spiritual significance to the Native Americans. It was sacred, and was used for ornamentation, gifts for friendship and courting, and as grave decorations to ease the dead's way to heaven. It transported the energy of the beaded belt's maker to the wearer. It indicated by its patterns a tribal affinity or a clan relationship. Oddly, the bead was made predominantly by whites in Dutch colonial wampum factories, which brought regularity in shape and color to the product. Prior to the use of beads, and among tribes that had little access to beadwork, the dyed porcupine quill served the same purpose. The quill workers (usually women) would chew the quills to soften them. Inadvertently they would swallow parts of the quill, which could lead to early death from internal bleeding.

What of the purchase of Manhattan Island? It did take place. Although the absence of the actual contract (so important to the Dutch administrators that they bought the island twice, once from the sly-dealing Canarsees and another time from the actual owners, the Manhattans) does not allow us to know the actual items exchanged for the land, Francis asserts that it was just as likely that gold was used as it was that trade items such as mirrors and trinkets were used. The wampum beads traded at the negotiations served to seal the agreement as a holy token of friendship and fair dealing. They had no cash value in themselves.

Quakers in Pennsylvania, Criminals in Georgia

Many a British American colony was set up to preserve the religious freedom of its founders and/or to give voice to some experimental social idea popular with its original sponsors, the notions of which often collapsed under the pressures of the realities in the New World. Two of the more interesting colonies in this respect are Pennsylvania and Georgia.

Pennsylvania (meaning Penn's woods) was established by William Penn, whose father had helped restore King Charles II to the throne and who bridled at the idea of the King naming the colony after him (in lieu of paying the £16,000 the king owed him for services rendered). The colony was to be a place where the Society of Friends (Quakers) could settle and create a just government managed by nonviolent principles and biblical injunctions as a true Christian community. Although all religions and persons could find a home there, however, it was not governed under a democratic ideal—the Quakers were the first major group to settle there, and they kept power through a proportional system of representation that gave them a majority in the colonial legislature. This was the case until the French and Indian War, even though they were no longer the absolute majority of the population as early as 1710. Indeed by the time of the Revolution, Benjamin Franklin estimated that the population was divided in thirds between Germans (Pennsylvania Dutch), Scots-Irish, and all other groups, including descendants of the original Quakers.

Part of Penn's and the Quakers' guiding faith was just treatment of the Indians, and this fairness kept Pennsylvania totally free from the usual colonial wars that interrupted the lives of the other 12 colonies and Canada. It was not until Virginia initiated the French and Indian War by sending George Washington into the area around current-day Pittsburgh that the colony's pacifism was effectively challenged. The dissidents were the frontier-living Scots-Irish who bore the brunt of the attack in the west. The change came about when Indian raids for the first time spilled east of the mountains and threatened the German settlements. Traditionally pro-Quaker in their voting patterns, the Germans changed their stand and backed the Scots-Irish, ending Penn's Holy Experiment.

This process is usually personified by historians in the march of the so-called Paxton Boys upon the Philadelphia seat of government in 1764. Named after the town that gave them birth, the Paxton Boys represented true democracy in action, the melding of all persons, regardless of ethnic background, economic status, or religious preference, into an *ad hoc* committee that bypassed the traditional governmental processes of the idealistic Philadelphia-based legislature. They attempted to enact realistic solutions to actual problems they faced, in this case self-defense against the new Indian menace. As such, not only did they ultimately make Pennsylvania government more representative of all citizens, they started a process of legislation by committee (Committee of Correspondence, Committee of Public Safety, and so on) behind the backs of the legal government. This process was instrumental in backing the Radical position ten years later at the beginning of the American Revolution.

Georgia was established in 1732 as the last of the original 13 colonies, and like Pennsylvania it had as its motivating force a better society for its dwellers. Founder General James Edward Oglethorpe's guiding principles included creating a place free from slavery and the evils of hard liquor, a haven to all religions (including Judaism but not Catholicism), and a place that could double as a military base to halt the pernicious Spanish influence creeping up from Florida. One of its more interesting precepts was that the colony be a settlement where British debtors could start a new life.

Under the British laws of the time, those who could not pay their debts were criminals who were jailed until the amount in question was paid off—hard to do while languishing in jail unless friends or family (usually as poor as the victim) came to the rescue. Oglethorpe and his investors believed that the New World was a place such persons could start over. Although this was a stated principle behind the colony's founding, few debtors or criminals of any kind figured in the settlement of Georgia—by one account probably no more than a dozen. The majority of the inhabitants were poor without debt, either self-sustaining freeholders from England, Scotland, and Germany or people brought over at the investors' expense.

Regardless of their origins, the settlers chafed under Oglethorpe's restrictions, and by 1747, after the general's recall to England under the accusation of misuse of colony investments, both slavery and drinking were finally introduced. Until then, with settlers pulling up stakes and heading elsewhere, Georgia had been the only British colony on the continent to actually lose population.

Yes, We Did Burn Witches

It would be safe to claim that the historical site in Salem, Massachusetts, that receives the most visitors today is the Witches' House. The origin of this modern attraction goes back to the events of 1692–1693, during which several local young girls played magic with a female black slave named Tibuta, who regaled them with tales of Voodoo and even baked them a "witch cake." The fun soon got out of hand. The girls began to suffer fits, seizures, and other odd behavior, which in those days was deemed as evidence of their being bewitched. Seeking out the causes of the girls' torment, the community soon fastened on Tibuta and several old and despicable-looking (at least to the accusers) women. Hysteria spread, charges and countercharges occurred, and ultimately about two dozen people, including three males, were arrested to face charges of practicing witchcraft. By the end of the process, 19 people had been condemned and executed on Witches' Hill. Some were burned, others hanged, and one, 80-year-old Giles Corey, was stoned to death.

Modern medical historians often examine conditions of earlier eras or the symptoms of would-be patients from centuries past and offer modern analyses of relevant facts. Such a search into the life of English King Henry VIII, for instance, has resulted in the realization that he suffered from several maladies brought on by syphilis and his diet of red meat and wine. In the Salem witch hunt, current researchers have postulated that the bewitched young girls who allegedly saw the devil at work most likely suffered hallucinations after eating contaminated food. Bread (or the witch cake) had been made perhaps from flour contaminated by a parasitic fungus that resulted in ergotism, a condition to which the body responds much as it would if the girls had taken what we today know as LSD.

As for the innocent witches, they were caught in a dilemma posed by their own religious beliefs, a situation demonstrated in a popular modern play, *The Crucible*. To admit publicly to witchcraft and repent would save them from a horrible death and result in their forgiveness. To admit to such a lie, however, would condemn their souls in the eyes of God. Better to take their chances in a stacked court proceeding with its risk of an unjust, fiery death than for their souls to be denied entrance to heaven and condemned to burn in everlasting hell for the convenience of a temporal lie. So they went to their deaths, believing in eternal salvation.

Where from Those Cajuns?

Any modern traveler who heads west out of New Orleans soon

winds up in a part of Louisiana called Cajun Country. The name of a local ethnic group, the term *Cajun* is now fairly well-known. It has been popularized as a music genre by singers like Doug Kershaw and as a culinary style by the television work of Paul Proudhomme and Justin Wilson as well as by published cookbooks. Indeed, in Lafayette, Louisiana, even the local university teams are the Ragin' Cajuns. Here one finds an ancient form of French culture and language thought to be originally part of the French Empire; but the questions arise: What is Cajun? What makes these people different from the French Creole culture of New Orleans? Where did these Cajuns originate?

The history of the Cajun people began in what is today called Nova Scotia, Canada. In the seventeenth and eighteenth centuries, before the arrival of the British, Nova Scotia was known as Acadia and the French settlers were Acadians. During the many colonial wars of the period, France and Britain contested for the Bay of Fundy and the mouth of the St. Lawrence River, which marked the northern and western boundaries of the French province of Acadia. By 1714 the Acadians had the misfortune of being dealt to the British in the Treaty of Utrecht, which settled the War of Spanish Succession (Queen Anne's War, to the Americans).

For the next 40 years the Acadians resentfully lived under the rule of the British crown, refusing to take the standard loyalty oath to the British king, stubbornly maintaining their Catholic religion against British Protestantism and their French language and culture against the encroachments of English traditions. By 1755 a new conflict, the Seven Years War, engulfed Europe, and France and England prepared for the war's spread to the New World, where it would be known as the French and Indian War. Right in the middle of the impending conflict stood the Acadians, still patently disloyal to the British government and in a good position to aid any French and Indian attack. English colonial officials, deciding they had been diplomatic enough with the Acadians, now demanded that they take an oath to the English king or face expulsion. Again the Acadians refused.

The British believed they had no other choice but to round

up all French-speaking inhabitants of Acadia and disperse this disloyal element among the 13 colonies or to Louisiana, the closest French colony, where they would be no threat. Consequently in July 1755, British Governor Charles Lawrence, British General Robert Monckton, and American militia General John Winslow sent troops to round up all Acadians and prepare them for expulsion. To force those who fled into the woods to surrender, the soldiers burned all the villages and destroyed unharvested crops. In October 1755, the English embarked about 6,000 Acadians, many of whom wound up in the swamps of south central Louisiana, where the name Acadian was eventually shortened to Cajun.

Henry Wadsworth Longfellow based his epic poem *Evangeline* on the expulsion of an Acadian woman and her search through the colonies for her lover, Gabriel, from whom she had been separated during the forced exodus. Late in her life, she finally found him. Legend has it Evangeline awaited Gabriel's arrival beneath a large tree now immortalized as the Evangeline Oak in St. Martinsville, Louisiana. Here Huey Long delivered the famous speech in 1927 that gained him the Cajun vote and made him governor. For Evangeline it was too late; Gabriel had died.

Franklin, the Industrious Marvel

There is no other way to describe Benjamin Franklin's life than to term it marvelously industrious. Born in Boston, where his father was a tallow maker, Ben was the 15th of 17 children and a school drop-out by age 10. He never let his studies flag, though he was curious by nature and inquired into knowledge for its own sake, turning vegetarian as a teen so he could save his money to buy more books. He was apprenticed to an older brother as a printer, and when his brother was arrested for criticizing the colonial government, Ben took over the press and won his brother's release through a series of essays written under the pseudonym Silence Dogood.

At age 17, Ben ran away from his apprenticeship and gravitated to Philadelphia, where he set up a print shop of his own and had established the *Pennsylvania Gazette* by age 22. To emphasize that Philadelphians could stay abreast of the news only by reading his sheet, he would publish out-of-date information that he said he gleaned from the pages of his rivals.

The paper became known for its ability to treat serious subjects with a dash of humor. Franklin wrote his material under a variety of pen names such as Alice Addertongue, Anthony Afterwit, Celia Single, and Miss Polly Baker, who wrote a speech defending herself for having a fifth child born a bastard. Franklin had fathered his own son out of wedlock, and he acknowledged and supported the boy, who became a British colonial administrator and gained revenge of sorts by staying a Tory during the American Revolution while his father was among the first rank of rebels. Franklin never married, although he had a common-law wife he left at home during his numerous travels and affairs of the heart.

Franklin's most notable literary work, in a popular sense, was *Poor Richard's Almanack,* which had the usual facts and material on crops and weather—he was the first to note the appearance of a nor'easter meant a storm along the North Atlantic coast. This was spiced up with numerous homilies that have become a national treasure of human frailties through wit. He wrote the poem "For want of a nail the shoe was lost, for want of the shoe the horse was lost," etc. Other Franklin witticisms include: "Keep your eyes wide open before marriage and half-closed after" (one wonders if this were not advice for his own wife), "Fish and visitors stink after three days," "He that feels in love with himself has no rivals," "Old boys have their playthings as well as young ones; the difference is in their price," and "She that paints her face thinks of her tail." Franklin suggested that young men take older women as mistresses, because "they are more discreet . . . and so grateful." He once even suggested that perfume be included in basic food preparation so that flatulence could become a social grace. The volume became popular worldwide, especially in France where Poor Richard was known as Bonhomme Richard, a name later given to the famous ship commanded by John Paul Jones, the father of the U.S. Navy.

Wise investment allowed Franklin to retire at age 42 and

devote himself to his intellect. He was what was known in Europe as a *philosophe*, epitomizing the man of the Enlightenment, and was on a level with such intellectuals as Montesquieu, Rousseau, Diderot, and Voltaire. Indeed his life demonstrated the fundamental concepts of the Age of Reason—faith in the reality of the world as revealed in the senses, distrust of the mystical, confidence in progress through education and experience, humanitarianism, energy, ingenuity, and the ability to reason all problems to a correct solution.

He made the famous electrical experiments with a kite—they should have killed him, they were potentially so dangerous—the publication of which led to his induction into the Royal Society of London and the Royal Academy of France. He founded the first police department, fire department, public library, and department of city streets, the first secular college, which became the University of Pennsylvania, and the first worldwide antislavery society.

His inventions included bifocals, the lightning rod, a new ship anchor, a burglar alarm, swim fins, a glass harmonica (for which Mozart and Beethoven wrote music), and the Franklin stove, which is still popular today. His home was one of the first in the colonies (and elsewhere) with indoor plumbing, and he even invented a two-story privy, sort of an early think tank that allowed him to clear the air, so to speak, according to one modern admirer.

Franklin was also a key contributor to American politics. In 1757 he was sent to London to represent the colony of Pennsylvania (and eventually most of the other colonies) and petition Parliament to help end the influence of the Penn family and protect the frontier from Pontiac's Rebellion. He stayed until 1775, becoming the American expert consulted by any English governmental authority who wanted to understand conditions and feelings in the colonies. It was during this time that Franklin developed the idea of "no taxation without representation," although he had no idea that colonies simply did not want to pay taxes to London. His most famous defense of American policy was the essay "Edict of the King of Prussia," in which Franklin argued humorously, using ancient German immigration to England as an example, that no truly benevolent mother country could afford to treat her colonial children arbitrarily and tyrannically.

During the Revolution, Franklin helped Thomas Jefferson write the Declaration of Independence, and he acted as the American minister to France, where he was instrumental in securing the French alliance so crucial to the American victory. He was one of the American negotiators of the Peace of Paris (1783), a treaty that recognized the claim of the United States to the western lands that would make the nation what it is today. When he returned to Pennsylvania he was elected with only one dissenting vote to two terms as president (governor) of the state—the dissenter was Franklin himself, who commented, "I have not the firmness to resist the unanimous desire of my country. . . . They engrossed the prime of my life; they have eaten my flesh and seem resolved to pick my bones." Later he was a Pennsylvania delegate to the Constitutional Convention, and he supported the idea of a Bill of Rights, although he died before it was adopted. When asked why he had never finished his autobiography, Franklin replied that he was too busy living his life to write about it. The true marvel was that with so much influence and success he managed to have himself seen as a mere printer, always the simple rustic in the homespun brown suit who loved to pinch the girls and write romantic letters to women around the globe. These qualities of humility and earthiness gave him his fame, which he has retained to this day. In the end, witty as ever, he suggested his body be pickled in a cask of his favorite wine.

CHAPTER II

The American Revolution

Massacre by Lobsterbacks in Boston

By 1768 the political air of Boston was full of tension. British authorities chose to enforce various imperial commercial regulations and duty collections largely to counter smuggling, they alleged, but this was carried out in a fashion the colonists deemed as bordering on deliberate harassment. Animosity was heightened in September of that year when two regiments of redcoats arrived, ostensibly for frontier protection. Few troops went west, however; most remained in the coastal ports to protect and assist customs collectors in their duties, a process that had by then degenerated into blatant corruption. By 1769 local conventions of colonials had met and moved to boycott British goods as an act of defiance. In Boston fistfights broke out between citizens and soldiers on leave, and the local courts harassed British officials in the execution of their duties.

Thus the essential ingredients for a bloody confrontation were well in place by March 1770, when crowds in the square before the customs house commenced to taunt and ridicule the lone guard on night duty there. Calling the redcoat sentry bloody back, lobsterback, and coward, the people began to throw snowballs (at times loaded with rocks) and chunks of ice at the guardhouse. The sentry called for support, and a whole guard detachment of eight men and the officer of the day, Captain Thomas Preston, responded. The officer attempted to

17

disperse the crowd and keep his men's conduct in hand, but when one of the soldiers was clubbed in the head and knocked off his feet, someone (not the captain) yelled, "Fire," and the whole guard detachment opened up on the rioters. The musket volley killed three men instantly and wounded eight, two of them mortally. American protesters had their massacre, which was immortalized in a Paul Revere engraving shortly thereafter.

The trial of the redcoats, accused of murder, provided the element of historical irony. Defending the soldiers was John Adams, who later became second president of the United States and whose cousin Sam had incited much of the propaganda that led to the shootings. Before a jury—a uniquely British institution—he argued that the British had been grievously provoked by a "motley rabble of saucy boys, negroes and mulattoes, Irish teagues, and outlandish Jack tars." Adams blamed the mob's conduct upon Crispus Attucks, an African American who had led the crowd, and "to whose mad behavior, in all probability, the dreadful carnage of that night is chiefly to be ascribed." Conveniently, Attucks was one of those martyred on the night in question, and could not reply in his own defense. The court bought Adams' assertions, and found Captain Preston and all but two of the soldiers not guilty. The two who admitted to firing first were convicted of manslaughter and branded with an "M" on their right hands, in the custom of the day. The Boston Massacre is a lesson, ignored to this day, of how a well-intentioned peacetime military occupation often produces more problems than it solves.

The Fictional Headless Horseman of Sleepy Hollow

While colonials served as militiamen during the many frontier conflicts with the French and their Indian allies in the seventeenth and eighteenth centuries, there was a sharp contrast between these simple, homespun militiamen and the tough, British regulars alongside whom they fought. This contrast was particularly acute with the militia from the Bay Colony

(Massachusetts). All Americans resented the class distinctions between the British and themselves, but the Puritans especially disliked the degree of cursing, whoring, drinking, and disregard of the Sabbath they viewed among the British redcoats.

Such attitudes merely added to the friction that sprang up over varied tax measures and led to the armed break with England in 1775, later confirmed in the Declaration of Independence in 1776. By then word had arrived that King George was to pay foreign mercenaries from various German states to thwart the revolutionaries in America. Since the bulk of the 30,000 foreign volunteers came from Hesse-Kassel, Americans applied the term *Hessian* to all of them. They made up the main force that General Washington surprised Christmas morning at Trenton and much of the army Gentleman Johnny Burgoyne surrendered to General Horatio Gates at Saratoga.

Their presence was immortalized in American literature by one of our best-known early authors, Washington Irving. In his *Legend of Sleepy Hollow,* a headless horseman prowled the dark places in the countryside. He was a Hessian soldier who, legend said, relentlessly searched for the head he had lost during the Revolutionary War.

A White Man Takes Scalps: George Rogers Clark at Vincennes

No two figures of the Revolution have had more opposite historical reputations than George Rogers Clark, the heroic fighter who valiantly saved the frontier of Kentucky and won the West for the new United States, and his British opposite, Henry Hamilton, the beastly lieutenant governor of Detroit. Hamilton allegedly incited vicious Indian attacks against innocent American men, women, and children, accepting as proof of his red allies' successes hordes of scalps, an activity that earned him his nickname, the Hair Buyer. It may be, however, that neither historical estimation is entirely true; they may be the product of able Rebel propaganda.

Everyone knew that the Native Americans would take part in the American Revolution—after all, they had fought in every colonial conflict in the New World for a couple of hundred years. The real question was on whose side these savages, as Europeans gratuitously saw them, would fight. In this question, the British had a real advantage: they could point to the Royal Proclamation Line of 1763, which prohibited white settlement beyond the Appalachians, and label Americans as intruders in violation of the law. Henry Hamilton used this dichotomy to become a skillful negotiator for his king. He had an interest in the American Indian that included drawing portraits and learning their culture. He was not the usual stuffy, aloof British colonial representative, nor did he have any qualms about plying tribesmen with liquor, once to the tune of an astonishing 17,520 gallons in one year.

Hamilton recognized the Indians' own efforts at an intertribal alliance to stop the Virginians, as they characterized all frontiersmen. The British governor did his best to provide assistance to further the red men's goals and drive the Americans eastward. He truly shuddered at the prospects of Indian warfare, having experienced the sight of torture and murder as a French prisoner during the French and Indian War. He did his best to ransom American prisoners whenever possible; but in the eyes of George Rogers Clark and other Westerners, he did his duty of setting the Indians on the settlements only too well. Hamilton did accept scalps from the Native American warriors, and he rewarded them for their bloody efforts.

As much as Clark and his men may have hated the Indians, they accepted their notion of how a warrior should fight and travel. They also took scalps as tokens of victory. Clark encouraged both this and outright revenge murders, which appalled Hamilton when he heard of it. Clark also took on a forceful style of negotiation with the tribes that emphasized the real threat of force if a truce could not be arranged. In 1778 he attacked in the Old Northwest, taking Vincennes in present-day Indiana and the Mississippi River towns of Cahokia and Kaskaskia (which interrupted Hamilton's lines of influence) and making contact with the pro-American Spanish at St. Louis. Hamilton immediately made a countermove out of

Detroit and retook Vincennes, effectively cutting Clark off from the East and threatening his lines of communication.

In a daring midwinter campaign forced by Hamilton's brilliant maneuver at his rear, Clark led his men across river bottoms (flooded to their necks for days on end), surprising Hamilton inside Vincennes in February 1779. Clark had fewer men than Hamilton and no supplies to enact a siege, and he had to get a quick surrender lest Hamilton's Indian allies come to his assistance. Clark had already captured four of Hamilton's Indian supporters, whom he now brought within sight of the fort. Under Clark's direct order, his frontiersmen savagely tomahawked and scalped the unfortunate captives with the helpless and sickened Hamilton looking on from the fort walls. Then Clark told Hamilton that, if he refused to surrender immediately without terms, the whole garrison would meet the same fate. Hamilton gave up shortly thereafter, reopening the West to the Americans.

Clark considered Hamilton to be a criminal for inciting Indian tribes against the Americans, but in his own methods he revealed himself to be very much of the character that he condemned in the British governor. Clark's victory, however, allowed him to send the condemned Hair Buyer back to a Virginia prison and upset British and Indian plans for a unified front against the settlers. This made him a hero to the westward movement, the Revolutionary cause, and American history. If anything, the actual record proves Clark to be the real savage, while Hamilton was merely an instigator of savagery.

The Swamp Fox, the Gamecock, and Bloody Ban

The American Revolution was never more bloody or vicious than in the internecine clash that took place in South Carolina. Although the Carolinians had defeated a British fleet that had outgunned their little fort on Sullivan's Island in 1776, the stalemate in the North after 1778 caused the British once again to turn their attention to the South. Here were the richest colonies with the most Tories (Loyalists) and the raw materials (indigo, rice, and tobacco) most important to the mercantile system of economics that ruled the empire. The redcoats quickly subdued Savannah and Charleston, and prepared to move inland under General Charles Lord Cornwallis. Since British troops were small in number, Cornwallis gave his subordinates much leeway in forming independent Tory commands, which they conducted on separate missions. The result was a horrid civil war featuring three interesting men—two Americans and one Britisher—whose exploits became legend.

The first American was Colonel Francis Marion, a short, muscular man of Huguenot extraction. Unlike so many officers of exalted rank in the South, Marion earned his rank in the Continental Line, Washington's American regular army equivalent, and had just made a daring escape from the capitulation of Charleston. His mild-looking, polite exterior concealed the tough inner core of a man who could kill from ambush, violate flags of truce, court-martial a friend who failed in his duty, and meld both enslaved black and free white Americans into a viable fighting force. His ability to cross rivers and hide his camps in wet, swampy terrain; his sharp, darting attacks and maneuvers throughout the Carolina lowlands; his willingness to break off or avoid fighting until he could win with few losses; his threat to British supply lines into the interior; and his ability to fight with as few as 20 to as many as several hundred men (his men often came in to fight a few weeks and then went home, some to return, others not), earned him the apt title, the Swamp Fox.

The other American was Brigadier General Thomas Sumter, for whom the fort that saw the start of the American Civil War was later named. Indeed Sumter may have been even more famous than Marion at the time, but historically he lacks the Huguenot's advantage of having had a 1960s television series (starring Leslie Nielson) named after him. His home burned by pro-British raiders, Sumter, who had already fought in the Patriots' 1775 assault on Canada, helped defend Sullivan's Island and defeat the Cherokees in 1776. He then fled to North Carolina, where he organized a militia dedicated to harassing the British and their Tory allies. His fame was great and men "ready to scalp an Indian, to hug a bear, to fight the fiercest Tories or the best-equipped British dragoon" (in the words of one historian) flocked in from all over to join him. Sumter's courage and determination in facing the British earned him his sobriquet, the Gamecock, because he and his men liked cock-fighting. The general also reminded them of a plucky rooster they all knew and admired—a rooster that had never lost a fight. To this day, the image holds in South Carolina, and the University remembers Sumter and still uses a gamecock as their mascot.

The third man of interest in the southern war was none other than the feared British regular army cavalry leader, Banastre Tarleton. A red-headed egotist, Tarleton had resigned a promising career in England to purchase a lieutenant colonelcy to help suppress the American rebellion. Attaching loyal New Yorkers of Cathart's Legion to the British Sixteenth and Seventeenth Light Dragoons, Tarleton led his group (Tarleton's Legion, as it became known) to the Carolinas, where it became the main mounted force of British soldiers in the region, a force noted for its plundering raids on suspected Patriot homesteads.

Tarleton received his sanguine nickname and his unit its evil reputation when they caught up with Colonel Abraham Buford's Third Virginia Regiment, which had fled the vicinity of Charleston upon its fall. Tarleton demanded Buford's surrender, but the Virginian refused. Although outnumbered, Tarleton's green-coated legion made an immediate charge and hit the American infantry before it could form a square, defeating the companies in detail. When some of the survivors sought to yield, while others kept firing, Tarleton used this as an excuse to continue the attack, butchering all where they stood. Then the legionnaires went back through the fallen, and hacked them again to make sure all were dead. The few running survivors were so cut up that Tarleton did not even bother to take them prisoner. Thereafter he was known as Bloody Ban or Bloody Tarleton, and the refusal to allow surrender in the South became known as Tarleton's quarter. It was a tactic used by both sides, as demonstrated by the Patriots at King's Mountain, where they murdered and scalped surrendering Loyalists under Lt. Col. Patrick Ferguson, inventor of a successful breech-loading flintlock rifle.

While his legion terrorized Patriots, civilian and military alike, throughout the Carolina upcountry, it was Tarleton's inability to stop the Swamp Fox that actually gave Marion his nickname. At one swampy road junction after a seven-hour chase, a disgusted Tarleton allegedly turned to his men and said, "Come, my boys! Let us go back, and we will soon find the Gamecock; but as for this damned old Fox, the devil himself could not find him." The result was the drawn Battle of Blackstock's Plantation, where Sumter was seriously wounded and carried from the field. (He would return to the army and survive to reach age 98, the oldest of all revolutionary war generals.) Marion was never caught, and Tarleton followed Cornwallis to Yorktown, where he and his Loyalists surrendered with the rest of the British army. Although South Carolinians wanted Tarleton and his men tried for war crimes, the Loyalists escaped a final reckoning by leaving aboard British ships before formalities could be completed.

Did Women Fight in the American Revolution?

Despite all of their aid and comfort during the American Revolution, few women faced direct combat. Some did, however. Margaret Corbin followed her husband to war, and when he was shot down she "manned" his cannon, losing her arm to wounds. Mary Ludwig Hayes did the same. Visibly pregnant, chewing tobacco, and employing the same vulgar language as other troops, she carried pitchers of water to the men under fire, earning the nickname Molly Pitcher. When her husband fell in the Battle of Charleston, she took his place at the cannon, helping to drive off the attacking British fleet.

Far more interesting was Deborah Sampson. Formerly a school teacher, she prepared for her military role by cutting her hair, binding her breasts, and donning male clothing. A height of 5'8" was to her advantage in disguise, but drinking with the boys loosened her tongue and revealed her secret. Undaunted by an immediate discharge from the service, she journeyed to a neighboring village and pulled the same stunt again, under a different name. She served with the 4th Massachusetts Regiment for more than two years and was wounded in action twice. She also served as an orderly to General John Patterson and earned the nickname Blooming Boy from comrades. She was finally "exposed" while being treated by a more-careful-than-usual doctor for a bout of fever. She was discharged honorably, and left her analysis of the episode in an 1802 speech, words that sound hauntingly modern: "I burst the tyranny bonds which held my sex in awe and clandestinely, or by stealth, grasped the opportunity which custom and the world seemed to deny as a natural privilege."

Was General Anthony Wayne Mad?

One of George Washington's better subordinate officers during the Revolution was Anthony Wayne of Pennsylvania. Although his troops were surprised once at Paoli when the British General, Charles "No Flint" Grey, made a silent bayonet attack into his sleeping garrison, Wayne learned quickly to copy the successes of others. Two years later he repaid the British at Stony Point, New York, with his own bayonet attack, the success of which was guaranteed when he ordered every dog within hearing distance killed to insure complete silence the night of the assault.

Wayne had seen solid service—with Benedict Arnold at Quebec in 1775–1776, the American siege encampment of which he called Golgotha because of its horrors; with Gates at Saratoga in 1777, where Wayne was instrumental in defeating Cornwallis; with Washington from Brandywine to Yorktown, where his division was always in the forefront of the attack or defense; with Nathaniel Greene in the South, where he cleared Georgia of British presence in 1782–83; and with the post-war army, leading the final bayonet charge at the battle against the Northwestern Indian Confederation at Fallen Timbers in 1794, a battle that won President Washington the Treaty of Greenville.

This, combined with his daring, gave him a reputation for recklessness on the battlefield that was later symbolized in his sobriquet, Mad Anthony, a name popularized in his nine-teenth-century biography written by Washington Irving.

Wayne's nickname did not originate from his battle exploits, however, but instead from a minor incident in 1781 that concerned a Pennsylvania neighbor of his known as Jeremy the Rover—a frequent deserter. Jeremy asked Wayne to intercede with the command system and obtain his release from jail. Wayne, never sympathetic with deserters or mutineers, refused. Jeremy, shocked at this streak of unneighborliness from his close boyhood friend, muttered in disbelief to his jailers: "Anthony is mad. He must be mad or he would help me. Mad Anthony Wayne, that's what he is. Mad Anthony Wayne." Given Wayne's courage in the face of the enemy, the appellation stuck, and he has been Mad Anthony Wayne ever since.

CHAPTER III

A New Republic

The Newburgh Incident—George Washington Achieves Immortality

No single incident is more important and yet more forgotten in the foundation of the American Republic than George Washington's Newburgh Address. It was preceded by events very common to a democratic social upheaval secured by war, but in the case of the United States the result was so different and so profound as to catapult Washington into the forefront of American heroes and truly make him the Father of His Country, or in the oft-quoted words of Richard Henry Lee, "first in war, first in peace, first in the hearts of his countrymen." Hence a look at the events preceding the Newburgh Address, named after the Hudson River town in which Washington maintained his headquarters in 1782, is appropriate here.

By the end of 1782, the British had been defeated in their attempt to crush the American Revolution. Under such circumstances, the Continental army was no longer needed. Worse, Congress was broke and considering disbanding the army without paying it fully for its past services. Several army officers spoke of the need to make past salaries part of the national debt for immediate payment. Should Congress fail to act, these men proposed that the army march on Philadelphia and take over the government.

Attending the meeting, Washington was deeply moved by the sincerity of the officers' position, but he could not support their wish to use force to achieve their goals. To accept the easy road to military dictatorship, Washington concluded, would deny the nation and the world the opportunity to see "the last stage of perfection to which human nature is capable of attaining." Washington then read a letter from a friend in Congress to the crowd, promising to pay the army as soon as possible and explaining the problems the new nation faced financially. He stumbled in the reading, squinted his eyes and adjusted the paper to no avail. He could not see it well enough to read. He reached into his coat and pulled out a pair of spectacles. Few knew that he used eyeglasses. Noticing the murmurs of amazement, Washington reassured them, "Gentlemen, you will permit me to put on my spectacles, for I have not only grown gray but almost blind in the service of my country." He finished the letter and left. The cabal had failed.

As Washington knew, there are two roads that lead out of any great social upheaval. One is easy to travel, offers quick solutions, and emphasizes personal power. The other is lengthy, full of difficulties, and emphasizes popular participation in government. The former is well-traveled; in the words of Washington biographer Thomas Flexner, "From the road to absolutism, there rises the dust of marching crowds: newly crowned kings and emperors, perpetual presidents, duces, führers, generalissimos, protectors, party secretaries, dictators of the proletariat: they advance to band music over the prostrate body of political freedom with their bodyguards, their legions, their storm troopers, their people's militias." The other road, Flexner finished, had but a solitary figure, George Washington, who like the Roman Cincinnatus forsook the power of the sword for the greater power of civilian life and popular rule.

Washington later reinforced his stand by establishing the two-term tradition as president, voluntarily stepping down in 1797 when he easily could have been reelected. (This is also why Franklin D. Roosevelt was wrong to have run for his third and fourth terms, a mistake rectified by the Twenty-second Amendment to the Constitution). It is this image, personified forever in Washington's Newburgh Address, that makes the United States the milestone it remains today, a unique experiment in popular government. It is all that essentially distinguishes us from the rest of the Americas, and it is the essence of why we have a flood of new immigrants every year.

Demigods of 1787

Demigods was Thomas Jefferson's term for the collection of 50 or more individuals who at one time or another debated and produced the Constitution of the United States. Though not a religious document, throughout our history it has been awarded a greater reverence and aura of sanctity than any other modest-sized composition. Some facts about the so-called demigods and the resulting document are listed below. (Jefferson was our representative to France at the time and was not present to contribute to the final instrument.)

1. The most common profession among these men, though not necessarily the basic means for earning a living, was law, whether they be lawyer, judge, or legislator.

2. Half or more were also gentlemen farmers, a role that would include professional surveyor George Washington. Owing to the character of educational curriculum of the time, many could double as preachers as well, a talent only Jimmy Carter, among today's leaders, can boast.

3. One was a physician, another a professor of law, still another a professor of mathematics. Many had served as officers in the Continental army and in the Confederation legislatures. Several were men from finance and commerce.

4. The spread in chronological age ranged from 27-year-old Jonathan Drayton of New Jersey to 81-year-old Benjamin Franklin of Pennsylvania.

5. It has been most common for American historians to judge Alexander Hamilton as the most brilliant man present, but "Little Jimmy" Madison as the wisest. All seem to agree on Franklin as the "American Socrates."

6. The Constitution itself is but a 7,000-word document that has

served as an invaluable tool for more than 200 years. Excluding
the Bill of Rights adopted with it, the original document has
been amended 16 times—once every 12 $^1/_2$ years. That speaks to
the adaptability of the Constitution to the explosive political,
social, and economic changes that have influenced the problems of government in the nineteenth and twentieth centuries.

7. The general practice in European countries has been to have an
   oath pledged to the ruler in power. Conspicuously different,
   Americans have always taken an oath to a collection of written
   pages and a flag. Breaking the oath is no simple act, as Confederates found out after the Civil War, when the Fourteenth
   Amendment disfranchised all persons who had taken an oath
   to support the United States Constitution and then repledged
   their support to the Confederate Constitution until such time
   as Congress removed the disability of disfranchisement. One
   might conclude that when the eminent British philosopher
   Edmund Burke declared it dangerous to place all civil security
   in a paper document that could be torn to shreds tomorrow, he
   was wrong in at least this one historical instance.

8. As pointed out by historian Forest McDonald in his *Formation
   of the American Republic*, the Founding Fathers were good politicians. Utilizing a convention called merely to amend the
   Articles of Confederation to write a new document of government, they concealed its real centralizing purpose through a
   masterful series of propaganda essays called the *Federalist
   Papers*. Written by James Madison, John Jay, and Alexander
   Hamilton, these works emphasized the supposed dual nature
   of power shared by states and national governments. (The
   formation of the first political parties and Hamilton's centralizing economic and political moves as secretary of the treasury
   during the Washington administration promptly proved this
   wrong, much to Madison's dismay). They undercut their opposition by declaring the Constitution in force in all 13 states
   when any nine of them approved it. They also assured that all
   states would approve it through a ratification process that
   came to include self-interest (Delaware and New Jersey needed
   the interstate commerce clause to protect themselves against
   tariff discrimination from New York and Pennsylvania, while
   Georgia needed the national defense clause to help them in
   their Indian wars), close votes in state legislatures calling the
   necessary ratification conventions (South Carolina and Mary-

land), often unfulfilled political deals and dirty tricks (Massachusetts, Connecticut, and Pennsylvania), outright monetary
bribery (New Hampshire), the promise of a Bill of Rights (New
York and Virginia), the actual passage of the Bill of Rights
(North Carolina), and threatened economic and military coer-
cion (Rhode Island).

9. It was a close fight, won by the supporters of the Constitution.
(They called themselves Federalists, implying a division of
governmental powers between the states and national levels.)
Their opponents were not merely Antifederalists, as supporters of the Constitution successfully named them (implying a
stance against the Federalists' more "reasonable," cosmopoli-
tan position). The Antifederalists included some of the most
able men of the day (Patrick Henry, George Mason) who feared
a strong central government as an extension of the tyrannies
imposed by England, as well as men who were powerful in
state government (John Hancock) and simply did not wish to
share that power with the upstart Federalists. All sides agreed
that the American Revolution was good, but they disagreed on
how much power could be entrusted in a national government,
or any government, with such a potentially strong executive
branch as the Constitution created. The Antifederalists feared
an imperial presidency (a recreation of King George III) and
unresponsive, corrupt, incumbent-controlled congresses (the
embodiment of the pre-Revolution British Parliament) that
have figured in so much of modern Washington, D.C.

In this light the Constitution represents the Federalists'
successful takeover of American government from the
Antifederalists by installing a new level of government above
them. Then the Federalists, like all winners, wrote the history
books to justify their deeds by decrying the Articles of Confederation as unworkable and their opponents as unpatriotic
divisionists, radicals, and immoral slaveholders—never mind
the illegal usurpation of power by the new government that
compromised the original states rights ideals of the Revolution. It took until the twentieth century before this concept was
seriously challenged by historians Charles Beard (*An Economic
Interpretation of the Constitution*), Merill Jensen (*The New Nation*), and Jackson Turner Main (*The Antifederalists* and *Political
Parties Before the Constitution*), indicating just how well the

Founding Fathers did their job. However, they would not recognize the modern 26-time amended version of their original intent. As Gordon Wood (*The Creation of the American Republic*) concluded, the Founders created "a political theory that was diffusive and open-ended, . . . so diverse and scattered in authorship [and] without a precise beginning or an ending, . . . so much a simple response to the pressures of democratic politics" that it remains utterly unique in the history of Western thought.

What To Call George?

In an age of monarchy, with a republican form of government quite unknown except to students of Classical history, Americans in 1787 found themselves facing the need to choose the proper title to be worn by the chief executive under the new constitution. Washington was duly elected, but what should he be called short of a monarchical title? Trappings of kings were in obvious bad taste after a generation of struggle—led by the likes of Thomas Paine, John Hancock, and Patrick Henry—against tyranny. Suggestions for the American president included His Excellency, Elective Majesty, His Serene Highness, Elective Highness, and the effusive His Highness, the President of the United States and Protector of the Same. Ultimately Congress adopted the plain title, Mr. President, and regardless of suggestions regarding the second man of the executive, John Adams was sworn in similarly as Mr. Vice President.

Facts about President Washington

In his diary Washington complained often of dental problems. Finally after several attempts, a French dentist and immigrant to New York produced for him a set of false teeth from rhinoceros ivory. Spiral springs held them together and port wine was used to give them a more natural color. They always caused discomfort, hence Washington's usual stern appearance in pictures. For the pleasant countenance we all see in the famous Gilbert Stuart portrayal, the artist had him remove his false teeth and substitute soft padding.

While president, Washington marched briefly at the head of a three-state militia force to crush violent resistance among Pennsylvania farmers to a new seven cents per gallon excise tax on whiskey. Because of the large-scale action required to force collection (the 12,000-man army was bigger than Washington's Continental army during the Revolution), Richard Armor in *It All Started with Columbus* referred to it as the whiskey "exercise tax." Washington soon left the field command to Secretary of the Treasury Hamilton, who was disappointed that the whiskey rebels dispersed and their leaders fled to Louisiana before any battles could be fought. Then, to Hamilton's further chagrin—he had expected a mass hanging—Washington sagely pardoned all of the suspects Hamilton had arrested and dragged back to Philadelphia in chains.

A tight-fisted Scotsman named David Burns owned a farm where the White House now stands in the District of Columbia, and President Washington, who took a personal interest in the development of the nation's new capitol, asked him to donate ground for the presidential residence, saying, "Had not the Federal City been laid here, you would have died a poor tobacco planter." The crusty Burns replied, "Yes, for if it hadn't of been for the widow Custis and her niggers, you would still have been a surveyor and a very poor one at that."

Early American Graffiti

Friction between the new American republic and Great Britain continued long after the peace that ended the Revolution in 1783. Issues of contention included rights over Atlantic fisheries, British aid to frontier Indian groups, trade restrictions, and of course impressment of American merchant seamen. In an attempt to resolve some or most of these problems, the George Washington administration sent John Jay, one of the authors of the *Federalist Papers*, to London in 1795, where he negotiated a treaty. It was less than a perfect treaty as far as many of the critics of Jay and the Federalist-dominated government were concerned.

The age-old spirit and practice of writing graffiti—which was seen at Pompeii and the Egyptian pyramids of the ancient world—remained alive and well in New York after publication of the Jay Treaty. Someone wrote the following on a city wall: "Damn John Jay, damn everyone who won't damn John Jay, and damn everyone who will not put a light in their window and sit up all night damning John Jay." Pretty heady stuff for someone who had to work with a brush instead of a can of spray paint.

Aaron Burr: Murderer? Traitor? Adulterer? Con Man?

Whether one consults the solid biographical study of Aaron Burr by Milton Lomask or the fictionalized popular treatment by novelist Gore Vidal, only a few facts about this fascinating historical figure should be enough to intrigue students. Consider the following:

1. He applied for admission at Princeton at age 11 and was refused. He then read on his own, pestered the faculty, was admitted, and ultimately delivered the commencement address at graduation.

2. He served in the revolutionary army, was elected to the New York legislature, became a notoriously successful lawyer, organized the northern half of the Jeffersonian Democratic-Republican party, and went on to become Thomas Jefferson's vice president after the 1800 election. First Burr tried to claim the presidency, as both he and Jefferson had the same total of electors. He turned to the Federalists in Congress for help, many of whom relished the idea of denying Jefferson the chief executive position, but Alexander Hamilton recognized Jefferson's superior decency (despite their political differences) and intervened to stop this ploy. This fracas resulted in the Twelfth Amendment to the U.S. Constitution, causing electors to vote separately for president and vice president rather than giving the latter post as a consolation prize to the one with the second highest number of votes for president. It also ruined Jefferson's faith in Burr forever.

3. His honor slurred by the former Secretary of the Treasury Alexander Hamilton's reference to possible and despicable relations with his own daughter, Burr challenged the prominent figure to a duel in 1804; Hamilton shot first and missed for what are disputed reasons, while Burr coolly cut him down. Usually Hamilton is seen as a noble figure, firing in the air to avoid a murder. Recently his dueling pistols, which both men used, were dismantled and examined. Surprised researchers found a hidden hair trigger on both weapons that could be engaged by pushing the normal trigger forward before firing. This allowed the owner of the weapons (Hamilton) to reduce the trigger pull from several pounds to mere ounces, allowing an extremely more accurate shot from his weapon than that of his unaware opponent. Historians now theorize that Hamilton engaged the hair trigger and, in his nervousness as he readied his pistol, fired prematurely by accident, thus losing his first shot in the trees above his head. Burr, unaware of the hair trigger (or did he find it, too?), then killed him with a single shot.

4. After fleeing possible prosecution and extradition, Burr reportedly sought to detach the trans-Appalachian West from the Union and form his own personal mini-empire, for which Jefferson had him prosecuted in 1807 for treason. While Chief Justice John Marshall ruled that the government (Jefferson and Congress) failed to supply adequate evidence to make a case of overt treason (evidence that was readily available), Burr, with further charges pending, skipped bail for refuge in France.

5. Burr returned to New York in 1812, practiced law to an old age characterized by vitality, and at age 80 was divorced on grounds of adultery.

All of this lends much credence to the observation of an old New Yorker that Aaron Burr's sole claim to virtue lay in the fact that he himself never claimed it.

The Almighty Dollar

Most students have heard the phrase, the almighty dollar, either in approbation or derision. They should also understand that most cultures, especially those considered civilized by historians, could not have achieved a level of prominence without the economic foundation of a stable means of exchange. This we call currency, be it coin or paper, and it is true whether we discuss Persians, Lydians, Egyptians, Greeks, or Romans. Exchange is crucial to the development of banking (the Medici family in Florence, the Rothschilds in northern Europe) and trade. The influx of precious metals from the New World transformed the history of Europe, while the mismanagement of funds contributed crucially to the French Revolution.

In 1785 the Congress of the Articles of Confederation decided that the monetary unit of the United States was to be the dollar, subdivided on the decimal system: half ($^5/_{10}$), double-dime ($^2/_{10}$), disme ($^1/_{10}$)—pronounced and later spelled "dime"—cent ($^1/_{100}$), and half-cent ($^1/_{200}$). The term *dollar* was derived from a corruption of the German *thaler*, which referred to silver coins minted in the Joachimsthal mining area of Bohemia (1517), the biggest silver strike in Europe before the discovery of the New World. Known as a *Reichsthaler* throughout Europe, the name was transmitted to the English by the Dutch as *rix-daaler*. By the end of the 1600s, the English had shortened the word to our *dollar*.

The new republic established under the Constitution organized its finances on the suggestions put forth by Secretary of the Treasury Alexander Hamilton in his 1790 Report on Public Credit. Embodied in the Mint Act of 1792, the monetary unit of the United States was to be the decimal-divided dollar, as before, but with a reduced silver content based on the traditional Spanish coins commonly known as pieces of eight. The Spanish coins had serrated edges that permitted them to be cut into smaller parts, from which the terms *bit* ($12^1/_2$ cents), *two bits, four bits,* and *six bits* came, and which caused the government to replace the double-dime. However, the silver amount of the American coin was hard to mint accurately and it was changed by the minter (contrary to the law), causing American dollars to be richer in silver than the Spanish piece of eight, with which it was supposedly equal. The result was that in 1803 Congress suspended the minting of the dollar, because most of the coins had flown to Spain. There they were melted down and recast as pieces of eight, with the Spanish government pocketing the difference in value.

For 34 years, the United States circulated no dollar of its own, although the term continued to be used in figuring monetary amounts and referring to the piece of eight, which was still legal tender. In 1837 Congress agreed to the minter's quality of the dollar and began reminting the coin. In 1857 Congress finally wised-up and declared pieces of eight were no longer legal tender. Americans who held such coins could exchange them for pennies (of copper/nickel) only, which quickly drove the Spanish dollars from circulation, with the U.S. government pocketing the profits of the turned-in Spanish silver.

The dollar symbol, $, so universally recognized today, has been in use for some time. There are several notions as to its invention. One story has the parallel lines // representing the Pillars of Hercules at Gibraltar with a superimposed flowing banner like the letter S and a Latin inscription denoting that the Spanish Empire extended beyond the pillars, farther even than that of Ancient Rome. Another has the symbol being a U with a superimposed S, the country's initials. Still another has the symbol coming from the Spanish sign that denoted silver minted at Potosí, Bolivia, the greatest silver strike in all the world, a superimposed PTS. Nonetheless, it was very common in the nineteenth century to write the amount $4.65 as 4 dos. 65 cts. No matter how one looks at it, $ is still the almighty dollar in any language.

John Q. Adams: The Naked President

To a degree similar to Theodore Roosevelt, John Quincy Adams believed in vigorous exercise for bodily health. To promote his physical fitness he often took an early morning swim quite naked in the then relatively unpolluted Potomac River, despite even the foulest weather. One day, well before the time when bodyguards were used to protect a president, he was alone in the water, clothes on the river bank, when a tramp happened along. Not knowing to whom the garments belonged, and probably not even caring, the tramp snatched the president's clothes and fled. Adams, busy with his exercise, took no notice until he emerged from the water and discovered his predicament.

Realizing immediately how it would appear should he attempt to reach the White House without his clothes, he returned to the water to hide his embarrassment, among other things. Fortunately a small boy came along shortly bearing a fishing pole. "Say, boy," Adams called out, "run to the White House and tell Mrs. Adams to send a suit of clothes to the President— I'll wait for you."

John Randolph of Roanoke: One of a Kind

In the early National Era no one epitomized firm adherence to the cause of states' rights and a weak central government based on strict construction of the Constitution than John Randolph of Roanoke, whose name was such as to distinguish him from the many John Randolphs Virginia produced in those times. A Jeffersonian who guided the Louisiana Purchase appropriation (his one break with strict construction) and much of Jefferson's first-term legislation through the House of Representatives, Randolph was dismayed to find that Jefferson and his advisors became more and more like the hated Alexander Hamilton in their reliance on the general welfare clause of the Constitution to justify actions that were plainly not intended by the framers' hallowed written document. When Jefferson asked Congress to bail out the investors in the Yazoo Land frauds, Randolph and others of his kind broke with the administration and formed a group to preserve the written Constitution. This group was called the Tertium Quids after the Latin for a substance that is apart from yet shares the qualities of two other objects (in this case, Federalists and Democratic Republicans). Randolph's opposition to the War of 1812 cost him his seat in the House, although he was returned in 1815 and later served briefly in the Senate.

As a national figure it was Randolph's speaking style that made him unique. Tall and thin (so much so that one wag characterized him as "the advance agent for a famine"), he suffered from a hormonal deficiency that caused him to speak in a distinctive soprano and be unable to have or desire sexual relations with women. (Some say this was result of scarlet fever, while others blame syphilis or claim that Randolph's testicles never dropped after birth.) His face was boyish at a distance, but closer inspection revealed that it was covered with fine wrinkles that gave him the appearance of an un-wrapped mummy. On a day in which he was to address Congress, Randolph would appear in the chambers late, fling open the huge doors with a bang, and let loose a pack of baying hounds down the aisles. Of course, the dogs would do as canines do on every leg that was not pulled up out of the way. Then Randolph would enter, throwing his cape over his shoulder with a flourish and announce his presence with a sardonic grin.

As he spoke he wandered up and down the aisles, a small slave boy following with a silver tray and a large stein of porter, from which Randolph lubricated his tonsils regularly. He owned 400 slaves, and this fact plus the way he made his points by cracking the side of his riding boot with a whip angered many a Northern representative who saw in him the epitome of what was wrong with the pre-Civil War South. His invective was brilliant, at times close to insane, but always vicious and rude. He said of one opponent: "He is a man of splendid abilities but utterly corrupt. He shines and stinks like a rotten mackerel in the moonlight." When he spoke in the Senate he would begin by alluding to the presiding officer, John C. Calhoun, as "Sir, Mr. President of the Senate and would-be President of the United States."

Randolph especially hated John Quincy Adams for his po-litical philosophy of loose construction and the so-called cor-rupt bargain that made him president. He also disliked Henry Clay for his support of Adams and his often-bragged-about virility. Referring to characters in the popular Henry Fielding novel *Tom Jones*, Randolph called them Bliffel and Black George, making Adams a secretly sinning, lecherous, stuffy Puritan and Clay a lewd, filthy blackguard. Insulted, Clay challenged him to a pistol duel, but both men missed. However, neither Clay nor Adams (whose family Randolph characterized as the American House of Stuart, the very embodiment of despotism) survived Randolph's destruction of their reputations. Some-time later, when an angry Clay met Randolph on the sidewalk, he refused to let the Virginian pass, vowing, "I never make way for a scoundrel." Randolph gracefully stepped into the muddy street and doffed his hat, replying, "But I always do."

Throughout his public service, Randolph held to the notions of Old Republicanism, those ideas that Jefferson believed when he originally challenged Hamilton's theory of expanding government—that political power tends to grow at the expense of human liberty, that human liberty in the United States depended upon resistance to the supreme central power of national sovereignty, and that this resistance could be best served by supporting the individual states in exercising their reserved rights under the Ninth and Tenth Amendments. "God did not mold Randolph to be in any majority," writes one historian, "He was only at ease in opposition . . . [and] confined himself to negative voting and destructive criticism." It but remained for John C. Calhoun to take these ideas and fashion a political defense of slavery and secession, a stance that firebrands would employ to break up the nation in 1861.

Jefferson's One-Man Stud Farm: Did the President Father Mulatto Children?

William Cullen Bryant, noted American poet and Federalist newspaperman of the early nineteenth century, even wrote about it:

> Go wretch, resign the presidential chair,
> . . . Go, scan, Philosophist, thy Sally's charms,
> And sink supinely in her sable arms;
> But quit to abler hands the helm of state.

The Philosophist was none other than the recently installed Democratic-Republican President Thomas Jefferson, author of the Declaration of Independence, and Sally was his female house slave, the beautiful, light-skinned quadroon (one-fourth black), Sally Hemmings. According to the stories, the widowed Jefferson did not need to find a new wife, he had one at home whom he made his concubine and by whom he fathered five children.

Where did Bryant get his information? Was there any truth in it? In *Thomas Jefferson: An Intimate Biography,* historian Fawn Brodie said yes, and built a large section of her biography of the Sage of Monticello on the alleged love between Jefferson and his servant. Since it does appeal to a prurient interest in all of us, let's take a look at it anew.

The story begins with an English publicist named James Callender, a man who excoriated King George III as one of the "ruffian race of British kings" in his tract, *The Political Progress of Britain.* In 1776 this was not a wise thing to say in England, and Callender soon fled to the sunnier clime of America just ahead of his arrest warrant. Eventually he joined the Jeffersonians against the Federalists and began writing propaganda in the political war that emerged from George Washington's first administration.

Callender did some good work for Jefferson. In his *History of the United States for 1796,* he revealed Alexander Hamilton's shenanigans in the Treasury and his illegal speculating in government securities and, outside of the administration, with Mrs. James Reynolds. Jefferson bought it all as the truth, which some it of undoubtedly was. Callender had a way of not letting fact get in the way of a good story, however, which should have caused Jefferson more concern than it did. After all, Callender wrote *The Prospect before Us,* the book that helped elect Thomas Jefferson in 1800 and got the publicist arrested under the Alien and Sedition acts. Jefferson had a right to be a little blind, but it cost the Virginian dearly.

He made his first mistake pardoning Callender and getting him out of jail, but the marshal refused to remit Callender's fine. Jefferson raised the money but Callender wanted more— he wanted a political appointment. Jefferson refused. Callender threatened to do him in, much in the same way as he had done to Hamilton. Still, Jefferson was adamant. Callender then got a job with a Federalist newspaper, the *Richmond Recorder,* and made it into a widely read Federalist scandal sheet. Unfortunately Callender never investigated anything; he merely published innuendoes, the sexier the better. He found a gold mine in Jefferson. Under the principle that the people must know, Callender asserted that Jefferson had fathered children not only by Sally Hemmings, but by a veritable "Congo Harem," the progeny of which he sold on the slave market to hush it all up.

One child by Sally Hemmings was Yellow Tom, a spitting image of the president. No one ever found Yellow Tom (Fawn Brodie said he was well-hidden), but there was an old slave named Black Tom Jefferson, whose death in 1800 temporarily fooled the Federalists into thinking that President Tom had died before his election. Defenders pointed out that the fathering of any black children at Monticello was done by Jefferson's two licentious nephews, Peter and Samuel Carr. While Jefferson was at Monticello nine months before the birth of her mulatto children, no one has looked up the whereabouts of the Carr boys at the same time. Jefferson had much trouble with his relatives: two other nephews were accused in Kentucky of killing a black man, his uncle was insane, and a brother-in-law was a well-noted tavern brawler. Polite persons, however, did not talk of such things in those days.

Virginius Dabney, author of *The Jefferson Scandal: A Rebuttal* (New York: Dodd, Mead & Co., 1981) and John C. Miller, author of *The Wolf by the Ears: Thomas Jefferson and Slavery* (New York: The Free Press, 1977), disbelieve this story. In Dabney's words, it is "unproved and unprovable." However, if it is true, Miller contends, then Jefferson stands condemned as one of the "most profligate liars and consummate hypocrites ever to occupy the presidency." Only one early public figure ever admitted to an open affair with a black woman; this was Richard Johnson of Kentucky, who was vice president under the Van Buren administration and the reputed slayer of Tecumseh at the Battle of the Thames in the War of 1812. (He never made it to the presidency because of the affair.)

One last word: Of all the Founding Fathers who spoke out against slavery and for the freedom of man, Jefferson was the only one not to free all of his slaves upon his death on 4 July 1825 (patriotic even in his passing, as was John Adams, who died the same day). Jefferson did free Sally Hemming's progeny, but not her. His daughter did that after Jefferson's death, but then her maternal grandfather John Wayles had originally owned and fathered Sally. This made the alleged sable paramour the half sister of Tom Jefferson's wife.

General Sir Edward Pakenham, Pickled à la Nelson

A popular country music recording heard on the radio by millions of Americans in the 1960s commenced as follows: "In 18 'n' 14 we took a little trip, down with Colonel Jackson to the mighty Mississip, We took a little bacon, and we took a little beans, and we caught the bloody British in the town of New Orleans."

This little ditty is obviously a popularized historical reference to the American victory won two weeks after U.S.-British negotiators had signed a peace treaty at Ghent, Belgium, to end the War of 1812 (it would take another month before the peace document reached Washington, D.C.). The song recounts how General Sir Edward Pakenham and 2,000 of his troops were riddled by the shots of General Andrew Jackson's motley, ragtag army of frontiersmen, Native Americans, French Creoles, Free Blacks, and Baratarian pirates. After the battle the British general's body was pickled in a barrel of rum and returned to the ship, where his distraught wife faced the agony of its delivery and adverse news of the battle.

At that time in history, pickling was the only way to preserve remains of the dead until the time of a proper state funeral and burial, a practice obviously reserved only for persons of political significance, like Pakenham. The same process had been applied to the remains of Britain's most celebrated modern naval hero, Admiral Lord Horatio Nelson, who was killed in 1805 at Trafalgar (after which London's most famous square is named). The process allowed that he might later be accorded a state cortege.

A historically apocryphal tale recounts that in Nelson's case, during his body's sea journey from Spain to England, ship movement from the thrashing sea caused the rum barrel lid to jar loose, presenting Nelson's good eye (he had lost the other in an earlier sea battle) peering eerily at a deck guard. The man was uncontrollably spooked and jumped into the Bay of Biscay to escape the dead Admiral's piercing gaze.

Andrew Jackson and the Longest Campaign

Among the four presidential candidates in the 1824 election, Andrew Jackson received the larger number of popular and electoral votes, but not enough for victory. By constitutional prescription the House of Representatives had to decide the outcome. Ultimately second-place John Quincy Adams received the support of fourth-place (and conveniently also Speaker of the House) Henry Clay, which guaranteed Adams the prize. Adams then obligingly appointed Henry Clay secretary of state in the new administration. Jacksonians immediately proclaimed the deal to be a corrupt bargain, a charge that was as unprovable then as now, but one that tainted his administration forever and led to a four-year election campaign against Adams.

As early as October 1825, the Tennessee legislature named Jackson as their choice for 1828. A series of jingles captured the mood of the Jacksonians. One told of "John Quincy Adams, who can write/Andrew Jackson, who can fight." Another well-known ditty entitled "The Hunters of Kentucky" lauded the General's conduct at the Battle of New Orleans. As the election approached, the tune was rewritten and renamed "The Voters of Kentucky." One verse went like this: "We are a hardy freeborn race/Who always fight for glory/And never gave our votes to place/as President a *Tory*."

Only the modern student of elections could imagine what a spectacle the 1828 campaign could present for today's media coverage. Consider some of the ingredients: Jackson supporters presented him as the Hero of New Orleans, the Peoples' Candidate, the Farmer of Tennessee—anything to enhance his image as an average man made good. Because of his toughness, he came to be known affectionately as Old Hickory (the first American president to have an endearing nickname), and at rallies and barbecues his Hurra Boys (campaign workers) handed out hickory sticks, canes, and hickory-handled brooms designed to sweep the corrupt Adams men from office and purify American politics once again. One did not put up a

Jackson sign in the front yard—a hickory pole sufficed. The corrupt bargain was a constant theme, fortified by Adams's use of gambling furniture in the White House. (He had bought a billiards table with his own funds, but such things get twisted around in the heat of an election.) The Adams family was characterized as the American House of Stuart, a reference to the high-handed British royal family thrown out in the Glorious Revolution of 1688.

Adams supporters stooped to dish out charges on the same level. They compiled a list of Old Hickory's sins—a rather easy task as he had so many likely ones: adultery, gambling (this one worked both ways, but the Adams charge had more potency), cockfighting, slave trading (which revealed Adams to be a Yankee with no sympathy for the South and its Peculiar Institution), bigamy (Jackson and his Rachel had married thinking her former husband had filed divorce papers, only to find out that they had jumped the gun rather than the broom), drunkenness, theft, lying, and, of course, murder. Indeed the list reads much like the charges levied against a deposed and excommunicated pope during the political storms of the Italian Renaissance—everything just short of sodomy. The Adams men even distributed a single-sheet Coffin Handbill bordered in black and picturing six coffins and names of six militiamen who they charged Jackson had murdered in cold blood (Jackson had executed them for mutiny).

It was further charged that Jackson was but one of several offspring of a common prostitute who was brought to the United States by British troops and who eventually married a mulatto man. Pro-Adams crowds paraded before a Nashville hotel where Jackson was staying, waving banners that read "The A B C of Democracy: Adulterer, Bully, Cuckold" and singing, "Oh, Andy! Oh, Andy!/How many men have you hanged in your life?/How many marriages make you a wife?"

Other Old Hickory Facts and Tales

Jackson's predecessors in the White House had all been men of better formal learning and generally polished manners.

Inaugurations had followed the demeanors of the men entering the presidential home; they tended to be staid, formal, and limited affairs. Jackson was the first real Westerner to ascend to the presidency, and his followers were of frontier stock or the common farmers and city dwellers of the East. Many of his supporters traveled hundreds of miles to see their president take power and hail the hero. A vast throng gathered to view the inaugural speech, although most could not hear it, there being no manner of amplification and Jackson being of too poor health to talk loudly. This mattered little, for Jackson was intentionally vague and his mollifying statements were not worth the hearing anyway.

Afterward, everyone repaired to the White House for the gala inaugural party. The crowd soon became a mob, consumed all of the food and drink, and nearly crushed the frail president in the rush to shake his hand. Roughly dressed backwoodsmen in muddy boots and moccasins stood on the richly upholstered furniture to catch a glimpse of their hero and lead a cheer. It was a heyday for breaking china and valued glassware. As the drunken, boisterous crowd departed they took souvenirs for the unfortunate folks back home who could not make the trip—pieces of curtain and upholstery removed with the casual swipe of a skinning knife.

The new president was known as a man of action out West and as a man of violence in the East. His reputation came from the many duels and gunfights he had fought, most of which involved snide comments made about the legitimacy of his marriage, a sore spot with Old Hickory. Jackson's most famous duel occurred with a noted pistol shot of the time, Charles Dickinson, a man who had slighted Jackson and his wife publicly several times, goading Jackson into the challenge (an easy endeavor, all things considered). Jackson, a frail, skinny man, wearing a loose shirt to conceal his true frame, took Dickinson's ball near his heart. The wounded president-to-be steadied himself and drilled Dickinson in the groin—a wound from which he died after days in agony. Jackson bled through several mattresses, but he managed to endure. He carried the ball next to his heart the rest of his life, and the wound bled and suppurated regularly.

The Dickinson duel made a reputation for Jackson. Legend has it that when a teacher asked her unstudied Sunday school class who killed Abel, she got no response. After much cajoling, pleading, and hemming and hawing, one glory-hunting scholar finally shouted out the obvious: "Andy Jackson done it!" It was also a reputation that made for caution in dealing with the president. When Vice President John C. Calhoun resigned to be reelected to the U.S. Senate over the Nullification Controversy, Jackson threatened to hang all involved in the scheme regardless of their station in life. Calhoun wondered aloud to Missouri Senator Thomas Hart Benton, a survivor of a Nashville gunfight with Jackson some years earlier and now an ardent Jackson man, whether the president was referring to him. He really did not know, Benton mused, but "when Andrew Jackson talks hanging, smart men get ropes." Under such pressures, the Compromise of 1833 soon followed.

Jackson's rough reputation did not help him any when, during a trip to New England to bolster party fortunes there, he was put up by party notables for an honorary degree at Harvard College. Then as now, the Cambridge institution was the alma mater of many better-educated persons of the time, most of them Jackson opponents who were disgusted at the thought of a noted duelist receiving an LL.D. from America's oldest and most prestigious institution of higher learning, of which Jackson possessed little. Tradition had it that recipients of honorary degrees were to make a small speech in Latin—and this seemed improbable from a president who could barely speak standard English. Jackson rose to the occasion stating, "E pluribus unum, sine qua non," to the hoots of America's upper crust who laughed that Jackson was not only an LL.D., but "an ASS!" The Whig opposition even made up a banner featuring a lazy ass sitting on its posterior with a mortar board hat and a collar tag labeled Harvard LL.D. However, the unlettered people who had put the old general in office were proud. "See, there now, Andy can even talk that fancy Latin stuff." As for the ass, a simple, humble, hard-working beast, it became a symbol for the common man in the Democratic party that was popularized by cartoonist Thomas Nast in the 1870s and has endured to this day.

During Jackson's last months in office, supporters in New York sent the president a 1,400-pound piece of cheese. The three-quarter-ton wheel was placed on public display in a White House corridor, where Jackson announced that it would be eaten by any and all visitors on Washington's birthday. Thousands lined up to take advantage of the offer, bringing their own utensils or gouging out chunks of the delicacy with their own fingers. The affair, which lasted only a few hours until the cheese disappeared to the last crumb, stands as America's most unique farewell party.

Legend has it that retiring President Jackson was asked by one reporter if he had any regrets. Wistfully Old Hickory admitted to having but two—he had not hanged John C. Calhoun nor shot Henry Clay.

Turnpikes, Freeways, Railroads

The student of medieval and renaissance warfare knows the pike to be a 16-foot wooden pole, pointed at the tip, anchored in the ground, and placed at an angle to thwart the thrust of a cavalry charge by armed knights. By the late eighteenth century, when the new republic of the United States commenced to macadamize eastern roads (surface them with crushed stone), the term *pike* received a new usage. The recently built Philadelphia-Lancaster highway required payment of a toll for passage, and entry onto the route was regulated by a long pole, called a pike, at the tollgate, which had to be turned to permit access. Hence we have the term *turnpike* yet today, usually designating a paid toll road like the famed Pennsylvania Turnpike.

Because of the difficulty of traversing even improved roads in the early days, canal and river travel was favored. At first the states and private companies invested in canals, the more famous being New York's Erie Canal, which diverted most westward travel through New York City and destroyed Philadelphia's domination of the nation's early economy. The expense of canal building caused many private companies to go broke. Others, like the Baltimore and Ohio Company, changed their investment to a new, cheaper form of transportation: railroads. The key, however, became for private entities to obtain government financing, and the issue of publicly financed internal improvements (as roads, canals, and railroads were called) was one of the hottest political footballs of the nineteenth century.

Some, like Alexander Hamilton through his Report on Manufactures and Henry Clay through his American System, saw the improvement of transportation networks as so beneficial to the nation that they should be financed by a tariff on imported goods. Some opposed public financing for constitutional reasons: no specific grant of power existed in the document for the federal government to act, and tariffs curtailed the import of cheap foreign goods in exchange for cotton, which motivated many Southerners. Others opposed the idea as being selfish: for instance, powerful New York politicians like Martin Van Buren opposed other states getting federal assistance to build systems that New York had financed alone and that would undercut the state's monopoly on western trade via the Erie Canal. Andrew Jackson, through his Maysville Road veto, tried to work out a middle way—no internal improvements unless they were truly national in scope. The result was that by the time of the Civil War few federally financed internal improvements were completed. The exception was the National Road, which ran from Wheeling, [West] Virginia, to Vandalia, Illinois and ultimately St. Louis, Missouri—currently parts of U.S. Highway 40 and Interstate 70.

Eventually, with the advent of the Republican party and the South's exclusion from Congress because of the Civil War, the internal improvements issue was settled on behalf of federal intervention in the form of the Transcontinental Railroad Act, which granted alternating sections of land to the utilities that built their steel rails westward. The land in turn was sold to immigrant farmers who provided the customers for the railroads' profit. As all European nations built rail webs at the same time, it is ironic that the terminology for the new choo-choo avenues differed. Only in English are they called railroads. In all other languages they are called ways of steel (*chemin de fer, ferrocarril, eisenbahn*).

Public financing of the nation's transportation system was

an established idea by the beginning of the twentieth century. It became the core of Franklin D. Roosevelt's program to spend the nation out of the Great Depression in the form of the Works Progress Administration. After World War II, Dwight D. Eisenhower proposed and Congress approved an entire system of interstate freeways that would modernize over-the-road travel; these were based on the German autobahns that Ike had seen when he helped conquer the Nazis. Of course, these roads do not come free—they are paid by a series of taxes on gasoline and road use permits, among others. They are an integral part of the concrete canyons that link our American cities today.

Where Did the Cherokees' $5 Million Go?

Under the terms of the Treaty of New Echota (1835), signed illegally by the so-called treaty faction of the Cherokee nation and unfairly made binding upon the rest of the tribe by U.S. authorities, the Cherokees were to remove themselves within two years to the area that is now northeastern Oklahoma. In exchange they would receive $5 million for their Georgia homeland. As the Cherokees held their lands in common, owning only the improvements built upon it individually, the monies received would be divided up on a per capita basis among the tribal members. In addition, President Andrew Jackson deleted the right of Indians who wished not to move west to hold any land in severalty, adding $600,000 to the final treaty terms. He obviously wanted all Indians to be removed and to end the problem once and for all. This much is in any history of the nation, but the question arises: What happened to the money? It is a germane question, especially since the tribal government was pretty much broke by the end of the removal process in 1840.

The story of the money revolves around intertribal politics. There were two factions in tribal leadership. On one side was the legally elected chief, John Ross. On the other was a group of middle-class Indians, those who had adopted the white man's ways, lived in houses, and farmed, using slave labor in many cases. Led by the Ridge-Boudinot-Waite families, they sought political power commensurate with their economic wealth. The majority of the Cherokees, however, sided with tradition and John Ross. Aware of this split, the U.S. treaty negotiators had recognized the dissidents as rulers of all Cherokees, obtained their signatures on the New Echota document, forced the papers upon the whole tribe, and then heartlessly abandoned the treaty signers to their fate—ultimate assassination by the enraged Ross faction. After the treaty was ratified by the U.S. Senate (by one vote), the recently elected Martin Van Buren administration funneled the money through Ross, again legally recognizing his paramount position in the tribe. It was a nice piece of double-dealing.

The first consideration is whether the Cherokees received any of the promised money, and if so how much? According to an itemized account of the federal disbursements, $500,000 of the original sum was deducted immediately for an additional land purchase in Kansas (sold back to the federal government 50 years later), and nearly $6.1 million was given out among the three elements of the tribe: $2.9 million to those in the East, $1.7 million to those known as Old Settlers (people already in the West, who had moved to Arkansas as much as 20 years before and were being moved again to the Indian Territories), and $1.5 million was doled out to various visiting Cherokee delegations in Washington, D.C. Because the expenses of removal exceeded the amounts appropriated by nearly $1.5 million, even before the mass of Cherokees left Georgia for present-day Oklahoma, much of the costs came out of their own pockets.

Therein lay the real problem. After all expenses and claims were satisfied, only $683,974 remained in the Cherokee tribal fund. The treaty faction, backed up by the Old Settlers, accused John Ross, his family, and cronies of fraud—pocketing large sums of cash for personal use. The United States had estimated that the Indians could be removed at a ridiculous $20 per head. After the federal government agreed to let the Cherokees remove themselves, Ross upped the ante to $65 per capita. In the end he charged the tribe more like $103 each. He also charged the tribal treasury 16 cents for each ration dispensed, items that had cost him 9 cents. His opponents claim that even

if federal estimates were a mite low, Ross never spent anywhere close to $103 per Indian for removal. He lent verity to
the charges when he returned $125,000 of his own funds to the
tribal treasury in 1843 to help subsidize the tribe during the
first lean years in the West. The doubts of the treaty faction and
the Old Settlers were reinforced by suspicions of Brigadier
Generals Winfield Scott (who escorted the Cherokees westward) and Matthew Arbuckle (who received them in the West,
but may have been unduly influenced by friends among the
Old Settlers), as well as by Governor Wilson Lumpkin of
Georgia (a removal advocate who hated Ross).

Ross managed to avoid the blame attached to him by his
opponents, partly through his own adroit politics and ability
to secure additional tribal annuities from Washington, partly
because his opponents all had blemishes of their own (at least
Ross had been against removal), and partly because no conclusive evidence of intentional fraud exists even to this day (Ross
refused to make a full accounting to anyone). The suspicion
still exists that Chief Ross may have profited by as little as
$832,000 to as much as $1.1 million. To his credit he never
considered the $5 million fund matter closed. Under his pres-
sure, for example, Congress voted over $600,000 to the Chero-
kees in 1850–1851 (about $92.79 per tribal member instead of
the nearly $3,000 promised in the $5 million fund). Ross called
this merely a partial payment and pressed on.

The rift in the Cherokee nation continued through the Civil
War, with Ross and his faction backing the North and the
treaty faction siding with the South (in fact, the Cherokee
Stand Watie was the last Confederate general officer to surrender in 1865). With Ross's death after the war, the victorious
Union imposed a new treaty against the tribe (all were blamed
for the Confederate activities of a few and their landed area
was reduced). This, along with the assumption of tribal leadership by the treaty party faction, united the Cherokee nation
as never before. Finally in 1906, after receiving persistent
complaints for 70 years, Congress voted to pay just over $1
million as the final installment of the amount promised in the
Treaty of New Echota in 1835. The $5 million fund was settled
at last.

Brimstone Hill and Saddlebag Evangelism

The new nation in America experienced a Second Great Awakening, or torrid religious revivalist movement, just after the opening of the nineteenth century. Commencing in some ways as a drive to cleanse the contaminating effects at Harvard and Yale as well as other tolerant tendencies in general, firebrand preachers stepped forward to battle infidelity. Timothy Dwight labored to resurrect godliness at Yale, yet he did so by restructuring the road to salvation that old-time Puritans had advocated. Dwight and others pushed religion in an Arminian direction, declaring that anyone who willed to do so could be holy rather than sinful. Much more a hit-or-miss proposition, this also minimized the Puritan emphasis on the intervention of the Holy Ghost. Detractors saw this as heresy and labeled the influential Dwight as Pope Timothy. Meanwhile Jedediah Morse's new Andover Seminary (1808) became such a vigorous champion of reinforced biblical orthodoxy and the revival spirit that it soon became known as Brimstone Hill.

For the frontier, the Methodists may have employed one of the more effective methods of delivering the works of salvation and encouraging revivalism—the circuit rider. The method's founder was Francis Asbury, whose biographer indicates "when he came to America he rented no house, he hired no lodgings, he made no arrangements to board anywhere, but simply set out on the Long Road, and was traveling forty-five years later when death caught up with him." Asbury often preached to crowds of more than 10,000, and his activities formed but one chapter in a revival era that introduced the famous and exciting camp meetings. Even President Theodore Roosevelt in his own study of the era indicated how impressed he was with the unlimited energy of the converted pastors Asbury left behind, men who combined religious duties with the work of ax and plow in building communities.

Onlookers among the throng, which employed everything from brush arbors to wagons to massive tents for shelter, observed wild and spirited manifestations that included cataleptic trances, involuntary jerks, the uncontrollable "holy laugh," babbling in ancient or unknown tongues, mimickings of David dancing before the Ark of the Covenant, and even individuals who got down on all fours and barked like dogs to tree the Devil. Things went a bit more deeply than that, however. Using Dwight's new approach to willed salvation, these circuit riders soon took the next logical step: if one could will his or her individual salvation, then one could expand religious behavior to include all of society and remake the sinful earth into a perfect heaven on earth. The result was a host of secular reforms that swept the United States in the first half of the nineteenth century.

The swath cut by domestic reforms became so compelling that western New York State, a center of the enthusiasm, became known as the Burned-over District by the 1820s, an obvious reference to the religious heat and fervor that continually swept the entire area. Commencing with the career of Charles Grandison Finney, who claimed he had a personal "retainer from the Lord Jesus Christ to plead His case," the Burned-over District underwent scorching after scorching. Unlike established churches, the prepared sermon was not stressed. Finney and those who followed preferred the extemporaneous, the human guided by the Spirit or the Holy Ghost, a style still popular among most evangelists today and even utilized among some of the established denominations.

The waves of revival that swept the Erie Canal traversed regions of up-state New York and produced not only tent meetings but demands for secular reform and new religious sects. As settlers traveled westward into the Old Northwest, they spread their secular ideas throughout the North, with ominous consequence for the future. These ideas included religious tracts to be used in schools as texts (as opposed to the old system of biblical study, which was being secularized at the same time through McGuffey's readers); the beginning of regular Sunday school classes in the modern sense of religious study; the introduction of temperance on the local level, spreading to larger administrative divisions later; the inauguration of the so-called Blue Laws to enforce Sabbath observation by all in the community; the creation of new "scientific" dietary reforms to purify the temple of the human body; the installation of the popular democracy that marked the Jacksonian Era;

the beginning of humane treatment of the deaf, dumb, and blind; improvement of prison conditions; the first organized stirrings of feminism, in the form of legal, educational, property, and political rights; the rise of the public school; and the institution of intensified antislavery feeling to bring reform to all persons under God's hand.

Also important was the creation of new religious groups like the Latter Day Saints, where founder Joseph Smith's influential secretary, Oliver Cowderly, brought in much of the baggage of the Burned-over District to fuel the Saints' beginnings in Palmyra, New York. Another religious philosophy, Millerism, melded into the current Seventh Day Adventists with its original emphasis on Adventism or the Second Coming of Christ—a feeling so intense at the time that the sect actually predicted the day and hour for Christ's arrival and witnessed many believers climbing into trees hoping to fly up angelic-like to meet Him. Shakerism, with its own twist on the Second Coming and Adventism, representing a bisexual orientation of God through His sending Ann Lee as the new messiah. (Lee was dedicated to the orderly, clean, industrious communal personal life, and she eschewed war, politics, corporal punishment, alcohol, and tobacco.) Spiritualism, which grew beyond its roots of mesmerism (clairvoyance) and phrenology (the study of intelligence and character though the bumps on one's head), asserted that humankind had to go beyond the Bible to "science" and find true happiness through seances, in which they contacted the spirits of those who had died. Fourierism, which espoused the ultimate in the perfect society, was based on the notions of Fourier, the French philosopher who had organized society on a communal basis. His was a system so refined that the collection of garbage was placed in the hands of little boys, whose pleasure in getting dirty could be turned into a useful activity.

Politically, the reform movements that began in religion became a national phenomenon that led from western New York through its indigenous Anti-Masonic party to the Whigs and the Republicans. The Anti-Masonic party was begun when William Morgan, a Mason, was denied membership in the lodge at Batavia, New York, an area to which he had recently moved. In revenge, Morgan published the secrets of Masonry for all to see, was jailed on trumped-up charges, kidnapped from jail, and never seen again, evidently murdered. Public outrage merely increased when it turned out that Masons held what was considered to be a disproportional number of political positions—locally, statewide, and nationally—and could frustrate investigations and court proceedings instituted by simple people converted to the "true" religion of the Second Great Awakening. The result was the creation of a local political party designed to fight Masonic activity in government. Because Andrew Jackson was a Mason and John Quincy Adams was not, the party naturally gravitated to the Whigs and the opposition to Jackson's successor, Martin Van Buren, who ran the incumbent (and allegedly Mason-dominated) New York political machine.

The progressive wing of Whiggery, as represented by New York Anti-Masons like political organizer Thurlow Weed, perennial candidate William H. Seward, and publicist Horace Greeley, became the basis for the antislavery Conscience Whigs in the 1840s and the so-called Black Republicans in the 1850s, who very nearly won the election of 1856 with Mexican War hero John Charles Frémont. They were finally outmaneuvered in their political aspirations by a more moderate Midwest political machine of latecomers, which, in the election of 1860, backed a modest Illinois lawyer for the Republican presidential nomination—a homespun man named Abraham Lincoln, who took the prize. Much of this victorious political realism had to do with the transformed religious idealism of the Second Great Awakening.

Graham Crackers, Sex, and Temperance

Any historian who has observed the rise in the multibillion dollar business of health foods and widely advertised prescribed diets is likely to note that such a development is not the first of its kind and very likely will not be the last. Right on the heels of the great religious revival of the 1830s, a man named Sylvester Graham created a far-reaching reputation as a lecturer and spokesman for what and what not to eat. He insisted that a "vegetable diet lies at the basis of all reforms," and he went on to advocate only the consumption of grains, vegetables, and fruits, while condemning alcohol, coffee, tea, and tobacco. One of the legacies of his campaign still with us is the wholesome treat made from his patented concoction of ingredients, the graham cracker.

Graham went even further in his attacks on popular human practices and desires, many of which he charged were overstimulated by the consumption of "high-seasoned foods, rich dishes, and the free use of flesh." Items like cured hams merely served to "increase the concupiscent excitability and sensibility of the genital organs," and it followed that they led not only to moral corruption but to the diminishment of the intellect as well. Since Graham held that no sexual functions were desirable save for procreation alone, he maintained that a concerted effort must be made to resist the stimulus that improper foods deliver to all vital organs of the body.

The dietary mission of Graham fit well into a larger movement that gained momentum throughout the 1830s and by the 1850s saw many counties and states go dry or restrict the amount of spirits that could be produced. This movement, which had arisen and declined throughout our history, eventually culminated in national prohibition after World War I. One of its legacies flowed from the campaign of the Boston Society Promoting Temperance in 1826. The Society asked that all who took the temperance pledge to sign their names on a list and place a T after the signature, signifying Total abstinence. With that a new word entered the English language: *teetotaler.*

Tidbits: Presidential Wives (Tyler, Taylor, Hayes, and Cleveland)

Julia Gardiner Tyler, second wife of John Tyler (who left office in 1845), always remained devotedly loyal to Dixie. Even while a resident of New York City during the Civil War (1864) she bought Confederate bonds, distributed anti-Lincoln pamphlets, provided money and clothes for Confederate soldiers in Union prison camps, and worked for the repatriation of prisoners of war. It was known conduct of this kind that, within a day of Lincoln's assassination, provoked three local ruffians to crash through her door and demand surrender of the Rebel flag she allegedly displayed in her home. No flag was found, so the unknown invaders tore down a symbolic piece of drapery from her parlor and fled. Two days later an anonymous letter in the *New York Herald* charged the presidential widow (correctly) with passing both ways through the Union lines at her pleasure and reminded readers that her two eldest sons served in the Rebel army.

While contemporaries described First Lady Margaret Taylor as "a most kind and thorough-bred Southern lady" possessed of "feminine virtues" displayed with the "artlessness of a rustic and the grace of a duchess," as late as 1937 *The New York Times* carried a story portraying her as one who sat "peacefully smoking her corncob pipe in the White House, while Washington gasped." Actually this picture of a mild-mannered version of cartoonist Al Capp's Mammy Yokum probably shocked the *Times'* twentieth-century readers more than Mrs. Taylor's acquaintances, as pipe smoking among women, especially in the South, was fairly common. Andrew Jackson's wife, Rachel, had the same habit.

Lucy Webb Hayes has come down to us in history with the moniker Lemonade Lucy. The Hayes's White House exhibited a pronounced Wesleyan quality, with regular readings from the Scriptures, daily prayers, and Sunday evening hymns. Only once, shortly after the inauguration in August 1877, did the Hayeses agree to serve alcohol at an official function; they served wine at a dinner for the Russian Grand Duke, only after Secretary of State William Evarts insisted that it would be an affront of the most egregious type not to do so. Soon after that episode, President Hayes publicly announced a no-liquor policy from that day forward. Most religious and temperance groups attributed this stricture to Mrs. Hayes's influence, and her nickname has endured. Lucy and her lemonade became a joke to the supposedly more sophisticated Europeans. The British humorous weekly *Puck*, for example, ran a two-frame cartoon showing the first lady peeking out from behind a bottle of wine with a scowl on her visage, and from a jug of water with a beaming look of approval. The caption read: "How wine her tender spirits riles,/While water wreathes her face with smiles."

Frances ("Frankie" to Grover Cleveland) Folsom had enjoyed the informal guardianship of the future president since age 11, when her father (Cleveland's law partner) died and Cleveland promised to take care of his daughter. And how! Cleveland followed her progress to adulthood and through college with regular letters and flowers, more like the older suitor he was rather than a guardian, with the complete approval of her mother. While he was New York governor, Cleveland and Frankie were betrothed and wedding arrangements were made, again with the open cooperation of her widowed mother. All was to be kept in the strictest secrecy, but the press soon found out—Cleveland had already more or less admitted paternity to an illegitimate son, which merely heightened speculation about the real relationship between the new president (age 48) and his future child bride (age 22).

Married in a private White House ceremony, with John Philip Sousa and the Marine Band providing the music, the newlyweds retired to what they believed was the secret solitude of Deer Park, Maryland. Reporters followed, setting up observation posts near the honeymoon cottage, employing field glasses to observe all visible movements, and even writing about the cuisine delivered daily (which gives an idea about how much they really saw). For years afterward, Cleveland lambasted the press, once calling them ghouls with tears of anguish in his eyes (reminding modern readers of a similar lapse on the part of candidate Edmund S. Muskie in defending his wife from the press, which cost him the 1972 Democratic presidential nomination). The beautiful new Mrs. Cleveland, however, took it all in stride, becoming quite appreciated by the press as a capable, charming first lady, one of the most popular of all time. Cleveland's young wife outlived the president and remarried a man named Preston. In the late 1940s, shortly before her own death, she was seated opposite then-General Dwight D. Eisenhower as a guest of President Harry Truman's daughter, Margaret. She was introduced as a former first lady, and Ike evidently could not put all of the information together with coherent logic, for he asked her where she had lived while in Washington, and was most embarrassed with the response, "In the White House."

Mountain Men and Western Rigors

Although they were preceded by French and Spanish inhabitants of St. Louis such as Pierre Chouteau and Manuel Lisa, the mountain men were the earliest Americans to go into the trans-Mississippi West in any number. They were a tough breed. As one eyewitness wrote of them: "Habitual watchfulness destroys every frivolity of mind and action. They seldom smile: the expression of their countenances is watchful, solemn, and determined. They ride and walk like men whose breasts have so long been exposed to the bullet and the arrow, that fear finds within them no resting place." Mountain men dressed and lived like Native Americans, eating the best meat cuts first (often as much as nine pounds a day when the hunt was on) "for fear of being killed by some brat of an Indian before we enjoyed them." They roasted meat over a fire of buffalo chips— not only was wood scarce on the Plains, but dried buffalo dung gave the meat a nice spicy flavor they treasured.

They were vicious fighters, these mountain men, shooting their stubby, .50-caliber Hawken rifles, then closing with knife and tomahawk. They scalped all of their vanquished opponents, using two half-moon motions with the knife, grabbing the hair in both hands while wedging their feet on the unfortunate's shoulders until the hair parted from the head. Their scalping and skinning knives were trade goods from the British-Canadian Hudson's Bay Company. The blades had the royal crest flanked by the letters G R, for George Rex (George IV). Even literate mountain men (few in number) knew of only one GR, the Green River in present-day Wyoming. So when they urged their friends on in the all-too-common knife fight, they would yell, "Give that child [their usual term for each other] Green River," meaning the knife to the hilt. Some of the better known and more colorful mountain men are listed here.

1. John Colter, a veteran of the 1804–1806 Lewis and Clark Expedition, is generally recognized as the first man to go into what is now Yellowstone National Park. His stories of the geysers and hot springs there earned the region the nickname of Colter's Hell. It was that and more; Colter himself had barely escaped to tell the tale. Captured by Indians who had a sporting outlook on life, Colter was disarmed, stripped, and told to run for his life. He did. When one fleet warrior outdistanced the others, Colter hung back and killed the man with his own lance. He hid in a river, submerged and breathing through a hollow reed until danger passed—a trick that has become standard Hollywood fare. Colter never fully recovered his health and died in St. Louis of jaundice in 1813. Many of his explorations in the Rockies were not duplicated until decades later, when his wild tales of Western geography proved true.

2. Jedediah Smith was a mild-mannered, Bible-reading, well-educated Easterner who explored the West from the Mississippi to California and back, becoming the first white to cross the deserts to get to California by land. Smith survived ambush without a scratch in three of the biggest fights the fur trappers had: the 1823 Ree Massacre of the ill-fated Andrew Henry expedition, the 1827 Mohave (Mojave) Massacre, and the 1828 Umpquah massacre, where 40 men died around him. He also overcame fatigue, starvation, lack of water, and freezing snow for years, only to disappear on the Cimmarron Cut-off of the Santa Fe Trail. His pistols finally appeared, sold in the New Mexican town by a party of Comancheros (renegades who traded with the tribes). The traders claimed to have bought them off a band of Comanches who believed the weapons were bad medicine, having killed their chief.

3. Jim Bridger was also a veteran of the Henry Expedition, who unlike Smith was illiterate but well-versed in the classics, which he like to hear read and see performed. He thought William Shakespeare to "have had a bad heart and been as devilish mean as a Sioux to have written such scoundrelism" as some of the historical murders that sprinkled his plays. A partner in many prosperous fur deals, Bridger was run out of the fort that bore his name by Mormon militiamen in the 1850s, an incident that led to the Mormon War in 1858.

4. Jeremiah "Liver Eatin'" Johnson carried on a lifelong blood feud with the Crows who had murdered his family after he

unwittingly violated one of their burial grounds as a guide. His nickname came from the belief that he allegedly ate the raw livers of his victims. The Crows swore to it, anyhow, although Robert Redford cleaned up Johnson's image some in his film named after Johnson.

5. Hugh Glass, another Henry massacre survivor, faced the greatest horror of all to Western hunters—running into an enraged grizzly. It mauled him almost beyond recognition, and he was left for dead by his companions; after all, they believed "dead men war no account," as one put it. Glass survived by sheer nerve, sewed his ears and face together, and scared everyone witless when he showed up the following spring, with his scarred visage, to curse the men who left him.

6. Sent on a journey with a lone Indian companion, Charlie "Big Phil" Gardiner from Philadelphia (hence his moniker) became lost in a blizzard. He showed up to everyone's surprise alive and well some weeks later, but alone. Well, almost alone: He pulled his Indian friend's shriveled leg out of his pack, saying, "There, damn you, I won't have to gnaw on you any more!" and threw it away. His nickname then became Cannibal Phil.

7. Christopher "Kit" Carson trapped animals in the Southwest, making his headquarters in Taos, New Mexico. Barely able to read and write English, he spoke eight languages, including French and Spanish, and could give sign fluently. Famous for his scouting for Captain John Charles Frémont on expeditions into California and Oregon, Carson took part in the Bear Flag Revolt and was sent east by Frémont to tell of the glory of American victory. He led Colonel S. W. Kearny back to California, were he had to sneak out of the surrounded American camp at San Pascual to bring help and save the day. Later he became a Union brigadier general of volunteers during the Civil War, lost several battles to the Confederates, and gained more fame by defeating the Navajo nation in 1864. It was said he liked nothing better than "to kill an Indian before breakfast."

8. James P. Beckwourth (originally Beckwith), another Henry massacre survivor, was an African-American trapper (as was Peter Ranne, who rode with Jed Smith), the son of a Mississippi planter and his black paramour. He had been trained as a

blacksmith and left the trade and slavery for freedom and adventure in the West. He was known as the Gaudy Liar—a compliment among mountain men who spun tall tales to entertain themselves in lonely camps. His memoir, *Life and Adventures* as edited by historian Bernard DeVoto, is still a classic with more truth than fiction to it, if taken as it was told—with a grain of salt. He inherited an Indian squaw from a companion killed in an accident, and often passed himself off as an Indian who was captured as a boy and returned to the tribe. His welcome in village after village showed the potency of the tale, which gave him special trapping rights and a new wife every now and then.

9. Bill Williams trapped beaver on the Gila and supplemented his income by guiding military explorers and stealing horses in Santa Fe. He would drive the horses over the Old Spanish Trail through Utah and sell them in Los Angeles. Sometimes he stole them a second time and resold them back in New Mexico. Legend had it that when vittles got short, smart men never turned their backs on Old Bill.

10. James Kirker, known later as Don Santiago Kirker, King of New Mexico, was also a survivor of the Henry Expedition. He abandoned the failing, trapped-out fur business of the Southwest to become, in 1838, the premiere scalp hunter of the Rio Grande. Plagued by recurring Apache raids, the northern Mexican states instituted a policy of paying bounty hunters for each scalp they could bring in. It became quite a business, as Kirker found out. When it got slow, one could always kill a few Mexicans to raise up the till—after all their hair was as black as any Apache's. If the Mexican governors cut off the trade as they did on occasion, Kirker would trade in stolen livestock with the very Apaches he hunted before, a policy that caused him to flee with a price on his own hair to American troops entering the area during the Mexican War.

Kirker then led Alexander Donniphan's 1st Missouri Cavalry, the Wildcats, from Santa Fe to Saltillo, winning the pitched battles of El Brazito (near present-day El Paso) and Río Sacramento (near Chihuahua City) with tactics including men pretending to fall dead to lure in the Mexican militia to their own ends, and sharpshooters hidden in wagons (a favorite Hollywood ploy in westerns, or oaters, today). Needless to say, the Wildcats just loved his style. He wound up his life in California, where many former associates, all with Mexican prices on their heads, congregated to enjoy the sun and their ill-gotten gains.

Mexican War: Ironies of Death, a List of Firsts, Wartime Atrocities, the Battalion of St. Patrick, and Gringos

For some time before the direct military struggle with Mexican forces (1846–1848), the United States had wrestled with problems arising from expanded occupation of Texas lands and reprisals from the south. Resulting war carried the battles across Texas, into Mexico, and ultimately to the Mexican capital.

During the administration of President James K. Polk, the actual war involved thousands of soldiers, a high percentage of whom died in the conflict. Many ironies arose from this episode in the two nations' histories.

1. For the United States, where figures are available, the statistics of 1,721 killed and 4,102 wounded are dwarfed by the larger 11,155 who died of disease.

2. For this price, plus $15 million in cash and the assumption of American damage claims against Mexico, the United States secured without dispute the territory that is now comprised of Texas, the northern halves of Arizona and New Mexico (the rest of these states was obtained in the Gadsden Purchase a few years later), Nevada, Utah, and present-day California, with its great Pacific harbors.

3. The war was, for the United States, the first seizure of an enemy capital, the first conflict in which West Point graduates played a decisive role, and the first one with war correspondents present on the battlefield.

4. At the decisive and bloody Battle of Churubusco (20 August 1847), the Mexican defense was spearheaded by the Batallón de San Patricio (Battalion of St. Patrick), made up of foreign volunteers, most of whom were American army deserters and many of whom were of Irish descent. Under a banner of Irish green adorned with the harp of Erin, the San Patricios nearly defeated their American attackers, fighting valiantly and with

a desperation of men who knew that capture meant court martial and death for desertion in time of war.

Mexican legend attributes the U.S. victory to a final charge in which the Americans drove a retinue of nuns, women, and children at bayonet point ahead of the assault regiments. The Americans, however, claimed the refugees bolted in panic down the road just ahead of the attack. Three times the San Patricios pulled down the white flag raised by the beaten Mexicans. Finally an American officer raised the white flag himself and the Mexicans surrendered en masse, leaving the San Patricios in the lurch. In the end, 65 San Patricios were taken, tried, and sentenced to death by hanging. General Winfield Scott pardoned 11 of them who had deserted before hostilities commenced, all of whom received 50 lashes, were branded on the cheek with a D, and then forced to dig the graves of the condemned. The execution took place as U.S. troops assaulted the well-known Chapultepec Castle, which housed the Mexican Military Academy. When the American flag flapped from the top of the buildings signaling victory, the trap was sprung and the San Patricios were no more.

5. One item attributed to wartime events is the term *gringos,* today usually applied to Yankees of a northern European heritage. Although the origin of the term remains in dispute (as does *mafia*), the more commonly accepted theory claims that U.S. troops, often encamped across the river from the Mexicans, engaged in singing the then-popular tune "Green Grows the Grass." The phonetic repetition led the Spanish-speaking soldiers to subsequently refer to the American enemy as "green grows," or as they said it, gringos.

CHAPTER IV

The Antebellum Era

Slave Revolts—Fears and Facts

The most dreaded form of slave resistance was armed rebellion. Organized gangs of runaways existed in most Southern swamps, blacks who established military-like colonies that occasionally raided plantations and made local travel risky. Usually these communities wanted merely to be let alone, but many slaves, enough to make it a feared possibility, wanted to purge the South of slavery through open rebellion. Hence the stifling of any debate questioning the Peculiar Institution, and the quick suppression and hanging of John Brown, lest slaves get too many bad ideas from white divisiveness. Blacks had more than enough impetuousness to revolt, stimulated in part by personal desires, past African memories and tales of freedom, and the Bible. American revolutionary philosophy was a factor: it caused slaves from South Carolina to New York to flee with the defeated British army in 1782, some of whom went back to Africa and were instrumental in the creation of Sierra Leone and others of whom established Blacktown in Nova Scotia. French revolutionary ideas played their part, as represented in the bloody example of the slave revolution of Saint Domingue, which in 1802 created the second free state in the New World after the United States, the black nation of Haiti. Indeed, open rebellion was the most feared form of resistance in the pre-Civil War South.

Historians disagree on how many slave rebellions actually

occurred in the United States from the introduction of slavery in 1619 to the Civil War. Fears and rumors would have had there be hundreds of instances, but most historians believe that seven major attempts were either barely nipped in the bud or came to fruition. The New York Conspiracy of 1712 (slavery was present in all 13 colonies until the end of British rule), cost the lives of a dozen whites and 28 conspirators. Six of these people wisely committed suicide rather than surrendering, others were broken at the wheel, hanged in chains and starved, hanged by the neck, or burned alive over a slow fire. The Stono River Revolt of 1739–1740, on the coast of South Carolina below Charleston, was stopped by white regulators in a pitched battle. When continued rebellion was feared, 50 more blacks were hanged for suspicion, and another vigilante movement swept St. Johns Parish farther north on the coast. The New York Conspiracy of 1741 might have been completely fabricated by Mary Burton, a white indentured servant bargaining for her freedom. Nonetheless, 144 blacks were arrested, of whom 13 were burned to death, 18 hanged, and 21 transported to the West Indies. In 1800 two slaves near Richmond told of the plan of a General Gabriel to lead local slaves in revolt. This incident, known as General Gabriel's Henrico Plot, resulted in 41 hangings. The Placquemines Rebellion of 1811 occurred near New Orleans, where about 500 blacks revolted but were ultimately defeated by white militia. The survivors were executed; all the dead were decapitated and their heads were stuck on poles along the Mississippi as a warning to others. Denmark Vesey's Charleston Plot of 1822 was betrayed, and Vesey and many of his lieutenants were arrested along with 131 others. Of these, 37 were executed, 43 were sent to the West Indies, and 48 were released after severe whippings, although to this day one historian believes that the informers made it all up to secure their own freedom.

If there is doubt of the veracity of the Vesey's plot, there is none about Nat Turner's Southampton Rebellion of 1831, which has captured much attention and became the basis of the 1960s bestselling novel *The Confession of Nat Turner* by William Styron. Turner's revolt occurred at a time when Virginia was debating the validity of the slave system in its legislature and constitutional convention, the state was suffering from continued soil depletion and migration of its best sons to the Southwest, David Walker's *Appeal* (a native North Carolinian's criticism of slavery) was published, and Abolitionists and their burgeoning antislavery pamphleteering efforts (through the U.S. mails) was on the rise. It made for a tense American South.

A mystic and a Christian minister who believed he was marked at birth by God, as evidenced the many scars over his body (Northerners later said they were the scars of ill-treatment, and Southerners maintained they came from his many knife fights), Turner was influenced by an eclipse of the sun on 12 February 1831 to schedule the revolt for July 4. God ordained that he be sick that day, though, which caused Turner to wonder about his ordination until he received another sign: for three days in August the sun rose with an unusual green haze (still called the Blue Days in local lore). Back in God's grace, Turner gathered his followers on 21 August, a Sunday, and after much ritual planning and eating, the group struck that evening, beginning with Turner's own master and his family (who had treated him well as a slave, a disturbing thought to whites). They vowed to kill all whites they encountered, of whatever age or sex. Within 48 hours his gang had grown to 70 members and the death toll reached 55.

Soon resistance began to grow in the form of forewarned whites and troops from Virginia, North Carolina, and the federal government. Several days of fighting dispersed the African-American forces, but Nat Turner remained at large another two and a half months. In the meantime, over 100 blacks had been killed and another 53 had been arrested. Of the latter, 20 were hanged, 12 were sent to other states, and 21 were acquitted. Once arrested, Turner was tried and convicted, although he steadfastly maintained that he felt guilty of nothing. Before his execution he spoke with his lawyer, Thomas R. Gray, who published Turner's words in book form. The *Confession* later became the basis of William Styron's novel, which in turn was criticized as unfair to Turner, as it was embellished with references to his alleged sexual preference for white women and other negative stereotypes.

The South was never quite secure after Nat Turner's

Southampton Revolt. Rebellion scares regularly swept the region during the Panic of 1837 and at election time, especially during the 1860 contest that resulted in the victory of Abraham Lincoln. Despite the example of Nat Turner, African Americans opted to protest their enslavement during the Civil War by fleeing to the Union lines and enlisting to fight for their freedom in the armies of the North—a humane approach to centuries of injustice.

Who Was Sambo?

African Americans have the dubious honor of being one of the most psychoanalyzed groups in American history—particularly by whites, which gives ill-meaning to the current IQ craze that asserts that black Americans rate one standard deviation below other ethnic groups present in the United States. That African Americans find this all too insulting is based on more than a mere slap in the face—it has its deeper meaning in the travail of slavery and how historians have interpreted the slaves' psychic response to the Peculiar Institution. Did the slave internalize his feigned laziness and inabilites until they became reality (as plantation owners wanted to believe), or was every slave a Nat Turner, fighting the system with guile and dignity (as African Americans forcefully state today)?

Numerous black historians, from the eloquent W. E. Burghart DuBois to Joseph Carroll and the popular Joel A. Rogers, have asserted the African Americans' nobility as an enslaved people. One of the better known proponents of this idea is the white Marxist historian, Herbert Aptheker. In his *American Negro Slave Revolts,* Aptheker paints a picture of a continually resisting slave population that attacked the Peculiar Institution in a variety of ways, from sly day-to-day resistance to outright armed rebellion. Aptheker would prefer to use as his working definition of rebellion the one adopted by the antebellum Texas Supreme Court—an assembly of three or more armed slaves intending to take their freedom by force. However, he feels that ten or more, intending to assert their freedom and being portrayed in contemporary literature as rebels, is a better definition, one that could also include revolts in the trans-Atlantic slave trade. As such, he finds there were at least 250 slave revolts from 1526 to 1865 that affected American Negro slavery. However, he has been criticized for arguing beyond the evidence and failing to distinguish between rumor, discontent, and actual rebellion.

One of Aptheker's critics is another white Marxist historian, Eugene Genovese, author of the monumental study *Roll Jordan Roll: The World the Slaves Made*. Genovese thinks that black and leftist historians of the twentieth century have been too impressed by the notion that the masses are noble and ripe for revolt, and if not, can be educated to be so. He notes that it is a sacrilege to suggest that slavery was a social system in which the vast majority lived in relative harmony, but he believes the record shows there was little organized, massive resistance to the slave regime.

Genovese points out that there were bloody slave rebellions in the Caribbean and South America that lasted for decades, had thousands of participants, and cost hundreds of lives. Yet the record for the United States in the nineteenth century includes only the Louisiana Revolt, Nat Turner's attempt, and two others that were snuffed out before they got off the ground. There was no rebellion between 1831 and 1865, despite the occurrence of the Civil War. He dismisses most of Aptheker's 250 revolts as panicked newspaper reports.

Genovese traces this alleged lack of a black revolutionary tradition to three factors: 1) the type of African involved in the slave system, 2) the ratio of white to black population, and 3) the treatment of slaves by their New World masters. Slaves in the United States came from Lower Guinea and represented more complex civilizations that previously disciplined them to servitude and class distinction, while slaves in Latin countries were more often Angolan and Congolese people who lacked these traits. Moreover, after the 1808 ending of the foreign slave trade, the United States had the only homegrown African slave population in the world, a group that was even more acculturated to the New World. In the United States the white-black ration was decidedly in favor of the white master class (most Southern plantations had fewer than 20 slaves and few had over 50), which more actively patrolled and isolated blacks and put them at the mercy of white law. Genovese finds treatment of slaves to be better in the United States than elsewhere, involving more food, leisure time, family units, better housing, and less corporal punishment, epitomized by the feeling of duty and responsibility that saw the slaves characterized as "my people" by their owners. Genovese also concludes that the American slave system was so repressive and yet so benign that revolt was impossible and impracticable.

Even more controversial than Genovese's theory is the one put forward by Stanley Elkins, based on earlier work by his mentor, Frank Tannenbaum. Rather than seeing the U.S. slave system as the most benign, Elkins posits that it was the most repressive—so much so that it literally brainwashed the normal, varied psyche of the enslaved African into a new, warped personality, one of childlike meekness, humility, optimism, happiness, and a readiness to laugh and joke. This character, whom Elkins calls Sambo, to the disgust of modern African Americans, is easily satisfied and full of emotion rather than reason. The personality change was caused by the shock and detachment of the previously free Africans through removal from their traditional milieu—their capture, march to the coast, sale and transport to the New World, resale and seasoning as slaves, and the need to internalize the standards of their new masters as their own to survive. The isolation and closed nature of the new system, particularly in the United States, caused the crushing of Africanisms to the degree that the African American became a new racial type.

Elkins finds that the same regression to childhood and all the rest also occurred among European Jews incarcerated in Adolph Hitler's World War II concentration camps, which he sees as comparable to the American slave system. He also sees three psychological theories that explain how this happens. One is a modified Freudian approach, in which the supposedly fixed patterns established in childhood are actually broken and reestablished by the shock of enslavement. Another is Henry Stack Sullivan's impersonal theory, which showed how immigrants became Americanized by adapting to the standards of those who held the keys to their personal security. Also playing a part is the application of role psychology, in which the role and the self become confused through a system of reward and punishment. Slavery in the United States was so pervasive as to kill all chance of rebellion, says Elkins. He points out that the rebel slave is a general type in Latin America, while in the United States the individual rebel is a noted exception. Hence U.S. slave revolts are known by those who led them—individuals like Gabriel, Denmark Vesey, and Nat Turner, who developed personalities outside the norm.

What if the Peculiar Institution was not as closed as the concentration camp, but more like a minimum-security prison? The constant terror of the camps was not present in slavery. Execution was not the goal. In such a system multiple personalities (even a false one to fool the white man, and another real one for life in the slave quarters away from white supervision) would develop as in any normal society. This is what many historians think actually happened under the slave regime of the American South. Kenneth Stampp joins other critics of Elkins to find at least four distinct slave personality types: the true Sambo, yielding and accommodating (but the wise master knew that at any moment Sambo might become a rebel); another labeled Banzo, a slave common in ruthlessly exploitive and expanding slave systems like that in Brazil (from whence the name) or the American Old Southwest (Arkansas, Louisiana, Texas, and some parts of Mississippi), who was overworked and fatigued to the point of not caring about life or punishment; a third called Jack, a hard working, efficient, and trustworthy servant who gloried in the life of the slave quarters as long as he was treated with respect, honor, and trust; and Nat, the true rebel, a conspirator as well as an individual troublemaker (runaway, thief, arsonist, saboteur) who was never reconciled to the system. Naturally these types could be male or female, and all types, as well as others not considered here, could feasibly be found on a single plantation.

In conclusion, it seems the slaves did not internalize Sambo, but played different roles in different communities. They acted as adults in the quarters regardless of how much they played the role of a child for their owner in the big house. They vied with each other to put one over on ol' Massa, even to the extent of cooperating with him to more easily fool him in the end, a process author Joel Chandler Harris immortalized better than anyone in the cornered Brer Rabbit's clever cry: "Please, doan throw me in that ol' briar patch!"

Dysaethesia Ethiopica *and* Drapetomania

About two decades ago, Bill Cosby, the embodiment of black success in the modern media industry, hosted a television special that examined the content of American language (literature), and especially pop entertainment (radio, TV, film), that contributed to what we call the black stereotype. Film clips of Step 'n' Fetchit, the most-employed black movie star of the 1930s who epitomized the dumb, fawning "cullud man" whites historically love so well, provided a centerpiece.

As Cosby's treatment showed, the issue of the slave system's effect on the psyche of present-day African Americans is one that is hotly debated by historians and participants. Some hold a racist theory that blacks possess innate racial characteristics that mitigate against protest. It's a comforting theory to a slaveholder, but one that the history of the ongoing civil rights movement pretty much discredits. Others, especially local commentators, often allow that slaves did resist their white masters, but not in their particular geographic area of study. Still others find that, during the brief time span they investigated, nothing occurred. Blacks, of course, had a concept of freedom that was rooted in the traditions of their African past and American present, a concept deeply presented in their religion, legends, and songs. No matter how many blacks were enslaved in the South, there were always enough free men and women of color to show that African Americans did not have to be chattels to live in the New World.

Even if black persons could not totally escape the demands of slavery, there were ways in which they could mitigate the system through passive and more active forms of resistance— a common enough occurrence to cause Southern whites to label their chattels, in the words of historian Kenneth Stampp, "a troublesome property." Whites classified all misdeeds as slave "crime" and took it as a matter of course that their black charges would at least shirk work and responsibility. The real problem was intent. Slaveholders never could agree whether the smart slaves or the stupid ones were the most exasperating—nor could they agree if the alleged stupidity was real or feigned.

More recent observers, however, point out that a suppressed people achieves self-respect by attacking its oppressors, whether this resistance is planned and obvious or subconscious and more subtle. In this light much of the slaves' inability to work as their white owners desired makes much sense. In his famous tour of the South, New York landscape architect Frederick Law Olmsted (the originator of Central Park) commented on how a long line of slaves hoeing a cotton field would stop work each time the overseer turned away, only to chop weeds with renewed vigor each time he faced their direction. Other blacks, chopping up cotton as well as weeds, seemed too dumb to catch on to the task at hand. This inability to learn extended to all tasks—a form of resistance that led whites to disparage all black work even to the present day and to ignore the obvious contribution of African Americans to the building of America's economic wealth.

Still other slaves faked illness, the most noted example being a Mississippi slave who convinced his master he was blind, only to emerge as the best farmer in the county after Emancipation—with perfect vision. Women used female complaints to beg off work, something no man regardless of his medical abilities seemed able to predict or cure. A good whipping was not the solution that first glance gave it. A field hand or house servant whipped for no good reason led to the whole gang slowing up its work and forgetting how the tasks were done. Mysterious work habits—mysterious to whites anyway—led the South's famous quack Negro doctor, Samuel Cartwright, to describe it as a disease, *dysaethesia ethiopica*, which was peculiar to Africans. Slaveholders preferred to call it rascality, but the result was the same—broken tools, lame livestock, the shuffle-walk, thieving, lying, and feigned sickness and stupidity.

Another protest against slave conditions also arose from

Dr. Cartwright's imaginative pen: *drapetomania*, a disease of the mind the first sign of which was unusual sullenness. He recommended removing the cause of discontent. Failing that, whipping the devil out of the slave's psyche would do wonders, the doctor opined. The secret was to catch *drapetomania* before it manifested itself in its most pernicious form, running away. Runaways were a constant plague in the plantation South (newspapers were full of such notices), and they were blamed on abolitionist propaganda or the activities of the underground railway and "conductors" like Sojourner Truth and Harriet Tubman. Although some ran away to escape to freedom, particularly in the Upper South along the Mason-Dixon Line and the Ohio River (estimates hover around the 60,000 figure for the period 1790–1860), running away in the Deep South was most often a form of negotiation, very much resembling a modern labor strike. After two or three weeks the recalcitrants would come back, the disliked condition would change, and usually some form of punishment was agreed upon to help Massa save a little face.

About Old Rough and Ready

With a long military career that drew him to locations all over North America, it is not particularly unusual that Zachary Taylor never voted until he was 62 years old. In 1848, as a recent hero of the Mexican War, Taylor was approached by Whig party leaders desiring a man of his reputation as their presidential candidate. They asked him if he was a Democrat or a Whig. Taylor replied that he did not know, never having given the matter much thought. When they offered him the possibility of the presidential nomination, Taylor declared himself a Whig on the spot. He easily secured the nomination at the Whig convention and won the White House shortly afterward.

Taylor died on a hot Fourth of July after ceremonies were held to lay the cornerstone of the Washington Monument. Returning to the White House, he consumed vast quantities of cold milk and fresh cherries. For decades his death was listed as *cholera morbus* (an acute gastroenteritis, with diarrhea, cramps, and vomiting), but in 1991 a Taylor scholar began to suspect that the president might have been done in by opponents who either saw his stand for free soil in the territories as traitorous to his slaveholding South (he owned plantations in Louisiana) or feared that his intransigent stand against the proposals that would become the Compromise of 1850 would lead to civil war. After acquiring the proper clearance, Taylor's body was exhumed and the remains tested for arsenic poisoning. Results: no foul play.

After Taylor died in office, Vice President Millard Fillmore found the White House both dirty and bare. The second floor Great Room was covered with a rug of woven straw grown heavy and stained with the spittle of Old Zach's regular tobacco chew. Who knows where the first lady chose to knock out the ash of her corncob pipe.

John Brown, Man on Fire: Raid and Song

By the time any 1940s farmboy in heavily Republican Kalamazoo County, Michigan, was six years old, he had already become familiar with the melodious refrain "John Brown's body lies amoldering in the grave . . . his truth goes marching on" (same tune as "The Battle Hymn of the Republic"). Like all Americans, Civil War participants and others, schoolchildren assume the song referred to the John Brown of Harper's Ferry Raid fame. In reality, the song was a jibe by the Twelfth Massachusetts Volunteer Infantry at their own Sergeant John Brown of Boston, a big burly man who had trouble fitting into his army-issue clothes and equipment. (One verse ran: "John Brown's knapsack is strapped to his back, It is filled with leaden bullets and moldy hardtack." Another line is more familiar: "They will hang Jeff Davis to a sour apple tree.") The sergeant, who was accidentally drowned as his regiment crossed Virginia's Rappahannock River in 1862, has become lost in the fog of history; the famous abolitionist John Brown, however, the "Man on Fire" in the words of one biographer, lives on, memorialized by the misinterpreted Civil War song and

popularized in the role stunningly and darkly played by actor
Raymond Massey in the 1940 film *Santa Fe Trail*, frequently
shown on modern movie channels.

Born in Connecticut in 1800 and raised in Ohio, the historical
abolitionist John Brown (as opposed to the sergeant) exhibited
the conduct of a man evangelically obsessed with breaking the
teeth of the wicked. For him the most evil men were Southern
slaveholders and those who carried out any conduct that supported or acquiesced in the continuing practice of enslavement
of fellow human beings, a belief that quite naturally brought
him to the center of the pre-Civil War struggle over slavery—
Bleeding Kansas.

In the territory of Kansas in 1856 there had occurred repeated intermittent violence and destruction between residents in contention over free or slave status for that territory's
admission to the Union. In apparent response a pro-slave
attack on the major free state stronghold (popularized in the
Northern abolitionist press as the Sack of Lawrence), John
Brown and his gang set out for Potawatomie Creek and murdered four men of Southern antecedents. Unknown to Brown,
these men had migrated from the South because they had
opposed slavery.

Three years later Brown attempted to seize the federal arsenal and munition works located at Harpers Ferry, Virginia, on
the Maryland line at the head of the Shenandoah Valley.
Although he captured the arsenal, the first casualty of the fray
was a local free Negro, Heyward Shepard—a mere bystander
shot by Brown's guerrillas. Brown and his 19 cohorts were
quickly surrounded by local militia. Soon U.S. Marines appeared, sent up from Washington by President James Buchanan.
Leading the marines were two army cavalry officers who were
home on leave in Virginia when the alarm sounded—Lt. Colonel Robert E. Lee and Lt. J. E. B. Stuart. The federal force
stormed Brown's position, killed ten men, and dispersed the
others, arresting Brown.

In October 1859 Brown was tried by Virginia courts and
convicted of committing treason against the state of Virginia
(not the United States), the only man so tried and convicted in
the nation's history. He was hanged at Charlestown on

2 December 1859, becoming a martyr to the antislavery cause. Oddly, a member of the watching crowd was John Wilkes Booth, future assassin of Abraham Lincoln. Today, near the lovely confluence of rivers that comfortably slide by the restored town of Harper's Ferry, one museum offers film and still slides of the whole episode, narrated by Ossie Davis and backed by the Howard University choir belting out "John Brown's Body" just as it must have been sung by Yankee soldiers over a hundred years ago.

A Mid-Century Bestseller

Out of the agitation against the Fugitive Slave Law of the Compromise of 1850, which so repelled the North, came Harriet Beecher Stowe's book, *Uncle Tom's Cabin*. It did something no politician could: it brought the issue into the heart of the ordinary citizen in a poignant, down-to-earth manner. Not bad for a woman who had never written a popular work before and who wrote about an institution she had seen for a few hours in Kentucky 17 years earlier. She had read Theodore Dwight Weld's *Slavery as It Is*, and she instinctively knew how to construct a gripping story. The interest raised by a short article appearing in *National Era* magazine involving Uncle Tom's death whetted public appetite and soon led to Stowe's book-sized manuscript.

Her real stroke of genius was to make Tom's owners well-meaning impoverished Southerners and the evil Simon Legree a Yankee by birth. She also knew enough to allay Northern fears of freed blacks by having hers go to Canada or colonize themselves back to Africa. It mattered not if her blacks bore little similarity to the mass of African Americans in bondage or that they thought and acted as New England whites; this was a political statement that effectively addressed political issues of the day—her real purpose. It hit the keystone of slavery, destroying the widespread notion so prevalent among whites North and South that African Americans were lesser beings, destined by their own innately inferior moral and mental insufficiencies to remain slightly above the brute in the order of things—legally, cattle that walked upright. Her plot was simple, it was gripping; the fact that it concerned slavery was unimportant to its success. It had an appeal in and of itself to readers who agonized over the trials, triumphs, crimes, kindnesses, and sufferings of its characters.

The impact of Stowe's volume cannot be slighted. It was translated into several foreign languages and rewritten into uncounted plays (she even did one herself) that gave Northerners an emotional bond based on a stereotype of the evils of slavery, if not an antislavery program. People here and in Europe read it aloud by the fireside. (After reading the powerful Russian language version, several Russian landowners freed their serfs.) It was even rewritten for Southern audiences, albeit slightly altered in emphasis (they loved the Yankee background of Legree, for example). In the South the book was criticized as being of incorrect dialect, with poorly drawn and grotesque characterizations and an overemphasis on slave maltreatment. Stowe answered these jibes the following year in a new book, *The Key to Uncle Tom*. A decade later in the midst of the Civil War, Harriet Beecher Stowe met President Abraham Lincoln. Smiling and extending both hands in warm greeting, he cut through all the pretense and stricture surrounding *Uncle Tom's Cabin*. Referring to the impact of Stowe's antislavery novel, Lincoln said, "So you're the little woman who wrote the book that made this great war." With a million copies sold in the United States and another million in Britain, *Uncle Tom's Cabin* was the first real worldwide bestseller in the modern sense of the word.

Pre-Civil War Anger—Bully Brooks and His Cane

On 19 May 1856 Republican Senator Charles Sumner of Massachusetts took the floor in the capitol building at Washington, D.C., and for two days he spoke out against what he characterized as "the Crime Against Kansas." An ardent abolitionist, Sumner was angered at attempts by so-called Border Ruffians, pro-slave men from Missouri, to bring the territory of Kansas into the Union as a slave state against what he saw as the will of its free-state people. Sumner had memorized the whole speech so as to be able to concentrate on the impact of its delivery.

What a delivery! This ascetic, scholarly Bostonian had a real talent for personal invective. He referred to Stephen Douglas's doctrine of popular sovereignty as a cover for popular slavery. He called the Kansas-Nebraska Act a swindle. He said the apologists for these atrocities had four faulty arguments based on tyranny, imbecility, absurdity, and infamy. The proposed solutions were nothing but more tyranny, more folly, more injustice, and possible civil war. He suggested that Kansas be made a free state immediately, a solution he labeled a remedy of justice and peace.

As he spoke, Sumner castigated the backers of the Kansas-Nebraska Act by name. Most particularly he called Senator Andrew Pickens Butler of South Carolina the Don Quixote of slavery who "has chosen a mistress to whom he has made his vows, and who, though ugly to others, is always lovely to him; though polluted in the sight of the world, is chaste in his sight . . . the harlot, Slavery." Senator Douglas and others were shocked at Sumner's venomous attacks. Already characterized by Sumner as "the squire of slavery, its very Sancho Panza, ready to do all its humiliating offices," Douglas muttered prophetically to any who would hear, "That damn fool will get himself killed by some other damn fool."

That "damn fool" turned out to be Congressman Preston S. Brooks of South Carolina, Butler's cousin who heard Sumner's invective from the Senate gallery. Considered a moderate by Northern standards, Brooks was believed to be very national by Southern standards, too ready to compromise. He was also a believer in a strict code of chivalry, and since Senator Butler happened to be absent, Brooks took it upon himself to defend his family's insulted honor. No true gentleman would go to court over such a personal matter, and to challenge Sumner to a duel would elevate the Massachusetts senator to Brooks's high social level. So he decided to chastise Sumner as a social inferior.

Brooks took a gutta percha walking stick—an inch in diameter at its big end, hollow cored, and weighing $11^{1}/_{2}$ ounces—and confronted Sumner sitting at his desk on 21 May. There were ladies present, so Brooks waited several minutes until they left. Then he came up and spoke. "Mr. Sumner, I have read your speech twice over carefully. It is a libel on South Carolina, and Mr. Butler, who is a relative of mine." Sumner sought to rise, but Brooks caned him over the head. He gave Sumner at least 30 stripes, as he called them, breaking his cane on the third one but continuing until he was exhausted, and Sumner lay in a pool of blood on the floor, his fixed desk ripped off the floor in his struggle. No one intervened, while several onlookers shouted encouragement: "Hit him again." Brooks was arrested, posted bond, and ultimately paid a $300 fine for assault, but he beat off an attempt to kick him out of the House of Representatives. He resigned his seat, instead. In the furor that followed, canes like the one Brooks used sold out all over the South, some carved with "Hit him again," or "Use Knock Down Arguments." Brooks was the hero of the hour. Everyone wanted a splinter of the true cane. His constituents bought him a new cane with a gold head, and reelected him overwhelmingly.

Meanwhile, Sumner spent three years recovering from what his biographer David Donald described as "only flesh wounds," which healed rapidly. Donald theorizes that, since Sumner had no concussion, he suffered a posttraumatic syndrome, a pyschogenic condition that manifested itself only when he tried to return to his public duties. His constituents, however, cared little for fancy analyses. They reelected "Bleeding" Sumner to his Senate seat. Throughout the North, he too became a symbol. Better yet was "the vacant chair of Sumner," which was eulogized in poem as a tribute to Southern violence. Sumner finally beat his psychic problems and returned to the Senate on 4 June 1860, where, at precisely noon, he began a four-hour speech on the barbarism of slavery. This time, he had nothing to fear from Bully Brooks. The South Carolinian had died two years earlier from an agonizing disease. As Sumner said to a friend, "The Almighty has settled this better than you or I could have done."

Dred Scott and the Extraterritoriality of Slavery

When South Carolina seceded in 1860, it was pushing to logical extreme the constitutional doctrine known as state rights or state sovereignty—a desire to minimize the power of the federal government *vis à vis* the states. What most historians fail to perceive is that this is not the same doctrine that the South had pursued between 1848 and 1860. As pointed out by Arthur Bestor in his essay on state sovereignty and slavery, secession was the alternative to, not the goal of, the Southern constitutional theory prior to the Civil War. The South seceded only when its program was threatened by the election of Abraham Lincoln to the presidency.

The Southern program was succinctly presented in John C. Calhoun's 1849 Southern Address, written by him in consultation with a Committee of Fifteen delegates, one from each slave state, and chaired by Alexander Stephens of Georgia (future vice president of the Confederate States of America). The document was in response to the proposal that slavery be eliminated from the District of Columbia with the approval of the white population there, a proposal based on the notion that slavery was incompatible with American ideals.

The real issue, however, was not the abolition of slavery. Indeed no political party, not even the nascent Republicans, sought to eliminate slavery from the Southern states. What Calhoun and the others came up with was a constitutional program that concerned the real issue of the 1850s and would lead to the Civil War. It involved the issue of slavery in the territories, of which the District of Columbia was one. Both sides realized that to exclude slavery from the territories would be its eventual death knell.

The question of slavery in the territories revolved around the fugitive clause (Art. IV, Sec. 2) of the Constitution. It states that no person "held to service or labor" in one state can, by escaping to another state or territory, be freed by the laws of that state or territory. This is the essential constitutional guarantee of the South's right to slaves, but it does more than that—

it gives the South an extraterritorial right in its slaves; that is, the law of slavery extends beyond the state of origin to encompass all of the states and territories, even those of free soil. Unless freed by his owner under Georgia law, a slave in Georgia, for example, is a slave in New York, Illinois, or the territory of Nebraska, even if they do not have slavery as an institution. Congress passed a Fugitive Slave Law in 1793 to enforce this concept, permitting slave catchers to arrest suspected Negroes and take them before a variety of state or federal officials, who would rule on their slave or free status.

At first no one seemed to care, but as the question of slave and free states grew in intensity, especially after the Missouri Compromise of 1820, the free states passed Personal Liberty laws, openly defying the Fugitive Slave Act. These laws gave state aid to suspected runaways, prohibited the use of local jails by slave catchers, provided jury trials for accused blacks, and often supplied a state-paid attorney. In 1842 the United States Supreme Court ruled that no state official could interfere with the federal right to enforce the Fugitive Slave Act (*Prigg v. Pennsylvania*). Northern states then simply proceeded to deny all assistance to federal fugitive agents, following the law to the letter.

The Compromise of 1850 included a new fugitive act that got around the Northern states' scrupulous ignoring of the fugitive problem. It created a series of special federal justice courts with sole jurisdiction in the fugitive question. The only evidence to be considered was the deposition of the Southern claimant. Black testimony was not allowed. If the Negro was found to be an escaped fugitive, the judge received twice the sum than if he ruled him free. No state writ of habeas corpus was valid in these cases. There was no appeal process; the judge's decision was final. The whole process was approved by the U.S. Supreme Court in 1859, when Chief Justice Roger B. Taney of Maryland ruled that states had lost their absolute sovereignty when they joined the Union and no longer had the right to interpose state authority to prevent the enforcement of any federal law (*Ableman v. Booth*). Ironically this same pro-Southern decision was used a hundred years later to negate Arkansas's attempt to interpose its authority to prevent school segregation at Little Rock (*Cooper v. Aaron*, 1957).

Southerners wanted more, however. They wanted the guarantee in slavery to apply to newly established western territories so they too could exploit the rich trans-Mississippi West. This problem had been solved for the Louisiana Purchase in the Missouri Compromise, but the addition of new territories after the Mexican War brought it up anew. Northerners proposed that slavery be excluded from all of the Mexican cession (Wilmot Proviso). The South, however, had fought the war with the most enthusiasm. This time, as Calhoun wrote in his Southern Address, the South would accept no division line of exclusion. The territories were to be opened for the exploitation of all citizens, slaveholders or not. They based their claim on the fugitive clause once again.

According to the Southern position, the Constitution recognized only the District of Columbia, federal forts, and dockyards as federally administered territories. It said nothing about Western lands. This meant the question of slavery in the territories came under the Tenth Amendment, a still-ignored provision of the Bill of Rights that states that all powers not specifically granted the federal government are reserved to the states and the people. It was a constitutionally guaranteed state right.

Since the Western lands were not yet sovereign (that came only with statehood), they themselves could not exercise the essential police power that gave slavery its authority. It had to be done for them. It made common sense that the few Western territories could not each exercise their extraterritorial police power. Accordingly, they allowed the federal government to administer police power on their behalf as agent or trustee for their extraterritorial rights, not as a sovereign policymaker. The only extraterritorial right recognized in the constitution, however, adhered to slavery alone; hence the federal government by implication had to protect slavery in the Western lands as well as in the states. This meant that free states had no extraterritorial rights to be protected, but that was life. Slavery had to be protected until the territory in question became sovereign—that is, until it called a constitutional convention and applied for statehood. Then as a sovereign power in its own right it could abolish slavery within its own boundaries.

Once this theory is understood and applied, the policies of the 1850s make sense. This was why squatter sovereignty and its Democrat supporter, Lewis Cass, were defeated in 1848. Cass maintained incorrectly, said Southerners, that a territorial legislature could rule on slavery. A territorial legislature, however, had no sovereignty, and a territory could not act until Congress passed an enabling act, a state convention was called, and statehood was proposed. This was why the Compromise of 1850 was passed and Franklin Pierce was elected president in 1852. The Democrats finally admitted to the Southern theory and backed popular sovereignty, regaining Southern votes. The essential difference between squatter sovereignty and popular sovereignty was not in the name, as most historians assert. Rather, it was in which stage of territorial government the decision on slavery would be made according to the Land Ordinance of 1787—the legislature or the convention; the administering federal trustee or the sovereign people.

The recognition of the South's extraterritorial right in slaves was why the Missouri Compromise was repealed by the Kansas-Nebraska Act and all territories opened to slavery in 1854. This led to the Kansas-Missouri border wars and "Ossawatomie" John Brown, who committed the brutal murders of several Southern farmers (who, oddly, were not slave owners, but fled the South to escape slavery's influences) in Ossawatomie, Kansas. It was why the U. S. Supreme Court ruled in 1857 that Dred Scott was still a slave no matter where his residence and that the Missouri Compromise was unconstitutional from its inception (Dred Scott v. Sandford). It was why challenger Abraham Lincoln forced Senator Stephen A. Douglas, Democrat party leader and backer of popular sovereignty, to deny his own scheme by proposing the Freeport question during the Lincoln-Douglas debates in the 1858 Illinois senatorial race. (Question: Can slavery be prevented in any territory? Answer: Yes, merely by doing nothing to support it in local law.) It secured Lincoln his party's nomination and victory in 1860, which threatened the whole house of cards. It was Lincoln as president who would have to enforce the extraterritoriality of slavery. Douglas, however, had already admitted no one really had to, which cost him the crucial Southern support he needed to defeat Lincoln in the 1860 election. As chief executive, Lincoln would get to appoint new Supreme Court justices. Conveniently, Chief Justice Taney, the architect of the Dred Scott decision, was obligingly nearing death, and several of his colleagues—all state sovereignty men—were near retirement.

So by 1860, Calhoun's scheme for Union based on his unique interpretation of the Constitution had failed in the eyes of the South. This was especially true when President-elect Lincoln refused to compromise any part of the Republican platform relating to opposing slavery in the Western territories. By moving with alacrity, the Southern fire-eaters went straight to secession, overwhelming the moderate voices that asked that Lincoln be allowed to make a false move first. The radicals offered decision, the cooperationists merely offered more of the same agony that had faced the nation since its beginning. The result was civil war.

CHAPTER V

The Civil War

Some Abe Lincoln Facts

Quite unknown until after his death, the bodyguard assigned to be by Abraham Lincoln's side at Ford's Theatre the night of the assassination had left his post to view the play, *Our American Cousin*, from behind the better seats in the front balcony. His supervisor did not report the fact at the time.

The diverse railway route that carried the president's remains paused and displayed the body of the fallen warrior for the Union in no less than 14 important cities. The parade that presented the casket to the train at the Capitol had included 200 recently freed blacks. Along the route, telegraph alerts brought forth nighttime bonfires from a saddened populace.

Most students learn that Lincoln was raised in circumstances close to poverty, was self taught, and read the law with a local attorney. He did not die a poor man, however. Most of his estate came from a burgeoning Illinois law practice. Even today with a $200,000 a year salary, a president cannot save much (nor is he really expected to) in expensive Washington, D.C. Lincoln's salary was $25,000 annually, the same amount that had been paid to all presidents from George Washington's time, yet he was a man of such simple and frugal habits that when he died he left uncashed salary checks amounting to nearly $8,000 and just over $17,000 on deposit at home in his Springfield bank. His total estate was valued, some three years after his death, at almost $111,000 (a figure equivalent to approximately $600,000 today).

A Confederate View of Lincoln

Because of the timing and nature of his violent death, Abraham Lincoln, leader of the victorious Northern crusade against secession, was put beyond the pale of ordinary inquiry and criticism, much like Franklin D. Roosevelt and John F. Kennedy in more modern times. The general consensus of American historians has been that our twentieth-century successes owe their continuation to the shedding of sacred blood from the Illinois rail-splitter, the dying god at Ford's Theater who, as he died to make men free, perished that we might have a new birth and a Second American Revolution. Even now over 125 years later, it is hard to challenge Lincoln's place in American history—to subject him to the criticism that puts him not apart from but a direct cause of America's present democratic (i.e., the theory, not the political party) confusion and distance from the republicanism (same warning) of the Founding Fathers.

It is quite possible, should this examination of Lincoln's career take place, that America's younger generation will be surprised to find that he will emerge not as the saving hero of the American political system but as its Cromwellian destroyer. To make such a reexamination, it is necessary to journey with noted Lincoln critic, the late Professor M. E. Bradford of the University of Dallas, through a Confederate interpretation of Abraham Lincoln's place in American history. Bradford finds his criticisms of Lincoln "sufficient to impeach the most famous and respected of public men." Magazine editor Thomas Fleming, another critic, characterizes Lincoln as "our Julius Caesar, our Cromwell," but nonetheless a man of greatness.

Bradford makes six basic criticisms of Lincoln's historical reputation:

1. Lincoln was dishonest in meddling with the nation's future obligations to the African American, slave or free. Indeed his political success came from an excellent ability to appear anti-Southern, without at the same time seeming significantly pro-African American or impious about the beginnings of the

Republic. Hence he could unite elements in the North that were ordinarily at loggerheads. He was willing to grant African Americans technical freedom without including any further reduction in the traditional racism of the North. It was only accidental that Republican leaders expanded this minimum grant of freedom with voting rights that applied to the South alone, and then so long as the blacks voted reliably Republican.

2. The corruptions of the Republican Era that mar the history of Reconstruction and the Gilded Age began with the Lincoln administration and were justified as necessary wartime measures. Lincoln reinstituted the economic policies that Alexander Hamilton and Henry Clay had failed to sustain against Southern and Western opposition led by the Jacksonians—policies supporting national banks, tariffs, internal improvements, homesteading, bounties for railroads that led to the Crédit Mobilier scandal, and heavy taxes, including the first income tax. The result was that for the first time in United States history creditors had the upper hand over debtors, and the developed East could exploit the developing West and defeated South.

3. Lincoln expanded the powers of the presidency in such a manner as to alter the basis of the Union. Indeed, historian Conrad Dietz compares Lincoln's actions to the Committee of Public Safety during the French Revolution—rationalizing all to preserve the revolution, or in Lincoln's case, the war effort. All that was lacking under Lincoln were mass executions. Unlike an external war, the internal Civil War became a machine that transformed the Union. Lincoln was our first imperial president, as he summoned the militia, expanded the U.S. Army, decreed an illegal blockade, defied the Supreme Court, suspended the writ of habeas corpus and created a Yankee Gulag called the American Bastille by his critics, transferred millions of dollars from authorized accounts to his pet projects, and pledged the nation's honor and credit to others—all without the constitutionally necessary participation of Congress, which he refused to call into emergency session. His actions were defined by the assertion that he would violate nine-tenths of the Constitution to preserve one-tenth. He did just that.

4. Lincoln led the North in such a manner as to put the domestic priorities of his political machine ahead of the lives and well-being of his soldiers in the field. No wonder we have wonderful propagandistic pictures of this great melancholy man leading

the nation to war. He had reasons for his guilty conscience. He fought and fought until he could find a Republican hero in a field general. The result was the firing of Democrats like G. B. McClellan, D. C. Buell, and F. J. Porter and the elevation of mere political hacks to army command, men like N. P. Banks, B. F. Butler, J. C. Frémont, and J. A. McClernand. The same held true of his cabinet, especially the original one, in which Simon Cameron stole the Union blind, a process Lincoln justified as necessary to save the Union. Even one of his hacks, H. W. Halleck, admitted such command decisions were "little better than murder."

5. He compromised the integrity of his office to further prosecute the war. Each time peace was in the offing, Lincoln upped the ante or stalled so as to make compromise impossible. Peace could come only on his terms, reasonable compromise take the hindmost. Lincoln's search for an expedient peace cost the nation over 100,000 lives. Worse, the war was his from the start, a responsibility Lincoln sought to transfer to Jefferson Davis by arranging to have the South fire the first shot. This occurred after several reasonable suggestions for compromise by politicians of both sides, attempts that failed due to Lincoln's refusal to consider them. These compromises included a willingness to pay for Ft. Sumter and other federal installations in the South (which Lincoln kept secret) and an offer to keep the Mississippi River open to Midwest commerce.

6. Lincoln altered the language of American political discourse so it was next to impossible to reverse the ill effects of trends set in motion by his executive fiat. He put it all in the rhetoric of Scripture (which was confirmed by his own assassination), making every good cause then and since a reason to increase the scope of government. One is not allowed to look behind the words of so august a presence as Abraham Lincoln. All that counts is the goal; the means to achieve that goal have become irrelevant.

Needless to say, viewpoints such as Bradford's and Fleming's have come under much attack from all sides. Bradford retorts that the myth his critics embody, the notion that there can be a second founding of the nation through the Civil War, is itself a heresy against the prescript of the original American Revolution of 1776. The Second American Revolution, however, is a powerful myth whose hero-martyr-messiah is Abraham Lincoln; all who question it are treated as if they were acting outside the American mainstream, even if their questioning is in the name of an older American orthodoxy—the original understanding of the Founding Fathers. Fleming concurs, preferring Lincoln's obviously corrupt opponent, Stephen A. Douglas, to "the not entirely incorruptible" Lincoln, and then posits the final question for Lincoln at the bar of history: not Was it worth it? but rather, Is it true that the political struggles of the 1850s were over right and wrong rather than sectional competition, tariff rates, and party politics?

Recently a different tack on Lincoln has been taken by distinguished Civil War scholar Kenneth Stampp. A historian more in the mainstream of historical interpretation than Bradford or Fleming, Stampp notes that Lincoln, as well as most Americans, had a blind spot in his political thinking that revolved around the notion of national self-determination. We support it when it applies to other countries, but deny its efficacy as a domestic ideal. Hence it was acceptable for a president of the United States, Woodrow Wilson, to propose the Fourteen Points in 1918, advocating nationalism among the numerous minority groups of the former German and Austrian empires, but it was anathema to suggest such a proposal might have domestic applications at home, as when the Black Muslim leader, Reverend Louis Farrakhan, called for a separate nation for African Americans in the Deep South. As Lincoln's war demonstrated 130 years ago, such notions spelled doom for the Confederacy from its day of creation, even if, as pointed out by historian Eugene Genovese, the concept of the Southern nation was based on the same principles of revolution that separated us from Great Britain.

A Hymn for Americans and Winston Churchill—and Just About Everyone Else

No historian has offered conclusive proof as to the original composition and early evolution of the melodic and moving

tune that serves as the vehicle for the "Battle Hymn of the
Republic." Bruce Catton, in the first volume of his trilogy, *The
Army of the Potomac: Mr. Lincoln's Army*, probably comes as
close to the truth as humanly possible. Originally an 1850s
Southern campground revival tune, "Say Brothers Will We
Meet You Over on the Other Shore?," written by an unknown,
but obviously very pious Charleston hymnographer, it was
picked up before the Civil War by the very impious U.S. 2nd
Infantry on one of its rotations into Southern coastal installations. Stationed in Boston's Fort Warren in 1861, the 2nd
Regulars taught the snappy marching tune to a green volunteer regiment, the 12th Massachusetts. The version they taught
the volunteers had words more appropriate to the Union's new
wartime mission: "John Brown's body lies amouldering in the
grave . . . and we go marching on." The 12th Massachusetts
learned the tune well, liked it, and brought it to the Army of the
Potomac where other regiments picked it up. The tune became
more or less universal.

Although the original songwriter remains anonymous, the
occasion under which the lyrics for "John Brown's Body" were
changed to the classic "Battle Hymn of the Republic" are better
documented. A Massachusetts woman, Julia Ward Howe, had
accompanied her husband to Washington, D.C., in November
1861, and with a sizable party watched some army maneuvers
south of the Potomac. The Reverend James Clarke, a member of
the group, aware of Mrs. Howe's poetic talents, and, like her,
hearing the marching men singing "John Brown's Body," suggested she write new words for the tune. She went to bed
pondering the idea, awakened at dawn, and in short order
wrote six stanzas, soon published in the *Atlantic Monthly*. She
received four dollars for her work.

Because its words combined the urgency of both patriotic
and religious ideals, offered a moving ode to freedom at a time
of national crisis, and harmoniously enjoined the evangelical
activism of that generation, the song ultimately came to rank in
popularity and preference with such counterparts as "My
Country, 'tis of Thee" and "America, the Beautiful." It has been
employed by religious crusaders from Billy Sunday to Billy
Graham, by suffragettes, prohibitionists, and a variety of other

reform movements, and of course in numerous political cam-paigns. As they flew toward combat drop zones in World War II, American paratroopers sang their own rendition, "Glory, glory, what a helluva way to die." Another special version, "Glory, Glory, Segregation," was used tongue-in-cheek by segregationists in the South in the 1960s:

> Mine eyes have seen the comin' of the NAACP
> They are mixin' whites and niggers where only whites
>   should be
> God bless Jefferson Davis and also General Lee
> The South will rise again.
> *Refrain:*
> Glory, glory, segregation
> Go to hell with integration
> Glory, glory, segregation
> The South will rise again.

Attesting to the eternal popularity of Mrs. Howe's tradi-tional version, the Mormon Tabernacle Choir's recording in 1959 sold 200,000 copies within a few weeks. A 1963 memorial service in London's Westminster Abbey, occasioned by the assassination of President John F. Kennedy, employed the aid of a large organ and choir to sing the "Hymn." In January 1965 it was sung in London's St. Paul's Cathedral at the funeral service of Sir Winston Churchill, in accordance with his ex-pressed wishes. Not surprisingly, Churchill was also one of only two foreigners in all modern history to be awarded hon-orary United States citizenship by Congress, the other being Raoul Wallenberg, the Swedish diplomat who saved nearly 400,000 Hungarian Jews from transportation and execution in the waning days of World War II, only to disappear into Russian captivity and oblivion.

Was Dan Sickles Temporarily Insane or as Crazy as a Fox?

Daniel Sickles was an ambitious man. He sought no less than the U.S. presidency, but he lived too hard, drank too much, loved too many, killed too publicly, and associated himself too openly with the graft and corruption that marked the New York City Democratic political society known as Tammany Hall. A lawyer and legislator, Sickles fancied himself a diplomat and served in the mid-1850s at the American legation in London, where he was implicated in the Ostend Manifesto mess. A states' rights Democrat, he was elected to the state senate and the United States Congress. Everything was looking good for his inflated career until he killed Philip Barton Key, son of Francis Scott Key of "Star Spangled Banner" fame.

As Sickles well knew, Key was a dabbler in Washington society and politics, captain of a militia company, dashing, handsome, and the family attorney. He became fast friends with Sickles's wife, a relationship that soon grew quite intimate. Sickles found out and shot Key dead on a public street, turning himself and his revolver over to Attorney General Jeremiah Black. His trial was the event of 1859, a real circus that rivaled anything a modern political family might experience today. His defense was provided by Edwin McMasters Stanton, later Abraham Lincoln's able, plotting secretary of war. The basis of defense was the plea of temporary insanity, never before used in an American trial, that the knowledge of his wife's assignations with Key drove him so mad that he had no responsibility for his actions. Of course, the prosecution pointed out that Sickles did no less himself, his affairs being legion and well known. However, a rousing speech by Stanton in pure gaudy Victorian style carried the day.

So far, so good. The whole country could identify with Sickles's alleged grief. Then he did the unthinkable—he took his wife back, thus condoning her actions in the eyes of the nation. He forgave her, and the country went wild. No one would associate with the couple. Mrs. Sickles would die eight years later in loneliness, but Dan Sickles went on to bigger and better things, hoping to restore his public reputation and appeal on the battlefields of the Civil War. Raising the Excelsior Brigade of five regiments, he led them, a division, and a corps, losing his leg to a Confederate cannonball on the second day at Gettysburg. The leg was pickled and kept on permanent display at the National Observatory in Washington.

Disabled from fighting, Sickles became a Republican, serving as military commander of the Carolinas and then as Minister to Spain, where evidence indicates he had a fling with Queen Isabella II, one leg evidently not being much of a problem in that task. He later returned to New York, where he became head of the Monuments Commission until he was fired for corruption. He was instrumental in beginning the Gettysburg National Military Park shortly before he died in 1914. Although Sickles probably never was temporarily insane, he certainly was crazy as a fox.

Shocking Statistics—Shiloh 1862

The Battle of Shiloh offers a fast statistical suggestion as to why the Civil War (the bloodiest war between the fall of the Napoleonic Empire at Waterloo in 1815 and the opening of the Guns of August at the Battle of the Frontiers in 1914) was particularly nasty when fought between fellow Americans from 1861 to 1865.

After his initial victories in the Western theater at Ft. Henry and Ft. Donelson in the spring of 1862, Major General U. S. Grant moved his army southward down the Tennessee River toward the Confederate base at Corinth, Mississippi. Because of the ease of moving men, equipment, and supplies by riverboat (from June 1862 to June 1863, for example, the army moved 338,000,000 pounds of military stores by river as opposed to 153,000,000 by rail), Grant used 153 transports to move as far down the Tennessee as he could to Pittsburg Landing near the Mississippi line, where he spread his army camp near Shiloh Church. Here on 6–7 April 1862, the first real battle of the Civil War was fought, as Confederates under Generals A. S. Johnston and P. G. T. Beauregard slammed into Grant's men in a surprise attack that cost the Rebels 10,699 lives (including that of General Johnston) and the Yankees 13,573 in killed, wounded, and missing (mostly captured).

Both North and South were stunned at the fury and destruction of the battle. This was no Manassas or Wilson's Creek, or even a Ft. Henry or Ft. Donelson, where there had been casualties (or rather, controlled losses). This was an organized massacre that devolved into pure mayhem. Even the soldiers were shocked. Grant numbly let weeks pass before revealing the true magnitude of the cost of victory at Shiloh. There were 8,000 wounded to be dealt with first, and no hospitals were available above the rudimentary regimental level. The day after the fight, nine-tenths of the wounded still lay where they fell, many having been there two days already. Five days later newfound casualties were still arriving. Medical theory of the day frowned on large hospitals, fearing raging epidemics. Even so, Dr. B. J. D. Irwin of Major General Don Carlos Buell's staff collected every tent he could find and constructed a gigantic medical complex under one roof, with each patient segregated by wound to assist in treatment. Because walls were nonexistent, air circulated freely and prevented the many deaths so common in shut-up hospital buildings of the time. The areas outside the tent, however, were appalling. Bloody stumps of arms and legs were piled on high, pools of blood coagulated in large ponds, and the dead lay in piles awaiting burial. The horrible stench of death and the pitiful cries of the wounded were on every breeze.

The casualty lists were so long that it seemed every home had to lose a loved one. The romance of war so evident on both sides in 1861 was gone forever. Gone too was another factor: It would be hard to compromise with an enemy who had inflicted such loss. The war took a desperate all-or-nothing tinge that was slated to grow as the battles, cost, and years passed. Even worse was the failure of either side to gain from the carnage. Major General Henry W. Halleck was placed in command of Grant's, Buell's and Major General John Pope's combined armies. They advanced on Corinth at the painfully slow pace of five miles a day, each night fortifying their camp against another Shiloh surprise. None came. The outnumbered Confederates withdrew deeper into Mississippi and waited until the Union armies broke up to occupy the vast areas of Tennessee and Mississippi. In the end, the whole affair degenerated into a mess that gained very little but the human cost of battle.

Abraham Lincoln, however, recognized that such costs had to be borne if the nation was to be made whole again. When news reached Washington of the drunkenness that commonly inflicted officers and soldiers of both armies and worsened their efficiency in the field (which particularly tarred Grant's reputation early in the war), Lincoln is reputed to have parried them by saying of Grant in particular, "I can't spare this man—he fights!"

A Brothers' War

How might we describe a brothers' war? Is it the embattled death of 2,000 French citizens in June of 1848, crushed at their barricades by the regular army? Is it the smashing of Chartist protesters at St. George's Field in 1830s England, or, closer to home, the use of the state militia to suppress the rebels in the 1840s Dorr War over constitutional government in Rhode Island? Whether or not these are considered brothers' wars, there is no doubt about the 1861–1865 American Civil War, which saw the most devastating slaughter of the nineteenth century and divided families and society in a most brutal fashion.

The spring of 1861 was a fateful moment of decision for Americans, and the man who ultimately led the military forces of the Confederate States of America shouldered a burden that typified that time. Robert Edward Lee was the son of revolutionary war hero, Lighthorse Harry Lee. He was married to a descendant of Martha Washington and was a veteran of 30 years' service in the United States Army. His wife owned and Lee supervised an estate called Arlington, which was located across the Potomac, facing Washington, D.C. (It was seized in 1862 by the federal government and turned into a Union cemetery, eventually becoming the National Cemetery.) In 1861 the army called upon Lee to assume command of federal troops to suppress the rebellious Southern states. Lee's home state of Virginia had conspicuously seceded and was housing the Confederate capital at Richmond. After an agonizing period of contemplation (during which he first felt out Confederate prospects before resigning his U.S. Army commission—a move that has led a recent historian to charge him with treason),

Lee went South to stand with his beloved Virginia. His emergence as the preeminent Southern general and hero proved the value the federal government had placed in his abilities at the war's outset.

As in all civil conflicts, the case of Robert E. Lee became magnified and duplicated by the hundreds across the dividing nation. Others not only separated from a social family as did Lee, but from their actual kin, making the Civil War truly a brothers' war. Historian George B. Tindall offers the following evidence: At Hilton Head, South Carolina, Percival Drayton commanded a federal gunboat while his brother Tom led the Confederate land forces. Franklin Buchanan commanded the Confederate ironclad *Virginia* and sunk the U.S.S. *Congress*, which had his brother on board. John J. Crittenden of Kentucky had a son in each army. J. E. B. Stuart's Confederate cavalry was opposed by federal horsemen led by his father-in-law, Philip St. George Cooke. Lincoln's attorney general had a son in the Confederate army, while the president's own wife had a brother, three half-brothers, and three brothers-in-law wearing Rebel gray.

The contest marked the beginning of modern warfare by developing telegraphic communications, aerial reconnaissance (by balloon), railroad transport, breech-loading artillery, breech-loading and repeating rifles, machine guns (Gatling guns), ironclad ships with revolving turrets, land and sea mines (called torpedoes then), trench warfare with accompanying entanglements, and total mobilization of the military and civilian population through conscription. Thus it requires little imagination to visualize the number of close friends and relatives who eventually faced each other in a conflict of such broad scope.

Juleps for the Few, Pellagra for the Crew

At the end of the nineteenth century, with the failure of Southern agriculture and the Populist movement, white farmers of the South and their families increasingly found jobs working in the coal mines, steel mills, and cotton factories that dotted the landscape. In company-owned towns, made famous in Tennessee Ernie Ford's best-selling song "Sixteen Tons" (referring to the daily task of one coal miner), their diet was limited to cornmeal, molasses, greasy pork, and coffee—much as had been the diet of slaves and Civil War soldiers. The result was an unbelievable insufficiency of vitamins and minerals essential to good health, weakness in physical strength, and the rise of diseases like hookworm, pellagra, and various other intestinal parasites. Rich mill and factory owners ate much better, of course, which led to the cynical Southern saying that life promised juleps for the few and pellagra for the crew.

By the mid-twentieth century, Southern living conditions had improved. Lloyd Lewis, a newspaperman-turned-historian who had just finished a biography of Union general William T. Sherman and was embarking on a similar, monumental study of U. S. Grant, got to thinking about the diet of the Southern soldiers and wondered if it had wider implications beyond turn-of-the-century economic conditions. Although Lewis died before he could finish the Grant study (it would be completed by Bruce Catton), he wrote regular letters to his editor that were collected and published for the benefit of other scholars.

Lewis found that Grant wondered how the Rebels would often win the first day's battle and then almost inexplicably seem to falter. This occurred at Gettysburg, Shiloh, Perryville, Corinth, Stone's River, Antietam—the names go on and on. He also observed how Rebel soldiers often went berserk when they captured Union camps and warehouses, looting the stores for the myriad of foodstuffs that Yankee quartermasters specialized in providing their troops. Lewis theorized that Southern ranks were undernourished even when supplied by their own commissariat, so much so that it affected their performance on the battlefield. Perhaps their defeats occurred because they tired quicker than the better-fed Union boys. The longer the campaign, the more likely a Union victory, especially as the war lengthened. "I wonder how much of it," mulled Lewis, "was pure physical weariness born of the lack of consistent food, imposed upon physiques not nurtured properly from infancy. They weren't lazy in battle, but they were called lazy in succeeding generations as visitors described them in their upland or swamp houses."

Perhaps one could carry Lewis' analogy a bit further and apply it to the black population wearied by generations of servitude to others. If the common white ate as Lewis describes, and it seems likely they did, then how much less nutrition was received by the average slave before secession or contract field hand after the surrender? Historians have pointed out the inadequacies of the slave diet for years. Could this be one of the many physical and psychological factors explaining why African Americans were described by whites as lazy? As demonstrated by their white Confederate counterparts, drive and desire can be mitigated greatly by a lack of stamina brought on by a lifetime of malnourishment.

The Battle of the Crater: Disaster in 1864

By the end July 1864, the Federal armies commanded by Lt. Gen. U. S. Grant had fought their way south from the vicinity of Fredericksburg, Virginia, to Petersburg outside of Richmond. This cost 100,000 casualties, almost exactly the number of men he began with two months earlier in May. At every step—the Wilderness, Spottsylvania, North Anna River crossings, Cold Harbor, and the gates to Petersburg—the Confederate Army of Northern Virginia led by General Robert E. Lee had thwarted the way. Grant's troops were worn out. Veteran officers and men who knew the ways of war were dead, wounded, or captured. The new Union soldiers were mostly fresh replacements with little experience. As the first assault on the Petersburg trenches had demonstrated, Grant's force was too weary and untrained to maneuver aggressively enough to defeat Lee's men, who shifted reinforcements to key points to meet each new Federal attack.

One of Grant's units was the Ninth Army Corps, commanded by General A. E. Burnside, the former Union commander at the 1862 Battle of Fredericksburg. His men were former sailors and miners from the New England and Middle

Atlantic states. They were hated by the rest of Grant's men, who unfairly blamed them for prior lost battles. By a quirk of fate, however, they occupied the point nearest the Confederate lines. As they looked at the Confederate works they had been unable to carry by assault, one of the regimental commanders got a bright idea—why not go under the Rebel lines, not over them? His regiment was from a Pennsylvania coal-mining region, and with the approval of Grant's staff, they began to tunnel under the Confederate trenches. The Rebels heard them digging, but counter efforts failed to find the Yankee miners. By late July, the Yankees had dug a shaft under the Confederate position in the shape of a tee, and packed it with four tons of explosives.

The big question was about who would lead the assault. Burnside's command had four divisions. The first three were worn out and undermanned from constant campaigning, but the fourth division—the first division-sized force of United States Colored Infantry committed to the Civil War battlefields—was fresh, fully staffed, and eager to do the job. Before then the black soldiers had been used only as laborers, and they wanted to prove their mettle in combat. Burnside agreed. He saw one big advantage to their use. As the blacks had not fought before, they were not seasoned fighters like his white soldiers and they would charge straight ahead over all obstacles. White solders had learned to go to the ground at the first shot fired. To make a successful attack in this fight required the men to charge through the Confederate position and take a hill to its rear, regardless of loss. Burnside trained his black soldiers to make the reckless drive forward and to split off columns to the sides as they ran to provide flank support to stop Rebel counterattacks. The weak white divisions would provide support and reinforcement. As Burnside saw it, everything was ready for a massive victory.

Then Grant and his staff learned about Burnside's proposed use of the blacks and objected. They feared that if the assault failed Congress would blame them for leading the blacks into a massacre to avoid white losses. So they ordered the whites to lead and the blacks to reinforce them. Unfortunately it was too late to train the whites on what to do when they reached the

Rebel lines. They wearily took the first rank as the blacks disappointedly returned to the rear. On 30 July at 3:15 a.m., the Pennsylvania miners lit the fuse. Nothing happened. Finally, two men volunteered to go in and see what had happened. The fuse had parted about halfway down the shaft, so they relit it and ran to cover. The mine blew up shortly after dawn. The explosion was so tremendous it took five minutes for the debris to stop falling, but the road to total victory was wide open before them. A half mile of the Confederate defense had disappeared.

The order to attack went out, and the three white divisions charged the Confederate line. When they got there all they saw was a massive crater in the ground and bits of wagons, caissons, and half buried horses and men. The attackers were poorly led; several of their general officers were in the rear, drunk in a dugout. The one general who got to the crater could not get the men to move on. Instead the Federal soldiers filed into the crater and began to dig up the half-buried men and equipment. Right on their heels came the black infantry. They could not get past the disorganized mass of whites, whom they joined in the crater. This confusion gave the Confederates the necessary time to organize a counterattack. When the Rebels saw the black soldiers they went berserk. They ran up to the edge of the crater and fired at the men inside. The Yankees were packed so tightly they could not raise their arms to fire back. A massacre ensued. Finally the men in the crater began to surrender. As black prisoners were pulled up many of them were summarily executed by Confederate soldiers. White prisoners were sent to the rear.

The rest of the Yankees retreated back to their original lines, and Confederate artillery open up and killed as many of them as surrendered inside the crater. About 4,500 men were lost all told. Politicians demanded an investigation, and Grant and his staff blamed the whole thing on General Burnside and his officers. In reality the whole attack was doomed to failure when Grant and his staff ruled that the black soldiers, who had been properly trained and were eager and fresh enough to make the assault, were relegated to a support role. Grant fired Burnside anyway, and settled down to a siege that would last until April 1865 and Confederate surrender.

The first use of black soldiers in division size had failed because of the racial politics of the day. It was not a mistake that would be repeated: blacks became a fixture of more and more Civil War combat armies and a permanent part of the regular army after the war.

The Heat of Retribution: Booth, Surratt, Mudd, and Wirtz

Though botched in some ways as badly as the modern Watergate break-in, the assassination operation that included President Abraham Lincoln, Vice President Andrew Johnson, and Secretary of State William Seward offered similar waves of aftermath.

While the attack on the president proved successful, the assassin assigned to kill Vice President Johnson got cold feet and wound up in a barroom in Johnson's hotel. Seward and his son were victims of nonfatal stab wounds. Had all gone according to plan and the attacks succeeded, the new president of the United States under the law of succession would have been Ohio Senator Benjamin F. Wade, president pro tem of the Senate and known as an ardent Radical Republican. He was the only real abolitionist who was not opposed to gunfights on principle, and who received his nickname, Bluff Ben, by accepting Southern duel challenges before the war and choosing rifles at 50 paces with a bull's-eye target pinned over each man's heart. There were no takers, Southern gentlemen considering this demeaning, and Wade thus bluffed them all.

Assassin Booth eventually was trapped and shot in a burning barn. Three collaborators, along with Mary Surratt (whose boarding house the conspirators had used as a meeting place), were tried by military tribunal and hanged. Although it seems likely she knew nothing of the plot, Mrs. Surratt has the dubious honor of joining convicted atomic-spy Ethel Rosenberg as one of only two women executed for treason in the history of the United States. In addition to the hangings, three men received life sentences to be served in the infamous Ft. Jefferson military prison in the Dry Tortugas off the Florida Keys.

Another more or less innocent victim of the purge that followed the assassination plot was Dr. Samuel Mudd, the Maryland physician who set Booth's broken leg the night he fled Washington, D.C. Even though he had no idea of the assassination or of Booth's part in it, Mudd received a life sentence and joined the others at Ft. Jefferson. Since 1865, when anyone says, "Your name is Mudd," they are referring to this incident and its damaging effect on the doctor's good name. Mudd redeemed himself quickly, though, when he became the only medical man to survive the prison's yellow fever epidemic of 1867, during which he valiantly tended to prisoners and soldiers alike, saving many lives. This act of selfless heroism earned him a pardon in 1869. The others were pardoned at the same time, as one of President Johnson's last acts in office.

Only one other execution was recorded in the aftermath of the Civil War, that of Major Henry Wirtz. He was the commandant of the infamous Confederate Camp Sumter prison at Andersonville in south central Georgia. Even though most Union soldiers at other prisons also died because of the intolerably poor sanitary conditions, overcrowding, and inadequate diet (although prisoners received the same cornmeal and beans ration as Confederate soldiers in the field, when they got them), retribution rose large in this particular case. In just over a year of operation 12,912 known deaths occurred in a total prison population of 32,899—leaving many witnesses for the prosecution. A foreigner (Swiss German), Wirtz was easily disposed of, and his superior, Brig. Gen. John H. Winder (Commissary of Prisons, in charge of rations) had died just before the Appomattox surrender. Wirtz naturally blamed Winder for the adverse conditions at Andersonville. In this case it seems to have been the truth; indeed, most historians believe that Winder would have hanged instead of Wirtz had he lived.

CHAPTER VI

The Reconstruction

When Did Andrew Johnson Learn To Read?

According to Hans Trefousse's *Andrew Johnson: A Biography*, the most recent study of the seventeenth president of the United States, Johnson did not learn to read from his wife but from James Litchfield, the foreman at the tailor shop in which he apprenticed in Raleigh, North Carolina. Johnson had a nagging desire for learning that he made up for, much like Abraham Lincoln and countless other poor boys who lacked a formal education, by reading every book he could lay his hands on. It is true, however, that Johnson's wife, Eliza McCardle, had a better formal education than he. She did assist him to further his own talents, but Johnson was literate when they met.

Tragically there are few items available to the modern researcher to amplify the relationship between Johnson and his wife. The few sources indicate that she was retiring and quiet, while he was volatile and outgoing. Their marriage endured for 50 years, however, through her constant illness from consumption, his frequent absences attending to his political career, the hectic days of the Civil War when he was a condemned traitor and she had to live behind the Confederate lines for a time, and the agony of his impeachment trial. Their relationship was marked outwardly with a tenderness of a picture-book marriage, making her his most valuable lifelong companion and supporter.

The Coming of the Klan

In late December 1865, six young ex-Confederate soldiers sat bored in the office of Judge Thomas M. Jones at Pulaski, Tennessee. They wanted something fun to do. One suggested that they organize a secret society. They thought it over all the next day and reconvened in the judge's office again the next night. They elected a chairman and a secretary, and divided themselves into committees to consider at length such things as ritual, rules, and a name for their club. The third meeting took place at a building one of the young men was house-sitting. Here they agreed to everything but a name. Thereafter the meeting house would be called a den, the den leader would be the Grand Cyclops, his aide the Grand Magi, the secretary the Grand Scribe, the greeter of initiates the Grand Turk, the den's two guards were Lictors, and the Grand Cyclops's two messengers became Night Hawks, while the rank and file members would be Ghouls. Finally one of the men, being a scholar of the Classics, suggested a name for the new organization, *kuklos*, which is Greek for circle. Eventually John C. Lester, John C. Kennedy, James R. Crowe, Frank O. McCord, Richard R. Reed, and J. Calvin Jones (the judge's son) settled on the alliterative Ku Klux Klan as the name of the new club designed to put some zip in dull old Pulaski.

The boys decided to put on Halloween-like disguises and celebrate the founding by galloping on horseback up and down Pulaski's streets. Funny how everyone was a bit uneasy about their antics and evil costumes, especially the African Americans. Maybe they even ran down a few blacks for fun. From here on out, the club required that all members wear robes and cardboard masks, some of grotesque size, and pretend to be the Confederate dead risen up from their graves at Shiloh and thirsting for revenge against Yankee soldiers, former slaves, Carpetbaggers, and Scalawags—the occupiers and alleged despoilers of the culture of the Old South. From this whimsical beginning came the society of white regulators that would terrorize the supporters of Reconstruction and operate in various forms until the present day. No one would have been more surprised than the six men who founded the Ku

Klux Klan as a lark. The Civil War that had been lost on the far-off battlefields of Virginia and Tennessee by the Confederates was about to be won on the back roads, swamps, and byways closer to home by a new guerrilla force that became as potent as the ubiquitous Mafia contingent in a more recent time.

Waving the Bloody Shirt: Preserving the Animosities of the Civil War

Waving the bloody shirt is a colorful phrase of post-Civil War politics that essentially meant accusing white Southern Democrats of wholesale slaughter of white Unionists and black Republicans in the South, and Northern Democrats of whole-hearted complicity in these deeds by opposing Republican congressional programs in Washington. The term came from cross-eyed Benjamin Franklin Butler, a Massachusetts politician otherwise known as the Beast of New Orleans. Originally a Democrat, Butler represented the poor Catholic mill hands in the southern section of the Bay State. He also fancied himself a military man; he wrangled a major generalship of the state militia and commanded several summer encampments, which gave him the distinction of having as large a body of men as Lt. Gen. Winfield Scott, the general in chief of the whole Federal army.

Calling himself a Jacksonian in opposition to secession, Butler led Union troops to Washington during the critical first days of the war. He was the first to classify as contraband of war the slaves who fled to the Northern lines, in effect freeing them. (These blacks have been known as contrabands ever since.) Eventually sent to the Department of the Gulf, Butler commanded the Federal occupation forces at the capture of New Orleans. His occupation of Gulf ports and southern Louisiana was highly controversial, even considered criminal, due to items sacked from alleged Confederate plantations. The theft of silverware was so common that Butler received a new pseudonym, Spoons. He never quite outlived his declaration that women of New Orleans who insulted Federal soldiers would be treated as "prostitutes plying their trade." This led to a death sentence being placed on his head in absentia by the Richmond government as well as to worldwide condemnation; hence the nickname Beast.

Butler was put in command of an army group that was supposed to cooperate with Lt. Gen. U. S. Grant's 1864 campaign on Richmond, but incompetency on his part led to his force being trapped on the Bermuda Hundred peninsula. With this, Butler earned a new nickname, the Bottle Imp. Grant and Lincoln fired him after the elections of 1864 to minimize his political influence. After the war Butler supported a harsh Reconstruction and helped manage the impeachment of President Andrew Johnson. During one debate on violence in the South, he waved a bloody shirt over his head, asserting that the victim was an Ohio Carpetbagger who had merely tried to obtain justice for African Americans in Mississippi. The antic was so successful in demonstrating Ku Klux Klan retaliations that the term came to be applied to any attack on Democrats that emphasized their support of Southern violence and subordination of legitimate black social and political aspirations.

Never one to let principle get in the way of practicality, Butler not only won elections as a Democrat and a Republican, but also as a Greenbacker; he unsuccessfully sought office as a candidate of the Anti-Monopoly party. He died in Washington in 1893, leaving behind a $7 million fortune and a record for audacity matched by few others.

White Terror—Klan and Rifle Clubs

After the more or less accidental organization of the Ku Klux Klan, the organization spread rapidly throughout the South. New levels of control were added, like the Grand Dragon and his staff of Hydras for each state, culminating in 1867 with the election of former Confederate cavalry general, Nathan Bedford Forrest, as Grand Wizard, the head of all the Klans, with a staff of ten Genii. Many names came to be used: the Knights of the White Camelia, the Knights of the Rising Sun, Pale Faces, the Invisible Circle, the Families of the South, and of course the

Knights of the Ku Klux Klan. Some organizations were more secret than others, but all had the goal of restoring political and social control of the South to the whites who held it before the loss of the war. This included the use of violence, if necessary, and it usually was. Who better to lead the Klan than General Forrest, the instigator of the 1864 Fort Pillow massacre in which surrendering black and white Union soldiers, former slaves and white Loyalists, were shot down as traitors to the Confederacy and the Old South.

The Klan specialized in terror tactics that included threats, beatings, whippings, and murder. Its stated goals were to protect the weak, especially widows and orphans of Confederate soldiers, to protect the Constitution as it stood before the Reconstruction amendments, and to prevent invasion from outside domestic and foreign enemies—in other words, to keep the South for native-born whites only. Over a half million men filled the Klan ranks in short order as their program went forth. The usual procedure was to issue a warning, administer a whipping if unheeded, and then resort to murder or exile of the major resisters.

Aware of the Klan's activity, Congress moved to allow the army to intervene in the states affected by passing the Enforcement Acts in the early 1870s, allowing the president to use troops to police the polls in federal elections. Recent scholarship has shown that most of the policing of polls, which ostensibly was to be used against anti-Negro terrorists in the South, was done in Northern cities to stifle the Northern Democrat opposition to Republican reelection. The Seventh Cavalry under George Armstrong Custer was pulled off the Great Plains and sent to the three states most heavily threatened—Louisiana, Kentucky and South Carolina—where they crushed Klan resistance. It was already too late: the Klan's terror program had succeeded in returning Democrat majorities in most Southern states.

After the Enforcement Acts dispersed the Klan, the Mississippi or Shotgun plan came into vogue. Organizations like the Redshirts and the White League, no longer secret and generally referred to as rifle clubs, actually fielded armies with cannons and fought openly against Loyalist blacks and whites

of the pro-Federal militia. The most spectacular example occurred during the election of 1876 when the Louisiana White
League defeated the Republican Metropolitan Police and loyal
militia led by none other than General R. E. Lee's former right-
hand man, Lt. Gen. James Longstreet, now a Scalawag political
appointee. This Battle of Canal Street, or the Third Battle of
New Orleans, guaranteed the redemption of Louisiana as did
the activities of similar groups in South Carolina and Mississippi. Recently there has been much political flak in New
Orleans, now about 80 percent black in population, over the
efficacy of maintaining the monument raised on the battle site
at the turn of the century.

Jim Crow Becomes Dominant; Octoroon Plessy

As Richard Wade points out in *Slavery in the Cities: The South
1820–1860* (Oxford University Press, 1964), historians generally fail to remember, or intentionally ignore nowadays, that
many of the white characterizations of African Americans
have a condescending vaudevillian nature about them that
was originally an intentionally concocted racial stereotype
designed to help relegate blacks to a second-class place in
American society. Many of these delineations stem from the
old minstrel shows so popular a century and a half ago (Hans
Nathan, *Dan Emmett and the Rise of Early Negro Minstrels*
[Norman: University of Oklahoma Press, 1962]). They are forgotten now, but two classic minstrel roles were fated to be
around longer than the rest of the minstrel genre: Zip Coon and
Jim Crow. Zip Coon was the urbane, sophisticated city Negro
who wore the latest fashion and perambulated about flashing
a big grin and spinning his cane. His name endures in a
derogatory term for African Americans. Jim Crow was his
country cousin, poor, dressed in rags, lacking the streetwise
demeanor and aggressiveness of Zip Coon. The more widely
known Jim Crow came to describe the initially informal and
later legal system of segregation that permeated American

society from the days of slavery to the middle of the twentieth century, when Martin Luther King successfully attacked its legal precepts.

Originating in the North, Jim Crow was designed as a system to replace slavery, which was gradually being eradicated there by the first wave of the American Revolution. It spread from the cities, because that is where traditional white control first broke down, a gradual process that continued until the Civil War in the South. By 1865, the end of formal slavery under constitutional amendments meant that a new social, political, and economic provision had to be made for African Americans. Few considered complete equality as the answer. The result was segregation, disfranchisement, and peonage. The key to this process was the willingness of the North to assist or acquiesce in the result. For this reason, it took 30 years after Appomattox to set Jim Crow in place, first by tradition and then by actual law (C. Vann Woodward, *The Strange Career of Jim Crow* [Oxford University Press, 1955]). Lynching helped in the former, Congress and the Supreme Court in the latter.

No instance has come to typify the Jim Crow reality by the 1890s better than the Louisiana case of *Homer A. Plessy v. Judge John H. Ferguson*. Louisiana had had a segregated system of street cars before and during the Civil War (called Star Cars because they had five-pointed stars to indicate Negro occupancy allowed), a system that had been integrated by a concerted effort during Reconstruction (Roger A. Fischer, *The Segregation Struggle in Louisiana, 1862–1877* [Urbana: University of Illinois Press, 1974]). In 1890, prompted by Congress's failure to pass a new civil rights bill designed to enforce renewed Southern compliance in black rights of citizenship, Louisiana state passed a new law segregating railcars by race. Unlike most of the South, New Orleans had a highly articulate, well-educated population of blacks and people of mixed blood, the later descended from liaisons between some of the best planters and their African-American concubines. The state also had a Latin concept of race that allowed such unions to be made more freely than anywhere else in the country. Plessy himself was classified as an octoroon, one-eighth black, and his participation in the case was no accident—it was an intentional setup, under the theory that an almost white person might advance the cause with fewer racial hang-ups in the higher courts than an easily distinguished black person.

These people were not about to be slighted by state law without a fight. Indeed the New Orleans blacks had tried to get an earlier case instituted by another light-skinned Negro, Daniel F. Desdunes, and won. Since Desdunes's destination was outside the state, however, the Louisiana Supreme Court ruled that the law could not be applied to interstate travelers under the interstate commerce provisions of the U.S. Constitution, which left the law intact inside Louisiana. So Homer A. Plessy took a train ride from New Orleans to Covington, purchasing a first-class ticket and sitting in a whites-only car. He was promptly arrested. In the ensuing trial, Plessy's attorney was Albion W. Tourgee, a former Carpetbagger in North Carolina who, disillusioned with Reconstruction, had gone to New York and written two novels on the subject, *A Fool's Errand* and *Bricks without Straw*. Blacks had brought Tourgeé to New Orleans specifically to plead Plessy's case. In court, the attorney maintained that the Louisiana law violated Plessy's rights under the Thirteenth and Fourteenth Amendments. However, Judge John H. Ferguson held that the case was a state matter and Plessy could be proscribed from riding in all but designated cars. Tourgeé appealed the case, eventually to the U.S. Supreme Court, as *Plessy v. Ferguson*.

There, on 19 May 1896, the highest court in the land ruled that states could separate the races legally provided that "separate but equal" accommodations were provided for all those so proscribed. Technically the decision only involved transportation, but other decisions expanded the separate but equal rule into all areas of American life. It would take half a century until African Americans could breach the wall created by the Plessy case, achieving that in the 1954 case *Brown v. Board of Education of Topeka, Kansas,* which dealt with another aspect of segregation, public school education.

CHAPTER VII

The American Empire

Massacre Out West: Fear and Reprisal

The Western Indian wars were marked by a constant interplay of misunderstanding, fear, and reprisal. Legend has it that the United States spent a million dollars for every Indian killed, not including women and children. Considering the following, it may be true.

1. Originally the Plains were called the Great American Desert and were believed to be uninhabitable. In the 1820s the U.S. Army built a series of ten small forts from Minnesota to Louisiana, creating the "permanent" Indian frontier, beyond which whites were not to pass. (Perhaps policymakers should have reread American history, especially that part about the Royal Proclamation Line of 1763, which did the same along the line of the Appalachian Mountains and now lay forgotten, half a continent behind the inexorably advancing reality of white civilization.) In the eyes of the Plains nations, the first thing whites did to violate the line was to relocate the Five Civilized Tribes (Cherokee, Choctaw, Chickasaw, Creek, Seminole) from the southeastern states to areas west of the sacred line. The result was years of warfare between the Plains natives and the woodland transplants.

2. The first interest in the Plains came from travelers wishing to cross them to Oregon, Utah, and California. This "right" was established at the Treaty of Fort Laramie in 1851, in exchange for the usual annuities. When a couple of hungry Sioux boys killed a stray cow along the permit trail, its owner, a Mormon

immigrant, demanded compensation. The Sioux offered $10.
The Mormon countered for $25. The Sioux said they did not
have that amount, and that no broken-down, half-starved cow
was worth that much. This point was made moot by an unwise
lieutenant who opened fire on the recalcitrant Sioux, igniting
an incident that cost the lives of his whole outnumbered command but one. (Why does one person always manage to escape
with the tale?) An ensuing military expedition hit a Sioux
village, killing 86 people of all ages and both sexes. Thus ended
the Mormon Cow War: the unfortunate massacred village was
from a different band than the beef connoisseurs.

3. In Minnesota during the Civil War, a Santee Sioux hunting
party, coming home without luck, picked up some eggs a stray
hen had laid by the roadside. When warned this was stealing
from a white man, taunts about who was brave and afraid were
exchanged, and four of the 20 hunters became warriors out to
prove their bravery, killing several whites coming home from
church. The murderers bragged of the deed to their chief, Little
Crow. A council was assembled and the topic debated. In the
end the tribe voted to go to war as all would be blamed for the
deaths anyway. Little Crow agreed reluctantly to lead them.

The warriors fell on every white unlucky enough to be
caught out, killing the men and children, gang-raping women,
and scalping all for 30 miles around. Twenty-three counties
were stripped of all human life. An attack on nearby Fort
Ridgley failed after 40 members of the garrison were dispatched, and the hostiles, now some 800 strong, hit New Ulm,
fighting house-to-house. The town was fairly well burned, but
the whites held on at the center square, finally repulsing the
attackers. The militia and several Civil War veteran regiments
counterattacked and defeated the Indians' main force, which
scattered.

Then the retributions began. Two thousand tribesmen were
arrested, 75% of whom had nothing to do with the war. Trials
lasted less than 10 minutes. In the end 306 were convicted of
murder, rape, and pillage. The local Episcopal Bishop begged
President Abraham Lincoln to intervene, and he pardoned all
but 36 convicted of actual statutory crimes. They were all
hanged in one spring of the trap at Mankato. Little Crow
managed to escape to Canada, but he was later shot from
ambush, foolishly having returned to the United States. His
surviving tribesmen, innocent and guilty alike, were sent to a
Nebraska reservation.

The Little Crow War marked a point of no return. After that, whites nationwide lost what little desire they possessed to live peacefully with red men of any tribe. It would hereafter be war to the knife, and knife to the hilt.

4. During the Civil War, settlers in Colorado demanded that the government assist in stopping raids on isolated homesteads. The usual punitive expeditions hit the usual wrong bands, the highlight of which was when the Cheyenne chief, Black Kettle, prevented his men from wiping out a military company that had attacked his peaceful village. In exchange a more vigorous expedition under Col. John M. Chivington struck Black Kettle's new encampment at Sand Creek in 1864, killing 163, of whom 110 were women and children. At the time of the assault, Black Kettle's lodge was flying the American flag, and he raised a white flag during the fray to no avail.

   Bad luck continued to haunt the old chief. In midwinter 1867 his camp along the Washita River was hit by the new Seventh Cavalry under Civil War hero Lt. Col. George Armstrong Custer, this at a cost of at least 100 lives, including Black Kettle and his wife. Nine hundred Indian ponies were killed and all the teepees burned, impoverishing the survivors. The only bright spot for the Indians was that their counterattack isolated a 20-man unit of the Seventh, which was obliterated. Custer refused to go to his compatriots' aid.

5. When gold was discovered in the mountains of Montana, the prospectors raced along the Bozeman Trail through treaty-guaranteed Sioux country to reach the mineral wealth. When the army began to construct forts to protect the trail, the Sioux chief, Red Cloud, protested and then went to war. Unfortunately the posts were poorly located and lacked firewood for winter warmth and cooking. The Indians easily suckered Captain William J. Fetterman's woodcutters' escort into a chase that cost them 80 deaths—the whole command. The fort lost another 60 men in various other skirmishes; but two incidents helped even the score for the soldiers (all infantry, by the way, and only a few, like those in Fetterman's unit, were temporarily mounted). In the Hayfield Fight, over 1,000 warriors hit a hay gathering party, which forted up behind its wagons and devastated the attackers using rapid fire from new breech-loading rifles. A day later, a woodcutting party did much the same in the Wagon Box Fight. The war proved too costly to the policymakers in Washington, however, and the whites sued

for peace and withdrew from the forts, which the Sioux promptly and thoroughly burned. This made Red Cloud a military genius of some note—the only chieftain to actually cause the United States to lose an Indian War. His visage is the one appearing on the nickel coin, on the side opposite the buffalo.

6. The Red Cloud War Treaty of 1867 was violated by the discovery of gold in the sacred Black Hills. As whites poured in and the Sioux refused to back off, the army planned a three-pronged punitive expedition to force a new treaty. The southern prong, under Maj. Gen. George Crook, was stopped by the combined forces of Sioux and Cheyenne lead by Chief Crazy Horse at the Rosebud in 1876.

Unaware of Crook's demise, Maj. Gen. Alfred Terry's eastern prong sent its mobile force, Custer's Seventh Cavalry, on ahead with orders not to bring on a fight. Custer ignored the cautionary command and unwisely divided his unit in the face of the Sioux-Cheyenne camp. As the famed medicine man Sitting Bull prayed for victory with old Red Cloud looking on, the warriors under Crazy Horse, Gall, and Rain-in-the-Face swarmed over the battalions accompanying Custer and killed 225 men—including Custer, two of his brothers, and a cousin. The only live being left after the 20-minute fight was the horse of Capt. Myles W. Keogh, Comanche. The rest of Custer's divided unit, under Major Marcus Reno, forted up on a hill and suffered another 32 dead and 44 wounded before being relieved. The western prong, under Maj. Gen. John Gibbon, never got into the fight. News of Custer's demise reached the east coast in the middle of the centennial celebrations of America's birth, which elevated its impact.

The campaign is still one of the most controversial in American military history, and one recent account based on Cheyenne Indian testimony asserts that Custer's men, mostly green recruits who had dismounted to fight on foot (a standard cavalry tactic Hollywood always forgets), panicked when surrounded. As their horses stampeded and the hideously painted warriors closed for the kill, they began to shoot each other and commit suicide to avoid being taken alive and tortured. "Save the last bullet for yourself" was a common Western saying, and it is also the title of a book by Thomas B. Marquis that advances this theory.

A postscript to the Custer affair was the 1890 ghost dance

religious outburst. Originating among the Paiute tribe in Nevada, the ghost dance was a nonviolent ceremony in which the prayed-to gods were supposed to bring back the buffalo and drive out the white man so the red man could live his former life of bliss. When it reached the Sioux, the ghost shirt (a new twist) was added—a vestment that would allegedly make the wearer immune to white man's bullets.

Again, stupidity gave the Sioux ghost dancers the opportunity to test out their more warlike version of the new religion. The panicking local Indian agent called in the army when the Sioux refused to stop dancing. Rumor even had old Sitting Bull become a convert. (By then, the chief had become even more famous for his extensive tours with the Buffalo Bill Cody Wild West Show.) Sending Indian police to arrest the chief, a riot ensued in which Sitting Bull was killed and the police routed. The Seventh Cavalry came in to round up other suspected ghost dance advocates, one of whom was Big Foot. He and his followers were located at Wounded Knee, and as the troopers searched the tribesmen for weapons, hysteria got the better of both sides and they opened fire pretty much simultaneously. Using artillery, the troopers killed 200 of the 350 Indians present, most of whom were women and children, at a loss of 60 dead of their own. The Plains wars were over at last.

7. Perhaps one of the most admired Indians in American history is Chief Joseph of the Nez Percé. Of him, and him alone, nothing but good has been written. Devoted to peace and with no prior military experience, he and his brother Ollokot (who died in the last battle) led their band in one of the most skillful campaigns ever fought against the U.S. Army. Naturally, the campaign began over the refusal of the band to leave their homes, where they lived peacefully raising cattle and the famed Appaloosa horses, and move to a new reservation. The army protested the orders; but Washington bureaucrats wanted neatness—everyone was to sign a treaty and move on to the reservation the bureaucrats had picked out—land that no one else wanted.

Meanwhile an Indian was murdered, an innocent white died in retaliation, and the war was on. Joseph was opposed to fighting, but under orders the army hit his camps at White Bird Creek and Clearwater River, Idaho. However, Joseph and 800 Nez Percé beat off the attacks and got away scot-free. Using captured weapons and rations, the Indians seemed to assume that if they could cross the Bitterroot Mountains to the east, the army would leave them alone. Blocked at Lolo Pass by a makeshift fort, Joseph boldly rode forward and persuaded the volunteers to let the tribe pass without a fight. The place has been called Fort Fizzle ever since. Later battles at Big Hole, Cammas Meadow, Canyon Creek, and Cow Island followed as the fleeing Nez Percé headed into Montana, seeking refuge in Canada. At each fight, the soldiers lost more than they gained.

Finally the army cornered the Indians in the Bear Paw Mountains near the Canadian border. In two days of battles, Joseph and his men beat back both infantry and cavalry attacks, before he raised the white flag and surrendered 80 warriors, half of them wounded, and over 300 starving women and children. During the surrender negotiations, Joseph made the famous speech that closes, "My heart is sick and sad. From where the sun now stands, I will fight no more forever." The five-month campaign had involved 2,000 soldiers, resulting in 180 dead and 150 wounded, and uncounted Indian casualties, all of whom probably wished the campaign had never started.

8. In the Southwest, the biggest threat to white incursion was the various bands of Apaches in Arizona and New Mexico. Fortunately, each band had no qualms at chasing the others, so the army used Apache scouts led by Al Sieber and Tom Horn to assist in its campaigns. For their part, although they did not really understand why it worked, the Indians skillfully used the Mexican border (the medicine line), to shake any serious pursuit until Mexican and American authorities authorized "hot pursuit" of hostiles across the international line.

Again the wars had foolish beginnings that belied their ferocity. In Arizona, for example, the Chiricahua Apaches, led by Cochise, hated Mexicans more than Americans. This changed when a brash army lieutenant executed Cochise's relatives in a mismanaged captive negotiation (some other band held the captives, as usual), and a war followed that effectively closed safe travel for a dozen years. In retaliation for these and other raids, residents of Tucson attacked the peaceful Apaches encamped at Camp Grant, whom they said sheltered the raiders. They killed somewhere between 86 and 150 people (the number is still disputed), raped the women, and carried 29 children into slavery. The war continued until a gutsy stage manager, Tom Jeffords, got the chief to let the mail through and to talk to Gen. O. O. Howard about peace. Impressed by Jeffords' courage to ride into his camp alone and by Howard's Christian sincerity, Cochise signed a treaty in the early 1870s that set aside a separate Chiricahua reservation in southeastern Arizona. A good piece of historical fiction on this episode is Elliot Arnold's *Blood Brother* (1947), which was made into a popular movie, *Broken Arrow* (1953), with Jimmy Stewart as Jeffords.

Things did not go so well with the Warm Springs Apache chief, Mangas Coloradas, who was described by one authority as, "beyond all question, the most famous Apache warrior and statesman of the century." He too was more interested in raiding Mexico until the Cochise debacle. Like most Apaches he thought the abandonment of the Southwest during the Civil War was his doing, and when the Union California Column came through, his men ambushed it at Apache Pass in southern Arizona. The soldiers were armed to fight Confederates, which meant they had cannon and breech-loading carbines—a new experience for the Indians, who broke and ran. Mangas Coloradas was among the wounded.

Soon after, for reasons still a mystery, Mangas Coloradas agreed to a truce talk, but he was arrested instead. "You have made more trouble than any other Indian. We have followed your trail 500 miles by burnt bodies and cut throats," said the white commander. As he lay resting that night, soldiers suddenly applied hot bayonets to his legs and feet. The startled chief leap up and was shot down without mercy. The imaginative official report alleged that he "made three efforts to escape and was shot on the third attempt." An excellent piece of historical fiction on Mangas Coloradas is Will Levington Comfort's *Apache* (1931).

The surrender of Cochise and the murder of Mangas Coloradas did not stop the wars. Geronimo, described by one soldier as "a thoroughly vicious, intractable, and treacherous man," and Victorio, a successor to Mangas Coloradas who was threatened with exile from his native New Mexico to San Carlos Reservation in Arizona, continued the policy of on-again, off-again hit-and-run raids for years. This lasted until Victorio was killed by Mexican militia south of the border in 1880 and Geronimo surrendered in 1886. The one-sided nature of the wars can be seen in one 1881 raid, where the aged, sick Apache leader Nana jumped the reservation and led 40 warriors on a two-month-long, thousand-mile raid during which his men fought 8 pitched battles, captured 200 horses, and eluded 1,400 troops. The Indians withdrew into Nana's Mexican hideout in the Sierra Madres without losing a single man. The Americans suffered 40 fatalities and uncounted wounded. Nana was not a Victorio or Geronimo, either—much less a Cochise or Mangas Coloradas! A better than usual Hollywood treatment of these wars, which ably demonstrates the how and why of Apache tactics, is the 1972 Burt Lancaster movie, *Ulzana's Raid*, written by Alan Sharp.

In the end, regardless of prior treaties, the whites transported all Apaches to San Carlos, a desolate, desert area where they lost all hope. Geronimo and his people were sent to Florida for a few years and later allowed to return to Oklahoma. (Their descendants, now called Fort Sill Apaches, were allowed to return to Arizona and meet the rest of the Chiricahuas only in the late 1980s.) Geronimo's surrender was not the end, however. Six of his number escaped and raided Arizona and New Mexico *ranchitos* into the 1890s. Everything seemed to be fine until a Mexican news report out of Sonora in 1930 shocked the now-complacent Southwest. In a fashion reminiscent of the nineteenth century, a small town had been hit by an Apache raid. A local posse trailed the renegades to their camp, attacking and killing all but two small children, who were let out for adoption among local families. General George Crook, who had led several campaigns against Apache renegades in the 1880s, summed it all up when he concluded that the Apaches "are the tigers of the human species."

John Henry, Steel Drivin' Man

No written documents provide conclusive evidence about the life of the singular Mississippi ex-slave, John Henry, who was well-known to several regions (especially Kentucky and West Virginia) for his prowess and vigor with a single-jack (one-man), nine-pound driving hammer. Many people interviewed in the post-Civil War era claimed to remember not only him, but also the essential details of a contest that made him a legend for all time.

John Henry was a steel driver, a tunnel-builder who struck his hammer against a steel drilling rod clenched between the hands of a fellow worker who twisted the drill slightly every stroke to aid in the penetration of rock. When the hole reached sufficient depth, a charge of black powder was inserted and a fulminate of mercury primer used to induce an explosion, lengthening the tunnel.

According to Alan Lomax's *Folk Songs of North America,* researched during the 1930s on a grant from the Works Progress Administration (WPA), the John Henry legend arises from an 1870s competition held at the Big Bend Tunnel on the Chesapeake and Ohio Railroad in West Virginia, where the rawboned, powerful African American was pitted against a new-fangled steam drill. During the contest, Henry bored two standard seven-foot blasting holes to the steam drill's one and one-third holes in 35 minutes. Wherever rail links spread, the story was repeated and often embellished. Indeed John Henry's power became so well reputed that it went into American black slang as a term for the prominent organ of a well-endowed male, and as a misnomer for one's signature, more correctly called a John Hancock. The famous ballad of his feat eventually reached 14 stanzas in number, 10 of which were once published by the University of North Carolina Press. In 1939, African-American singer Paul Robeson starred in the title role of a Broadway stage adaptation of the tale.

All versions of the story of John Henry, whether in the form of play, song, or prose, have been adapted to other geographical regions and conditions, such as the operation of a cotton-rolling steam winch. Several playwrights and authors of prominence have chosen to refer to the mythical John Henry as the black Paul Bunyan of the workingman. Even Illinois poet Carl Sandburg, the biographer of President Abraham Lincoln, has rendered the comparison in *The American Songboy.* The greatest tribute of all may have been the Chesapeake and Ohio Railroad's naming its last, largest, and most powerful modern steam locomotive the Jawn Henry in the 1950s.

Laborers Become Nasty—Molly Maguires, Strike Violence, and the Bombing in Haymarket Square

More than any other incident of the late nineteenth century, the Pinkerton National Detective Agency's suppression of the

Molly Maguires in the western Pennsylvania coal fields heralded a declaration of war on organized labor. Formed in
Ireland during the potato famine of the 1840s, the Ancient
Order of Hibernians was a terrorist society organized by Irish
tenants to oppose the encroachments of landlords. Since many
Irish people emigrated to the United States, where they often
were looked down upon and considered natural drinkers,
fighters, criminals, and plotters against the interests of so-
called decent people, many assumed that the anti-landlord
association, known colloquially as the Molly Maguires,
followed to do similar mischief against the capitalists who
employed them here. That such action might occur was understandable at a time when coal miners brought home $35 a week
while costs for the necessities of living, paid to the company
store, were $35.03. Mining was a dangerous occupation, as
well: in 1871 112 men were killed in mining accidents and
another 332 were crippled for life.

Since many of the coal veins were owned by railroad companies, it was natural for them to turn to Allan Pinkerton's
agency, which had helped them curtail the rash of train robberies during that era. When Pinkerton blamed the legendary
Molly Maguires for various incidents against railroad property, the Reading Railroad asked him to investigate further
and help bring indictments against the ringleaders. Pinkerton
eagerly organized his greatest infiltration effort up to that
time, using Irish operatives knowledgeable in the tenets and
secrets of the Ancient Order. There was a real problem, however, in that Pinkerton may have made up the entire scam. In
any case, his agent James McParlan joined the movement,
traced the activities of alleged leaders, and then appeared in
court to testify against them. The accused maintained that
McParlan actually had egged them on, taking part in some
violence and murders and planning others. The prosecution
held otherwise, and the jury voted likewise. The result was 24
convictions, 10 hangings, and the setting back of railroad
opposition in the coal fields for a few years, until the bloody
Homestead strike of 1892. Once again, the 300 Pinkertons hired
as strike police were assaulted as they moved to protect strike
breakers, forcing the use of the state militia to restore order.

Labor responded with more violence, seeing the law as a tool in the hands of their oppressors. In 1877, as depression gripped the nation, bloody railroad strikes hit all over the country, requiring the use of federal troops and state militia to suppress them. These violent eruptions were instrumental in increasing the membership of the Knights of Labor, led by Terence V. Powderly. As an industrial union, organizing all workers in a plant regardless of trade skills or lack of them, the Knights called for the eight-hour day, arbitration instead of violent strikes, various political reforms like a graduated income tax, and consumers' and producers' cooperatives. After a few successes, the Knights were destroyed by events growing out of the depression of the late 1880s, primarily their failed strikes against the Southwestern Railroad, the eight-hour-day strike in Chicago, and a lockout of Knights by employers in the packinghouse industry.

The key to their destruction was the 1886 Haymarket Square Incident in Chicago, during which some "anarchists" (no one was ever identified as the actual culprit) threw a bomb into the police ranks arrayed against them, killing or wounding 77. The ensuing trial resulted in the execution of four people and lengthy jail terms for others, two of whom had their impending executions postponed by Governor Richard Oglesby. Oglesby's successor, John Peter Altgeld, later pardoned three others, claiming that their trials had been unfair. Altgeld later protested against President Grover Cleveland's use of federal troops against the strikers led by Eugene V. Debs of the independent American Railway Union at the Pullman Palace Car Company, maintaining that it made the Democrats no better than Republicans. Debs was arrested for being in violation of a Federal court antistrike injunction, which became the preferred legal manner to attack strikers—even in opposition to standing state laws against their use—until the 1930s.

In protest, Altgeld wrote a treatise, *Our Penal Machinery and Its Victims,* which maintained that the poor unfairly lacked the protections of the law given to the rich. More than that, the violent failure of the late-nineteenth-century strikes demonstrated the inadequacy of the American economic system to meet depression and the lack of crowd control available to local political jurisdictions, problems that would not be more fully addressed until the advent of the New Deal.

Pinkerton: From English Radical to American Detective

Allan Pinkerton, founder of the famous detective agency that bore his name, was a Glasgow, Scotland, native who, in his youth, typified the very labor radicals he and his hired agents would chase down in the American industrial expansion of the late-nineteenth century. Legend has it that his father was severely injured (and eventually died from his wounds) in a Glasgow street riot sponsored by Chartist radicals protesting labor conditions during the British industrial revolution of the 1830s. No official record, however, exists of this. His son Allan, however, trained as a cooper, soon joined the Chartist movement as a street organizer, campaigning violently for the reforms of the Charter: equal electoral areas, universal suffrage, payment of members of the House of Commons, no property qualifications to vote, voting by ballot, and annual parliaments. As an agitator he took part in the assault on Monmouth Castle at Newport, designed to free another Chartist from jail. The Chartists were repulsed in a bloody encounter with the regular army, and Pinkerton fled with his compatriots, becoming a marked man. In quick succession, he fled the law, hid out for months, married his sweetheart, and slipped aboard a ship bound for the United States, finally winding up in Chicago.

After working as a cooper for a time, Pinkerton stumbled into the detective business by helping the local sheriff subdue a gang of counterfeiters. Others came to consult him and offer him more sleuthing work. His fame spread, causing him to open one of the world's first private detective agencies—Eugene F. Vidoq of France is usually credited with establishing the first. Adroitly using disguises and a bit of playacting, Pinkerton cracked case after case, eventually coming to the notice of the powerful Illinois Central Railroad, the chief civil engineer of which was a retired military man, George B.

McClellan. Pinkerton had one big advantage over local police of the time: he could cross any jurisdictional boundary. Besides, he was honest and efficient, rare qualities in the law officers of the day. He hired his operatives with skill and employed the first woman detective in history, Kate Warne. He also kept his radical qualifications intact by rendering monetary assistance to John Brown and his Abolitionist raiders.

During the Civil War, under the pseudonym E. J. Allen, Pinkerton protected the Lincoln entourage on its way to Washington for the inaugural and provided military intelligence for the Army of the Potomac, headed by Major General McClellan, his old railroad friend. As a military intelligence gatherer Pinkerton was a flop—he never could get the count of the Confederate army correct, usually magnifying it by two or three times to be safe, which helped make McClellan (who magnified the Pinkerton numbers a time or two again) an ineffective combat commander, although the general probably could have accomplished that on his own. Pinkerton also broke up the Southern spy ring headed by Rose O'Neal Greenhow in the national capital.

It was after the war that Pinkerton became a household name. Under his agency symbol—the eye that never sleeps, from which the modern term *private eye* originated—he chased and brought in the notorious Reno gang in Indiana, chased but failed to capture the Jesse James gang in Missouri, and provided secret information to the attorneys defending Andrew Johnson from the Senate's impeachment proceedings. Then he abandoned his radical leanings and went to work for big business as a strike breaker and destroyer of workingmen's unions, effectively employing infiltrators and turncoats to crush the Molly Maguires (used as the basis for A. Conan Doyle's Sherlock Holmes novelette, *The Valley of Fear* and H. G. Wells's novel of the same name). After his death in July 1884 his sons continued to operate the agency, which had become national in scope, crushing the Burlington Railroad Strike in 1888 and exacerbating the 1892 Homestead strike near Pittsburgh so much that the National Guard had to be called in to quell the violence. Each time the Pinkertons used the tactic of having their operatives sworn in by local lawmen who were elected with the support of the railroad and coal mine owners.

The Pinkerton agency has continued its activities up to the present time, although the emphasis on antilabor activities has given way to the chase of more conventional lawbreakers. From an English radical who fled Scotland under the threat of arrest, Allan Pinkerton shifted his loyalty from the common man to those with the ability to pay, becoming the quintessential American detective of his time. He was truly a representative of the nineteenth-century American man on the make, who rose above his rough beginnings to join the ranks of the refined and glory in the riches his support of the wealthy made possible—a real-life version of the fictional hero, Horatio Alger. In an age of robber barons, when getting ahead at any cost was the hallmark of success, Allan Pinkerton was their kind of detective.

What Were Robber Barons and What Made Them Tick?

As popularized by Matthew Josephson in his volumes *The Robber Barons* (New York: Harcourt, Brace, World, 1934) and *Politicos* (New York: Harcourt, Brace, World, 1938), American business suffers a bad reputation in the history books, a reputation marked by greed, corruption of government, and stacking the deck of free markets in their favor at the expense of the general public. This so-called Progressive interpretation, named after the trust-busting era upon which it draws, is the standard fare in almost every history text used in high school or college. It views the success of American businessmen and those who have benefited from their acumen as fraudulent. It sees the rise of big business as a Social Darwinistic survival of the fittest, public be damned, just as many early writers erroneously saw the rise of such giants as something heavenly ordained, an attitude that led to naming the late-nineteenth century the Gilded Age.

Often overlooked in the Progressive view are the jobs, technology, cheap by-products, and cheap gasoline that made the

United States the envy of the world. This other viewpoint has been provided by the business historians of the Organizational school. Their emphasis is upon the success of American business, but with a twist. They assert that what made the whole triumph of American business possible was not the individual entrepreneur but the bureaucratic centralization of the controlling power structure. The strategy of business was not a process of individual imagination as much as it was predetermined by the structure of industry. If John D. Rockefeller, Sr., had not created Standard Oil, someone else would have, runs the argument, which is both amoral and deterministic. It also has some limitations in that it assumes that anyone could have done what Andrew Carnegie did; namely, outproduce the industrial steel giant of the nineteenth century, Great Britain, in merely 20 years.

Burton W. Folsom, Jr., criticizes these two traditional approaches in his book, *The Myth of the Robber Barons: A New Look at the Rise of Big Business in America* (Herndon, VA: Young America's Foundation, 1991). Although admitting that the Progressives and the Organizationalists have valid points in their approaches, Folsom calls for an overall reexamination of the industrial era in the United States between 1840 and 1920. He presents his argument in three parts: a redefinition of the term, *robber baron*, a recognition that interference by the state inhibited economic growth, and the assertion that the absence of state involvement and a reliance on market forces probably was the key factor in true business growth.

Folsom divides the industrialists into two groups. The ones who innovated, cut costs, and competed in an open market he calls Market Entrepreneurs. He labels as Political Entrepreneurs those who tried to succeed through government intervention, creating monopolies and pools, engineering vote-buying, and manipulating stocks. He sees the former, men like John D. Rockefeller, Sr., Cornelius Vanderbilt, James J. Hill, and Charles Schwab, as builders of the American economy who strived to make a profit by cutting costs and beating foreign competition at the production game. They thereby created jobs and wealth for themselves and the country, making this nation the envy of the world. They also plowed much of their profit back into the national infrastructure through charitable donations and the creation of libraries and educational institutions. These men or their actions are ignored or misinterpreted by both the Progressive and Organizationalist historians.

The Political Entrepreneurs were men like Edward Collins, Henry Villard, Elbert Gray, and the builders of the Union Pacific Railroad, who corrupted business and government and dulled America's competitive edge. They were in fact the characters of the Progressive and Organizationalist histories and were correctly portrayed by them. Folsom of course finds the Market Entrepreneurs to be the heroes of American wealth, while he agrees that the Political Entrepreneurs need to be excoriated for their shortcomings. He notes that until the arrival of massive governmental economic intervention in the twentieth century, the Market Entrepreneurs generally destroyed the Political Entrepreneurs, not at the expense of the American people, but rather to their advantage by lower prices and better-quality products—something that the Japanese do today by studying American heroes so often forgotten by our own people.

Folsom finds further that the government did poorly as an economic developer. Indeed when the state tried to regulate the trusts, Folsom argues that such action merely punished the Market Entrepreneurs and entrenched the Political Entrepreneurs, the exact opposite as claimed in most American history textbooks. The men most hurt by the Interstate Commerce Commission and the Sherman Anti-Trust Act were Hill and Rockefeller, both of whom had reduced costs by operating efficiently. Their Political Entrepreneur competitors, then, used their allies in government to hinder the Market Entrepreneurs.

Folsom's final point is that the absence of governmental interference and the reliance on market forces is what allowed the Market Entrepreneurs to operate. He decries Alexander Hamilton's idea that a small tariff can assist fledgling industries gain strength so they can ultimately and freely compete in world markets. He shows that his Market Entrepreneurs operated without governmental assistance and under adverse conditions. Andrew Carnegie and Charles Schwab, for example, lowered the price of steel from the British standard $56 per ton to $11.50 per ton in the last 20 years of the nineteenth century using imported ore; the fabulous American Mesabi Iron deposits had yet to be mined. In so doing they allowed Hill to build the Great Northern Railroad with private financing and to fund advances in dry farming, thus providing jobs for the many immigrants who poured into the United States daily. Market Entrepreneurs also funneled their money back into society to benefit everyone. (Progressives sneer at Rockefeller's giving dimes to small children, and often ignore the fact that he gave up to 50% of his profits to charities and needy causes, one of which helped eradicate the boll weevil and save the American cotton industry.) Their main criteria for donating funds was not only need but the willingness of the receiving party to work and succeed. Their contributions far exceeded the income tax raised to provide governmental aid during the same period.

Folsom concludes that a serious study of the rise of business in the United States will have to sacrifice the morality play of the greedy businessman fleecing the public until stopped by the state. Any such study will have to recognize the real contributions of business to the overall triumph of the United States in the first half of the twentieth century, a heritage we threaten to destroy today by misreading history and blaming the Japanese.

Barbed Wire: Simple, Greatly Significant

It is a fair question to ask any student of nineteenth-century British history just how it came to pass that a citizen of Liverpool in 1876 could purchase a bushel of American wheat at a price lower than British wheat grown but a few miles down the road. The answer contains several ingredients, including widespread American railways (in which British investors contributed heavily), the effective use of steam shipping across the Atlantic, the end of the vast roaming buffalo herds, and the 1862 Homestead Act. Another very crucial part of the answer is the contribution of a simple invention: barbed wire.

If one combines the ability to confine cattle to a set range on the vast prairies of the inland United States and the ability to isolate millions of acres of flat land for dry farming, it is understandable how wheat could be grown as easily as a Minnesota front lawn. Barbed wire, the product that made this all possible, was the invention of Joseph Glidden of De Kalb, Illinois. Although there had been a half dozen or more predecessors who had tinkered with the idea of cheap, effective wire fencing on the treeless Plains, Glidden's was the first one that worked. He bought out his competitors, found and purchased a newly invented wire twister, and began twisting barbs inside double-stranded wire. His success was instantaneous. His only competition has been the twentieth-century electric wire fence, which in many areas is limited by access to electric power.

An early agent and promoter of Glidden's wire, John "Bet a Million" Gates, once gave a persuasive demonstration of barbed wire in San Antonio. Skeptical ranchers quickly observed how their meanest longhorns shied away from the fence, a commodity represented by Gates as "light as air, strong as whiskey, and cheaper than dirt." The open range had ended. In its wake, wire cutting wars were legion for a time, Gates had a get-rich monopoly on barbed wire sales, and Britain suffered an agricultural depression.

Can a President Fink on His Cronies?

After Reconstruction officially ended with the symbolic withdrawal of federal soldiers back to their garrisons as a part of the Compromise of 1877, Republicans divided into two factions, the Stalwarts and the Half-Breeds. The Stalwarts were headed by Senator Roscoe Conkling of New York, and they represented the decline of Republican Reconstruction idealism, a drive for spoils of office, and an amoral party loyalty on all issues. The Half-Breeds, representing the old Liberal Republicans and their reformist attitudes, were led by Senator James G. Blaine of Maine. The party stagnated in the 1880 convention over the nomination Blaine and the Stalwart desire

to renominate Ulysses S. Grant for a third term. Blaine outmaneuvered the others by shifting his support to a dark horse
candidate, Brigadier General James A. Garfield, former chief
of staff of the Army of the Cumberland and an 1863 Union hero
of the Battle of Chickamauga.

The Democrats went with their own war hero, Major General
Winfield Scott Hancock of Gettysburg fame. In a close race,
the Republicans managed to carry the day through the use
of "soap," slang of the time for the buying of votes and
the counting of gravestones. This was done under the protection of the U.S. Army, which operated through the Enforcement Acts that were originally conceived to protect loyal
blacks and whites in the South, claiming to use them for a
"higher purpose."

Garfield came into office as an ardent advocate of civil
service reform. He had to compromise with the Stalwarts,
however, to gain the nomination by taking as his vice president Chester A. Arthur, a noted spoilsman from the notorious
New York Customs House Ring and Conkling's right-hand
man. The interparty fight broke wide open when Garfield
appointed Half-Breeds to New York patronage spots. Fate
intervened just as Garfield and the Half-Breeds seemed certain
to win everything. As the president accompanied Blaine to the
Washington railroad station, two shots rang out, one of which
hit him in the back.

"Oh, my God!" Garfield muttered. Behind him the assassin,
Charles Guiteau (later declared insane but hanged anyway),
shouted out, "I am a Stalwart and Arthur is president now!"
Giteau put his finger on the exact quandary facing Garfield's
party supporters. What would Arthur, the Gentleman Boss, do
to them? The president hung on for six weeks before dying,
and the suspense of Arthur's takeover grew hour by hour. To
everyone's surprise, Arthur read well the public disgust on
spoils (as typified by the assassination), and he turned on his
former cronies—the really corrupt ones, anyway—and appointed good men of all factions to patronage positions.

There was more grief in store for the old-time spoilsmen
who once counted Arthur as one of their own. He supported
and got through Congress the first major civil service reform of

the century, the Pendleton Civil Service Act of 1883, which set up a commission to establish competitive examinations for hiring and a merit basis for promotion. Although the act really did little beyond insulating 10 percent of the officeholders from patronage appointments, it set the United States on the road to the modern civil service system—and this from one of the consummate spoilsmen of his time. The result so weakened the Stalwart faction that when Arthur sought to gain nomination and election to the presidency in his own right in 1884, the Half-Breeds dumped him for a real reformer, Blaine himself. Arthur got his revenge that fall when the Blaine ticket fell to the Democrats, led by their own reform-minded man, Grover Cleveland. (This marked the first Republican loss since the Civil War.) The advent of the respectability of reform owed much to Chet Arthur's own ability to rise above his past. However, this overlooks the cynical, realist tradition in American politics that a reformer is one who gives free to the capitalists what the real politician charges for dearly. This cynicism became the major criticism of Cleveland's democracy through his two disconnected administrations.

Was 1884 America's Dirtiest Campaign?

The cast: James G. Blaine—charismatic senator from Maine, most eloquent in speeches, known to gain patriotic support by "waving the bloody shirt," and criticizing the British by "twisting the lion's tail" (for the Irish vote locally)—and Stephen Grover Cleveland—self-read lawyer, sheriff, district attorney, mayor of Buffalo, and reform governor in his opposition to the Tammany Hall machine in New York City. Blaine was nominated earlier at a convention where he had been described as a plumed knight in his attacks upon all doubters of his wisdom and defamers of his honor, and he lacked support from leaders of his own party. (When asked to speak in favor of Blaine's candidacy, one replied, "Gentlemen, you have been misinformed. I have given up criminal law.") Cleveland, at 250 pounds and devoid of charisma, appealed to the public as an "ugly-honest man" or, as one said, "We love him for the enemies he has made."

The ingredients: Blaine had evidently received consulting fees for services to a railway firm, which, although explained acceptably earlier, later emerged as a *sub-rosa*, profitable lobbying activity. Democrats turned up an implicating note that included, directly over Blaine's signature, the order, "Burn this letter." Cleveland, on the other hand, may have been the father of an illegitimate child by a Buffalo, New York, woman of dubious reputation, but he did pay voluntary child support.

The dirt: Blaine faced Democratic campaign chants such as, "Blaine, Blaine, James G. Blaine, the continental liar from the state of Maine," and "Burn this letter!" On the other side, Republicans sang, "Ma, ma, where's my pa? Gone to the White House, ha, ha, ha."

The possible decisive mistake: The heated campaign, hanging heavily on the personal and the scandalous, tipped to Cleveland due to an incident at Delmonico's restaurant in New York City. Blaine and millionaire Republican bigwigs gathered for a large feast, and a visiting Protestant minister made a speech that included a reference to the Democrats as the party of "rum, Romanism, and rebellion." Blaine, who had always successfully courted the American Irish vote, neglected to offer some mollifying sentiment. This implicitly approved the linking of alleged Irish drunkenness and their Catholicism while ignoring their enthusiastic support of the Union during the Civil War. There were no Gallup polls to measure the impact of this incident, but Cleveland became president.

Big Show Entertainment in the 1880s

During the twelfth century in Europe, the highlight of a peasant's entire life was likely to have been a pilgrimage to a town or city that boasted a great religious shrine and the alleged relics of saints long dead. For rural Americans in the nineteenth century, it could very well have been attending a performance of the Greatest Show on Earth, what America's best circus was called after Phineas T. Barnum ("a sucker is born every minute") and James A. Bailey combined their operations in 1881.

However, Barnum and Bailey had a lot of competition in the

1880s from another type of public drama. This was the Wild West Show popularized by Col. William F. "Buffalo Bill" Cody, among others. Garbed in immaculate buckskin clothes, sporting a well-barbered goatee, all topped off with a ten-gallon hat, Cody, who had won the Congressional Medal of Honor while scouting for the army, came to epitomize the frontier for millions of Americans. This was true for Europeans also, for his show made several world tours. Cody's troupe was composed of cowboys, Indians (including the legendary Sioux medicine man and chief, Sitting Bull), buffalo, cattle, stagecoaches, and cavalry troopers all put together in scenarios that would later be embellished in twentieth-century Hollywood movies—the chase, gunfights, Indian raids with the cavalry arriving in the nick of time, and even cattle drives.

Some of the most exciting acts were the trick shooters. The best of these was a woman, Annie Oakley, who was called Little Sure Shot by Chief Sitting Bull. Raised in Ohio, she was part of a vaudeville act until Cody hired her for bigger and better things. At 30 paces she could perforate a tossed-up playing card a half-dozen times before it hit the earth. Her prowess with pistol and rifle became legendary; so much so, that a punched card or show ticket came to be called an Annie Oakley. She once shot a cigarette from the mouth of Germany's Kaiser William II at his request, a feat that millions would have liked to duplicate during the Great War with lesser accuracy.

The Rise of Team Sports

By the 1880s, the big ring shows had to compete with another entertainment phenomena, baseball, an activity immensely popular with spectators and players alike. All a town needed was an open field and an umpire. In the 1870s a league of professionals had formed, and by 1888 an all-star team from the United States toured the world, even using the famous pyramids in Egypt as a backstop. While boxing grew more popular during the decade, even more noteworthy for the future was the attendance of 50,000 spectators at the 1889 Princeton-Yale football game. American football today is a billion-dollar operation on both the college and professional levels (not to mention high school and league play), yet the athletic President Teddy Roosevelt threatened to press for its abolition at the turn of the century because of excessive injury and death from its play. His admonitions encouraged the introduction of rules and forms of physical protection that are currently part of the sport.

Pitchfork Ben Tillman—Why So Named?

Benjamin R. Tillman of South Carolina was one of the most vocal supporters during what has been termed the Populist Revolt. The movement's name came about from the desire of the common people to assert their political right to reform government they perceived to be dominated by the rich.

Representing the poor whites of the sand hill backcountry against the aristocratic Bourbon Democrats of the lowlands and Charleston, Tillman attacked privilege wherever he saw it rear its ugly head. Calling himself the One-Eyed Plowboy, he praised the virtues of the farmer and placed himself clearly on their side. "I am simply a clodhopper, like you are," he intoned. He called South Carolina's laughable public school system "an abominable humbug," butchered the image of high-toned Charleston society, asserted that the state university was the hangout of aristocratic agnostics, and maintained that the state's prestigious private college, the Citadel, was a "military dude factory." It did not help any when his cultured opponents referred to the self-professed plowboy as "the vulgar, profane, coarse, murder-glorifying, treason-uttering, scowling, vicious and uncultured Tillman," which only cemented the clodhopper's popularity in the eyes of poor whites. "Some of you expected to see hoofs and horns," he entertained one audience. "I have some peculiarities [but] I am what I am, and God made me what I am," he thundered, sounding something like an evangelical Popeye the Sailor Man. "I am left handed, and have written with my left paw. I am one eyed. Some say I can see more with that one eye than some men can see with a dozen."

Tillman went on to excoriate what he saw as the malignant alliance between the Republicans and conservative Democrats nationally, best depicted by the administrations of Grover Cleveland in the late 1880s and early 1890s. As much as he wished to replace the Democratic label with that of the Populists, Tillman recognized that in the South at least, because of Appomattox and Reconstruction, that would be hard to do. Better to throw the Clevelandites out and capture the Democrats for the people, Tillman said. It would be a difficult task to knock off the only Democratic president since the Civil War, but Ben Tillman set out to do just that.

He began his campaign for the U.S. Senate with this strategy in mind, and in the process he picked up a new sobriquet for himself, Pitchfork Ben. He labeled the president as "that old bag of beef" and "either the most dishonest or the most damnable traitor ever known," claiming he would gladly give $5,000 to go to Washington to "tell the old scoundrel what he thought of him." The key to his victory was the speech at Lexington. "When Judas betrayed Christ, his heart was not blacker than this scoundrel, Cleveland, in deceiving Democracy," Tillman shouted to his eagerly listening throng. "He is an old bag of beef and I am going to Washington with a pitchfork and prod him in his old fat ribs"—obviously referring to a farmer's use of the pitchfork's sharp tines to move cattle along in a crowded chute between corrals.

In Washington, Pitchfork Ben made his most important and tragic contribution to modern American history—his attack on African Americans, which included advocacy of total segregation and proscription of the Negro's basic civil rights. While governor of South Carolina he and his supporters had already curtailed black participation in state politics and social life. His policy had been tacitly endorsed when the United States Congress had failed to pass a new Enforcement Act to protect blacks in their political and civil rights. Now he went national with his program, using the recent American victory in the Spanish-American War as his launching pad.

Citing the American annexation of Hawaii and retention of places like the Philippine Islands, Tillman called for self-determination of local peoples and chided Republicans for their willingness to rule "our little brown brothers" overseas with the Krag (the army's standard infantry rifle of the time) while denying Southern whites the same privilege back home in the case of American blacks. He laughed that the Republicans and Democrats had seemingly changed places over human rights since 1860. He challenged the Republican's apparent hypocrisy on the race issue by their placing whites in control of colonial governments and suppressing the right of indigenous peoples. "I do not object to those white men . . . being protected, but do not protect them with hypocrisy and cant. Be men! Stand up! Come out and say why you do this thing." Tillman also took his campaign to the Northern voter and found much support for Southern views against the African American. It was the beginning of a tacit understanding among America's whites to let each locality determine its racial policies, a status quo that lasted until Rev. Martin Luther King publicized the Montgomery bus boycott in 1954.

New Orleans in 1891: A Mafia Lynching

Mayor Joseph A. Shakespeare of New Orleans was one of the more anti-Italian politicians of his time. In a letter from his office he castigated Southern Italians and Sicilians as "the most idle, vicious and worthless people among us." New Orleans was a crucial commercial depot for international trade and the geographic entry port for the inter-American river system. By 1890 a rivalry had developed between the Provenzano brothers and the Matranga brothers for control of the Mississippi River docks. When a murder investigation led to the trial of two Provenzano henchmen, Police Chief David Hennessey indicated that he would testify to and provide proof of the presence of an organized criminal society in the city. Shortly thereafter, as he left his office, he was blasted by a shotgun. As he lay dying, he gasped and said the "Dagoes" had done it.

The grand jury arraigned to judge responsibility for the Hennessey murder proved to be a farcical proceeding marked by intimidation and bribery and finding no bill (i.e., no one was indicted) against eight of eleven accused assassins. Unanimity came only when the jury ruled that an organized crime syndicate called the Mafia did exist. Returned to the city jail, the accused murderers were celebrated heroes of New Orleans's Italian section. The grand jury proceedings and the fiesta atmosphere greatly angered other citizens, who called a mass meeting two days later. Instigated by 60 men of substance, a mob marched on the jail and dragged the suspects from their cells. Two were hanged from nearby light posts, seven were shot by makeshift firing squads in the prison yard, and two others were riddled by bullets as they tried to hide in a doghouse built for the jail's guard dogs. This occurred during a time when lynching African Americans was legion, and it is ironic that several members of the execution mob were black.

While a newly written song entitled "Hennessey Revenged" became popular in New Orleans, President Benjamin Harrison's secretary of state, James G. Blaine, faced an international incident because several of the lynched men were still Italian citizens. Italy recalled its ambassador and severed relations with the United States. Eventually the affair was settled when Washington agreed to pay $25,000 to the dead men's relatives in Italy. The crime captains never forgot the lesson of New Orleans. Readers of Mario Puzo's *Godfather* (or viewers of the film) might recall how Michael Corleone's suggestion that he kill not only Sollozzo but also his police protector met with the following response from Corleone family *consigliere* Hayden: "Nobody has ever gunned down a police captain; why if we did that all of our protection would run for cover."

An American Irony: "Raise More Hell, Less Corn"

Writing to friends back in London from Boston in 1842, British author Charles Dickens observed that in the Bay City access to basic essentials was so favorable that, in contrast to European city poor, all the poor he saw in Boston had a blazing fire and meat for dinner each evening. In his words, a flaming sword tossed high in the air would not "attract so much attention as a beggar in the streets."

Yet by the 1890s, this mood had changed. Not only did protesters roam the streets decrying their poverty, but they were not alone in bemoaning economic conditions in the United States. Most issues of the post-Civil War United States involved the concentration of wealth in fewer hands while the classes Dickens noted as relatively prosperous had become destitute and poverty-stricken. Farmers and small businessmen joined laborers to form a multitude of activist political organizations that by 1896 had united under the banner of the Populist party. North, West, and South, transcending the animosities of the Civil War and even race, the common citizen attacked the America of big capital—big railroads, big oil, big banking, big business in all its glory—a place where single references like Wall Street could identify the opposition, if not the tormentor. The concentration of wealth in the late-nineteenth-century United States had spawned a movement of the little guy to take back control, using government and the new Australian (secret) ballot.

No period of American history produced more colorful and distinctive figures, ideas, and actions than the Populist era, as a list of some of the more notable figures (many of whom were elected to state legislatures rather than to Congress) and their issues reveal:

1. Mary Elizabeth Lease, according to the flamboyant press coverage of the time, exhorted Kansas farmers to "raise less corn and more Hell." A self-taught lawyer, her list of causes was shared by most Populists of her generation, and it was tied in some way to problems endemic in the agrarian Midwest and South. She sought agrarian reforms in credit, marketing of crops, free silver, prohibition, regulation of corporations, nationalization of railroads, and women's suffrage. The causes of other Populists merely varied in the emphasis they gave to a particular societal ill.

2. William Alfred "Whiskers" Peffer was a Kansas newspaper editor and Populist senator most prominent in the 1890s. He gave his greatest concern to farmer indebtedness and mortgages. Basing his arguments on census figures, he wrote and spoke about farmers and small town residents drowning in a sea of debt and taxes that threatened their homes and livelihood, a situation that grew while railroads and other corporations

thrived from properties valued at a fraction of their actual worth. He asserted that the average farmer had become a slave to debt and postulated an inflationary currency based on free silver to ease their burden.

3. Jeremiah Simpson was one of the more effective and colorful stump speakers of the outdoor lecture circuit sponsored by the National Farmers' Alliance. He gained national notoriety in the cause of Populism when in the course of demolishing a very urbane Republican plutocrat (Prince Hal Halloway), the humbly attired Simpson piously placed his fingers through his galluses and declared that "princes wore silk socks," but that he himself had none. From that day forth the hostile, big business-controlled press derided him as Sockless Jerry Simpson, forgetting that most of Simpson's listeners wore no socks either.

4. The list of flamboyant, angry protesters grew long, but always the concern was much the same. Arkansas editor W. Scott Morgan drew attention to land monopoly and growing absentee ownership, which ruined what he saw as the lost golden age of American agriculture and the secure independent farmer. Minnesota lawyer Ignatius Donnelly was also a farmer, lecturer, writer, reformer, Allianceman, and politician. Through his public career he rotated through the Republican, Liberal Republican, Granger, Greenback, and Populist parties. He even wrote a futuristic novel, *Caesar's Column*, on what he saw as the destructive trends of the times. Jacob Coxey of Ohio orchestrated the best known of many marches on Washington by the unemployed and disgruntled, all in the name of free silver and the farmer's plight. James Weaver, an Iowan whose political activities carried him vast distances, came from a varied work experience that included gold miner, storekeeper, mail carrier, lawyer, and politician—all this after he had succeeded to the command of his Civil War regiment on the battlefield and won a brigadier generalship. He ultimately became a presidential candidate on the Greenback ticket and later on the Populist slate.

A Farmers' Army Is Arrested for Walking on the Grass

The generation of Americans that experienced many protest marches, especially the march of 200,000 participants who listened to the Reverend Martin Luther King's "I have a dream" speech, can certainly sympathize with a protest event of the 1890s, the march of Coxey's army, or the Commonwealers. During the depression of the early 1890s, the greatest economic recession in the United States up to that time, the numbers of unemployed grew so fast that they decided to work together to gain some relief from their misery. Forming "armies," commanded by self-appointed "generals," the unemployed would march on various governmental entities demanding jobs, usually on public works. One of these groups, led by a Massillon, Ohio, Populist named Jacob Coxey, was better organized than the rest. He called his movement the Commonweal of Christ. In response to suggestions of one of his lieutenants, Carl Browne (a California publicist who dressed much like Buffalo Bill Cody), Coxey decided to march on Washington, D.C., leading eight nationwide armies, some from as far as the West Coast. They came to petition President Grover Cleveland for a nationwide, government-sponsored road building program to put the unemployed to work.

Coxey's army made the biggest march on the national capital since the Confederate Army in 1864. It heralded the infant beginnings of yellow journalism in the sensational press coverage given the march of the Commonwealers. Never ones to let fact get in the way of a good story, reporters printed everything from truth to fiction, the sexier the better. Nothing awed observers more, however, than the fact that Coxey was not a Populist crank, but a wealthy quarryman who owned three ranches and dozens of blooded race horses. Indeed, his own mount was valued at $40,000, enough to pay 80 laborers a year under going rates. Beside him on a white Arabian gelding rode his daughter Mamie, an utterly beautiful red-headed 17-year-old who was dressed in white as the Princess of Peace. She was so radiant that she unexpectedly stole the whole show as the crowds struggled to get a glimpse of her.

Although the Commonwealers wanted government road-building jobs, Coxey's real concern was with a deeper issue— monetary reform. As if to personify this interest, Coxey's wife and two-month-old son, Legal Tender "Leeg" Coxey, joined the march in a black carriage. It was Coxey's enthusiasm for monetary reform that plagued the whole Populist political movement at the turn of the century, driving all other issues into the background. Summed up in the words *free silver,* or the coinage of 16 silver dollars for every gold dollar minted (hence the slogan, 16 to 1), even knowledgeable reformers of the day saw it as the cowbird or parasite of the Northern Populist crusade. In the South, the cowbird was the issue of race, graphically illustrating the difficulty of attracting voters to a single-issue crusade. Such difficulties persist even today: gun control, abortion, school prayer, or the federal debt are a few of the so-called single-issue crusade controversies that come to mind.

After the Civil War, money supply in the United States had been shrinking with the declaration by the Supreme Court (*Hepburn v. Griswold,* 1870) that greenbacks were not legal tender in the payment of debts. This was later reversed in *Knox v. Lee* (1871), which led to more confusion and a ceiling on the amount of paper in circulation. Another repercussion of *Knox v. Lee* was the so-called Crime of '73, the demonitization of silver (omitting it from legal coinage). With farmers and other debtors wanting an inflationary monetary base to make it possible to pay debt with dollars cheaper than those borrowed, and with Western miners wanting to exploit the newly discovered silver deposits in the Rockies, Congress submitted to the pressure and passed the Bland-Allison Act (1878), which caused the government to purchase and mint between $2 million and $4 million in silver dollars a year, a policy known as bimetalism. Later, in the Sherman Silver Purchase Act of 1890, this purchase was changed to 4.5 million ounces a month (the estimated total monthly production of silver nationwide) with new paper dollars redeemable in silver or gold at the discretion of the redeemer.

The Sherman Act caused bankers to fear that silver would drive gold off the market (a theory called Gresham's Law by those in the know) and threaten the gold reserves. After all, one could borrow in gold and pay back in silver. This led to the Sherman Act's repeal in 1893 in the midst of the depression. Influenced by notable propagandists, the generally well-behaved Commonwealers had great appeal among the average onlookers. They were egged on by the likes of Chicago's

William H. Harvey and his *Coin's Financial School*, and Minnesota Farmers' Alliance leader Ignatius Donnelly with his *American People's Money;* by magazines such as *Arena* and the *National Bimetalist;* by the pro-silver platform of the new third party, the Populists; and by President Grover Cleveland's purchase of 3.5 million ounces of gold from the J. Pierpont Morgan-Agustus Belmont banking house of New York to buttress up the federal reserves, the generally well-behaved Commonwealers had great appeal among the average onlooker.

No one dreamed the Commonwealers would get across the Appalachian Mountains, much less to the District of Columbia, but there they were in the streets of Washington shouting, "Coxey, Coxey," and bearing banners reading, "Cooperation, the Cerebellum of the Commonweal" and "The Medulla Oblongata and All Other Parts of the Reincarnated Christ in the Whole People." Doubtless most of the marchers had no idea what cerebellum and medulla were; it was all Browne's idea designed to gain more press coverage. By now, Coxey had been forbidden to address the onlookers from the steps of the Capitol. He stepped up to speak anyhow, and he, Browne, and a Philadelphia-based organizer, Christopher Columbus Jones, were arrested for trespassing.

A later trial found the trio guilty of trampling on the grass and shrubs of the Capitol building in a harmful manner and illegally displaying banners in the form of their rather inconspicuous lapel pins. They were sentenced to 20 days in jail. Dissension, starvation, verbal persuasion, and official harassment drove most of the Coxeyites home, leaving the final 50 or so die-hards to face prosecution and conviction in Maryland, where they were jailed and then put to work on public roads. They got their government jobs at last, but with no pay beyond three months of room and board at public expense. In 1914 the ever-persistent Coxey finally received permission to give his speech from the Capitol steps, and in 1944, the 50th anniversary of his original march, he gave it again to those few government workers who had nothing else to do for lunch. He died in 1951, true to his cause to the end.

The Tuxedo

Most American males at some time in their life pay the price of a tuxedo rental. It has become a long-honored tradition that specific occasions demand that particular type of apparel. Its popularity dates to the late nineteenth century, but at that time it would have been accessible only to the elite.

An inordinately wealthy New Yorker who made millions in tobacco, Pierre Lorillard IV (ultimately producer of Old Golds and Kent cigarettes) spent heavily on elegant living and entertaining guests. In 1886 he opened a lavish walled retreat for his rich friends outside New York City, naming it Tuxedo Park. James Porter Brown, a friend who was not only rich but had recently dined with England's Prince of Wales, reported that the prince had appeared in an elegant tailcoat with the tails cut off. The style became an instant sensation and was copied by visitors at Tuxedo Park; the tuxedo has remained with us ever since that time.

War in Cuba: First Strike in Manila

On 15 February 1898, the battleship USS *Maine* blew up in Havana, Cuba, killing 260 officers and men. The ensuing investigation showed that the ship had been sunk by a mine, but it could not affix responsibility to any person or group. More modern research has pointed an accusing finger to the Cuban rebel movement led by José Martí, theorizing that the mine was brought on board by colliers hauling bagged coal. Spurred on by the so-called yellow journalism of prominent newspapers, Congress demanded war to intervene and settle the years-long Cuban Rebellion against Spanish rule. Even though the Spanish government gave in to all U.S. demands (an armistice in the local fighting and revocation of the concentration camp policy), President McKinley reversed his prior antiwar stance and requested forcible intervention in the Cuban embroglio. The war resolution called for the independence of Cuba and a withdrawal of Spanish armed forces. It also disclaimed any

U.S. territorial ambitions (the Teller Amendment) and authorized the use of the army and navy to enforce its provisions.

Despite denying any territorial ambition and avowing interest in Cuban independence, Congress and the president reckoned without the influential manipulation of American objectives by a strategically placed group of imperialistic politicians known as Jingoes. Foremost of these was Assistant Secretary of the Navy Theodore Roosevelt, backed up by Senator Henry Cabot Lodge of Massachusetts and the American minister to Great Britain, John Hay (formerly Abraham Lincoln's assistant private secretary, who later coauthored Lincoln's biography with John Nicolay). These men wanted the United States to become a world power in the pattern of the much-admired Great Britain, and saw this as the opportunity to further their goals at the expense of the Spanish. Their arm of choice was the navy, a modern steel fleet with 26,000 officers and men who were well trained and motivated for action. The minute that war was possible, these men got Roosevelt's boss (who was lukewarm on war and imperialism) sent away on a prefabricated excuse, leaving the politically safe Roosevelt in charge. Even before war was declared, Roosevelt had sent a message to the commander of the U.S. Asiatic Squadron (six ships), Admiral George Dewey, to be ready to move on the nearest Spanish naval force (14 ships) stationed at Manila Bay in the Philippines.

War was declared on 20 April, and Roosevelt ordered Dewey to take the Philippines. On 1 May 1898 Dewey steamed into Manila Bay and ordered his gunnery officer to open fire ("You may fire when ready, Mr. Gridley"). In a seven-hour battle, the Spanish fleet was destroyed—American losses were eight wounded, and the Spanish suffered 381 casualties. Dewey lacked the men necessary to take Manila, so he blockaded the city with the aid of Philippine rebels led by Emilio Aguinaldo. Upon the arrival of U.S. troops under General Wesley Merritt, the town was assaulted on 13 August and the Spanish surrendered the following day. Although it would take some years for the betrayal and capture of Aguinaldo and for the guerrilla warfare against Muslim dissidents (the Moros) on outlying islands to occur, Roosevelt had moved the country onto the

imperial stage by *fait accompli*. He did so with the belated full
support of President McKinley, who had approved of the
occupation of the islands and their eventual conquest.

Teddy in Cuba, Death Apart from Bullets, and Mr. Dooley

Like all nineteenth-century wars fought by the United States,
the Spanish conflict cost more men their lives off the battlefield
than on it. This was because the war took place in a tropical
climate, compounded by the poor sanitary conditions and lack
of immunity inherent when a large body of predominantly
rural men congregate in one place for the first time in their
lives. Serving aboard ship and more familiar with different
climes, men of the U.S. Navy and Marine Corps actually improved their noncombat death rates from the previous, peaceful year. The war lasted 114 days (leading Roosevelt's friend
John Hay to call it "a splendid little war"), and of the 26,102
sailors and marines involved there were 85 deaths—56 from
disease and 18 from combat. The rest were ruled accidental.

The army's experience was a little different. Of the 74,717
men who answered the call to colors or were already in the
regular army, 2,910 officers and men died. Of these deaths only
345 were combat related; the rest died from disease. Most
volunteers never saw the enemy or even left the continental
United States. No matter. At a camp on the old Civil War
battlefield at Chickamauga, typhoid fever ran rampant. Tampa
offered even more exotic diseases, but this situation was tem-
pered because the men moved rapidly through Tampa on their
way to Cuba. Those in Cuba had their worse fight after the fall
of Santiago. There, yellow fever decimated the regiments, causing
the army to quarantine homecoming troops on another hellhole,
Long Island's Montauk Point.

This did not stop Teddy Roosevelt from making the most of
his wartime opportunities. Eager to be at the point of action, he
left the Navy Department and volunteered for the army. He
then raised a regiment of cavalry from cowboy volunteers out

of the four territories — Arizona, New Mexico, Oklahoma, and the Indian Nations. Officially called the 1st U.S. Volunteer Cavalry Regiment, Roosevelt styled them the Rough Riders. He chose a rip-roaring theme song for them from a St. Louis brothel (which probably says something about the character of the rank and file): "There'll Be a Hot Time in the Old Town Tonight." In an unusual fit of modesty, Roosevelt accepted the title of lieutenant colonel, reserving the full colonelcy for Dr. Leonard Wood, a professional soldier. It was Teddy, however, who led the regiment in action, and his name became synonymous with the regiment's history. Although they fought on foot like all the cavalry regiments in Cuba (the horses never arrived in time from Tampa), the Rough Riders took part in the major Cuban battles and were noted particularly for their headlong charge up Kettle Hill, commonly called the Battle of San Juan Hill in record books.

A prolific writer like Roosevelt, who wrote everything from best-selling popular history to self-serving political commentary, would of course pen his memoirs of the campaign in time for the next elections. Roosevelt's account was in the first person, and the pronoun *I* dominated the story, much to the amusement of critics. Upon perusing *The Rough Riders,* humorist Finley Peter Dunne, who under the pen name Mr. Dooley was a famous newspaper columnist at the turn of the century, saw fit to speak to his equally fictional literary friend, Mr. Hennessey:

> "I haven't time f'r to tell ye the wurruk Tiddy did ar-rmin' 'an equippin' himself, how he fed himself, how he steadied himself in battles an' encouraged himself with a few well-chosen worruds whin th' sky was darkest. Ye'll have to take a squint into the book ye'erself to l'arn thin things."

> "I won't do it," said Mr. Hennessey. "I think Tiddy Roosevelt is all r-right an' if he wants to blow his horn lave him to do it."

> "Thrue f'r ye," said Mr. Dooley. . . ."But if I was him I'd call th' book 'Alone in Cuba.'"

In any case Roosevelt returned home the hero of the hour, and was ultimately elected governor of New York. Tom Platt, the state Republican political boss, soon saw him as a real menace—a good government man or goo-goo, as they were called then—who needed to be suppressed before he destroyed the influence of party bosses (like Platt) in managing state affairs. ("I want to get rid of the bastard," thundered Platt.) Platt begged Mark Hanna (better known as Dollar Mark for his penchant of buying politicians such as McKinley) and the national party bigwigs to banish the Rough Riders' noted reform-minded leader by making him vice president for McKinley's second term (thus making him into a piece of "ornamental impotency," as one commentator put it years later). "Don't any of you realize there's only one life between this madman and the White House?" Hanna shouted in response. Platt was adamant, however. Later when McKinley's assassination elevated Teddy to the presidency, Hanna wrung his hands crying, "Now look, that damned cowboy is president of the United States!"

Roosevelt was the youngest to serve as the nation's president (John F. Kennedy was the youngest elected.) His accession to the presidency cemented America's place in the world as an imperial power, something dear to Roosevelt's heart. Not all Americans wanted the honor, which many saw as dubious at best and a betrayal of the American mission of democracy at worst. Tongue in cheek, as always, Mr. Dooley probably summed the momentous events of the decade as only he could do: "They'se wan consolation; an' that is, if th' American people can govern thimsilves, they can govern anything that walks."

Boxers and Chinese Scholarships

In spring of 1900 an aggressively antiforeign group of Chinese nationalists, the Society of Harmonious Fists, rebelled at the growing and humiliating domination of China by outside powers. Known to outsiders as Boxers, this rebel force was actually commanded by various Chinese religious orders who routinely taught their followers a form of karate now known as Kung-Fu, or boxing as it appeared to Europeans. Foreigners, used to having their way in China, called upon the Empress

Dowager to suppress the movement, but she slyly professed to be unable to control them. The Boxer armies eventually cornered the various foreign legations and missionaries in the city of Beijing (Peking) and laid siege to their fortifications. A European army, joined by the Japanese and Americans, moved inland, and after several botched operations managed to raise the siege and defeat the Boxers. The Chinese government then appealed to the United States to use its good offices to deal with the powers.

In the Boxer Protocol of 7 September 1901, despite the contention of the United States that the Chinese government had been the victim of an illegal insurrection, the victorious powers laid a heavy indemnity of $332 million upon the Chinese government, the American share of which was deemed to be $24.5 million. The Americans accepted $4 million in payment to satisfy private claims and remitted the remainder as scholarships for the purposes of educating Chinese students in the United States. This, along with the Open Door policy of trade and nonoccupation, gave the Americans much good will that lasted until after the Communist takeover in 1949.

Tidbits: Presidential Wives (McKinley and Coolidge)

Ida Saxon McKinley, formerly a sprightly, devoted, and attentive wife, experienced severe physical and mental problems well before she became first lady. Childbirth proved difficult in 1873, to be followed by phlebitis, splitting headaches, and epileptic seizures both mild and major. The death of her four-year-old daughter from typhoid merely aggravated her own health conditions, reducing her to a near-invalid stage. Whenever President McKinley was forced to leave town on business, he wrote his wife daily. He always exhibited concern and tender comfort for her, even under the most delicate social circumstances. At dinner parties he would sit next to her, and if he observed her slipping into a minor seizure he would place a napkin or handkerchief over her face and continue visiting with guests. Once the spell had passed, the first lady would resume her role in the conversation as though nothing had happened.

Grace Coolidge and husband Calvin could not agree upon a name for their second child, born in 1908. Because of an Easter-time birth, Mrs. Coolidge referred to him as Bunny but continued to badger her delaying husband for a name. Finally Mrs. Coolidge demanded that a decision wait no longer, and insisted on an explanation for the delay. Her husband responded, "Well, my dear, I agree with you, but I thought that before we called him Calvin, I'd see if he knows anything." Thus the child became Calvin, Jr.

American Eyes and News in 1901

What would be some of the most reported events in 1901 for the average American newspaper reader? Consider the following:

1. Queen Victoria of England, reigning since 1837, passed away at the age of 82. Grief-stricken at the death of her husband in 1861 (Prince Albert, the one portrayed on the popular tobacco can), she had remained in some level of mourning for 40 years.

2. While a monumental oil gusher greeted the Beaumont area of Texas, Filipinos requested independence, and Italian composer Giuseppe Verdi passed away.

3. Carry Nation, along with 500 volunteers, laid waste to the saloons of Topeka, Kansas, with her keg-splitting and glass-shattering hatchet. Periods of time spent in jail did not slow her actions.

4. Steel magnate and philanthropist Andrew Carnegie died, Utah struggled to change its polygamy laws, and members of the Automobile Club of America were arrested in New Jersey for breaking the eight-miles-an-hour speed limit. The drivers, who faced a collective fine of $10, had been motoring along at excessive speeds often reaching thirty miles per hour.

5. Some 64,690 square miles of Oklahoma land was opened to white settlers, resulting in a land scramble by nearly 200,000 Boomers (legal settlers) preceded by an untold number of Sooners (illegals who had sneaked onto the lands before the

starting gun). Most of the original towns were tent cities, which lead to the ostentatious saying: Rome may not have been built in a day, but Guthrie, Oklahoma (the territorial capital), was.

6. Buffalo's Pan-American Exposition was darkened by the shooting of President William McKinley by Leon Czolgosz (pronounced Sholl'-gosh), making the dynamic Teddy Roosevelt the new president. Paris lost a special treasure with the death of Henri de Toulouse-Lautrec at the age of 36. One of France's greatest artists, he grew to maturity with an adult body and the atrophied legs of a dwarf.

7. The first Eastman Kodak Brownie camera went on the market and sold for just one dollar. Sweden's Alfred Nobel awarded his first prizes for physics and literature, Anna Edison Taylor successfully passed over Niagara Falls in a barrel (suffering only shock and minor cuts), and Great Britain signed the Hay-Pauncefote Treaty, surrendering exclusive rights to the United States for construction of a canal across Central America.

8. Guglielmo Marconi reached a level of perfection in telegraph technology adequate enough to send a message from England to Newfoundland, while King Gillette announced to the market a replaceable razor blade for so-called safety razors (not everyone shaved, which took some skill with the straight razors in vogue at the time). In popular music, Scott Joplin reached the highest level of audience appreciation in his life, becoming the King of Ragtime for his classic tune "Maple Leaf Rag." The reading public was treated to the release of *The Wonderful Wizard of Oz* and *The Tale of Peter Rabbit.*

Some TR Tidbits

By the time Teddy Roosevelt had become the very popular elected president, German Kaiser Wilhelm II had already established a grand reputation in international circles for verbal intemperance and for having the personality of a bully in diplomatic affairs. When he sent warships to the coast of South America to intimidate Venezuela into paying German debt claims, TR called in the German ambassador and informed him that if Germany did not submit to arbitration within ten days,

Admiral Dewey and an American fleet would be sent to prevent further German action. Although the German ambassador said the kaiser would never back down, Teddy said he was responsible only for his actions, not the kaiser's. A week later, Roosevelt informed the German ambassador that he had decided not to wait the full ten days but would send Admiral Dewey's fleet within 48 hours unless the kaiser submitted to arbitration. It was 36 hours later when the kaiser informed Roosevelt through the German embassy that he would agree to American arbitration, giving veracity to what would be called the Roosevelt Corollary to the Monroe Doctrine: If European nations had a complaint with any American nation, the United States would act as the arbiter.

Unique among presidents, TR had the opportunity to give away the bride at the marriage of a young woman who later became a first lady—Eleanor Roosevelt. She was a favorite niece of the president and married one of Teddy's distant cousins, Franklin Delano Roosevelt.

During his first term, Teddy created a mild scandal by inviting noted black educator and early civil rights advocate Booker T. Washington to dinner at the White House. Dining with African Americans was considered a no-no both in the North and South in those days, and few but the brave ever did it. When Roosevelt ran for the presidency in his own right in 1904, Republicans appealed to the black vote with Equality buttons depicting him and Washington at dinner. Democrats countered this with a racist slogan: "The Election of Roosevelt Means Booker Niggerism." Despite this mudslinging, TR garnered the most electoral votes and the largest popular vote of any president in American history to that time.

Like many overly enthusiastic persons, TR had a tendency to go off half-cocked, which caused more problems with the South. In 1906 he invited Thomas Sherman (son of William T. Sherman, the Civil War general) to the White House after the unveiling of his father's statue on nearby Pennsylvania Avenue. Sherman was a Jesuit priest (much to his father's chagrin—he had wanted another general in the family) who was the spitting image of his father. He accepted, and during his visit to the White House Teddy mentioned that certain West Point cadets had planned a tour of the various sites of his father's march across Georgia and South Carolina. Wouldn't Father Tom like to tag along?, TR asked. Sherman agreed, evidently hoping his presence would act as a peace feeler to the South from his family, who had long been embarrassed by his father's boast to "make Georgia howl" and prove "war is Hell." Calling the planned journey a "gratuitous remembrance [of] one of the most ghastly and repulsive features" of the late war, Southerners would have none of it, causing the plan to be hastily abandoned. Although rugged Teddy bounced back from this debacle with his usual élan, a disconcerted, perhaps overly sensitive Father Tom Sherman tragically went insane shortly thereafter.

The First World Series and Super Bowl

On 13 October 1903 the first inter-league series for the world championship in baseball turned out to be an embarrassment for the well-established, senior National League. Boston of the upstart American League upset Pittsburgh of the National League with a 3–0 victory to win the fifth of an intended nine-game series. The contest featured such Hall of Fame greats as Honus Wagner and Cy Young.

The first Super Bowl, in 1967, involved the National Football League's Green Bay Packers and the American League's Kansas City Chiefs (established in 1960 as the Dallas Texans). No surprise was anticipated for the outcome, and none occurred. The Packers gave the Chiefs a 35–10 whipping. However, after Coach Vince Lombardi's Packers achieved a second victory the following year over the Oakland Raiders, the pendulum began to swing the other way. In 1969 the New York Jets of the American League upset the National's Baltimore Colts by 16–7 before the nation's stunned television audience. This was after the Jets quarterback, Joe Namath, promised the press and fans an American League victory. Subsequently the National Conference dealt three of its teams—the Colts, the Browns, and the Pittsburgh Steelers—to the smaller American Conference to even up the competition, and a more balanced and professional united league saw the Kansas City Chiefs return to the Super Bowl in 1970 and repeat an American Conference victory over the powerhouse Minnesota Vikings. The audience draw was so great that the league soon expanded football into the present 28 teams, evenly divided between the two conferences.

Movies Arrive

Before the advent of film, nineteenth century novels and short stories had provided the most influential medium for conveying ideas and entertainment on a mass scale. However, the turn of the century witnessed a variety of new inventions that expanded the possibilities for visual storytelling and amusement. Audiences enjoyed their first story in movie form in the 1903 production of *The Great Train Robbery*. The first movie house opened in Philadelphia in 1905, and popular demand resulted in 10,000 more across the country within three years. The 1915 12-reel *Birth of a Nation*, a bigoted treatment of Reconstruction and the role of the Ku Klux Klan, grossed a full $18 million. (Today *Birth of a Nation's* success would be comparable to garnering about $500 million from a few million dollars in production costs.) With the addition of sound to *The Jazz Singer* in 1927, the full potential of film was realized. The visual offering continued to expand through the 1930s and 1940s, and with the addition of television and the VCR, film has become the most profound visual influence in American life. Now it is common to record weddings, for example, and have the video played before the end of the reception. Even more important, audiences can vicariously participate in a war at the front lines, as the coverage of U.S. activities in Vietnam and the Arabian Gulf so vividly have illustrated, changing the historical concept of an aseptic war forever.

Meat Flavored with Rat Dung: Teddy Responds

Most Americans today are well aware of the governmental role in regulating consumer products that might be poisonous or otherwise injurious to the user's health. With that in mind, we might observe a few lines from *The Jungle*, a 1906 novel by Upton Sinclair, as they describe food production in that period of American history: "It was too dark in these places to see well, but a man could run his hand over piles of meat and sweep off handfuls of the dried dung of rats. These rats were nuisances, and the packers put poisoned bread out for them, and the rats, bread, and meat would go into the hoppers [for sausage grinding] together."

At that time we had Teddy Roosevelt as president, a man who wrote dozens of books but read even more. His ethics and stomach challenged, he reacted immediately to Sinclair's words and dispatched special agents to Chicago, America's meat-processing capital, to verify what he had read. The agents wrote back: "We saw meat shoveled from filthy wooden floors, piled on tables rarely washed, pushed from rooms in rotten box cars, in all of which processes it was in the way of gathering dirt, splinters, floor filth, and the expectoration of tuberculosis and other diseases of workers."

Within the same year, under presidential leadership, Congress enacted the Meat Inspection Act and the Pure Food and Drug Act. Both serve as fine examples of the role of government as an independent regulator in activities where the general public might be harmed. This episode represents one of the finest examples in history of the problem-and-response role of concerned fellow citizens and, as a plus, the participation of the fine arts (in this case, literature) as a positive influence in society.

The 297 Pounds of Taft

William H. Taft was Teddy Roosevelt's personal choice as his successor for the Republican ticket, and from the outset of the campaign, Roosevelt provided Taft with regular advice on his conduct and popular image. He said, "Photographs on horseback, yes; tennis, no; and golf is fatal." However, candidate Taft's favorite recreation was golf, which the 297-pound campaigner continued to play while he told newsmen he was trying to shed a little weight. TR got smarter, too, proposing that Taft "cast aside golf and take an ax and cut wood," and he referred to the possibility of Taft sitting on a steed as "cruelty to the horse." Rather than the ax, Taft risked the horse. He took up riding, only to quit after one animal collapsed under the excess weight on his back. This is reminiscent of the Whig presidential candidate in 1852, General Winfield Scott (the victor over Mexico in 1848), who had to be lifted onto his horse with a sturdy A-frame hoist to review troops. Scott, however, weighed in at a reported 350 pounds. The best evidence of Taft's almost-svelte size (compared to Scott, anyway) is, of course, the fact that he installed a new larger bathtub in the White House after his election in 1908. There was no way to disguise the principle discovered by the Greek scientist, Archimedes, well before the time of Christ—the principle of water displacement!

The Birth of the NAACP

By the end of the nineteenth century and the dawn of the twentieth, African-American leadership had fallen into two schools of thought. One was represented by the foremost black spokesman of his day, Booker T. Washington, who, born a slave, became an educator of tremendous reputation, the founder of Tuskegee Institute in Alabama, an exponent of black self-sufficiency, and the only black in the United States who could boast of having had a White House lunch with President Theodore Roosevelt and tea with Queen Victoria at Buckingham Palace. Washington believed that equality was a privilege his race had to earn by becoming good workers and obtaining wealth and capital. He sought to give hope to Afri- can Americans, to appease hostile whites, and to prevent further restrictions in black civil rights. He stated his position most concisely at the 1895 Atlanta Cotton States and Interna- tional Exposition, using the theme that blacks and whites could be as united and cooperative as the human hand, and yet as separate as the five fingers. As the first African American to address a large audience of hostile Southern whites, Washington skillfully wended his way down the middle path, yielding here, standing firm there, trying to alienate no one. It was a more or less impossible goal.

Washington's speech was greeted with much enthusiasm by whites throughout the nation, but with less support among better educated blacks, who felt he had given up too much. Chief among his opponents was W. E. Burghardt DuBois, an African-American intellectual with a Ph.D. from Harvard University who was a professor of Sociology at Atlanta University. DuBois believed that black progress meant demanding the equal rights due all American citizens immediately and unconditionally. He maintained that merely being born in the United States made these equal rights part of the heritage of African Americans, and they did not have to do penance in any form for them, especially after their 350 years of enforced servitude.

To set forth his program, DuBois organized the Niagara Movement in 1905 in a meeting with 29 other black professionals who agreed with his basic tenets. Called radical by its critics, the Niagara Movement eschewed Washington's Atlanta Compromise in favor of a declaration designed to focus on black discontent and a clarion call to rise up and act to ensure equal voting rights and complete social equality. DuBois also saw no need to emphasize solely industrial and agricultural education, which tended to exclude African Americans from the more advanced economic opportunities in the professions.

As time went on, naturally, Washington and DuBois graduated from a respectful disagreement to outright hostility over each other's positions. DuBois pointed out that Washington's compromise had done little but enshrine current prejudice and discriminatory state and federal laws. Lynching was rampant (there were 3,539 known lynchings of blacks in the United States between 1885 and 1912), and blacks had been proscribed from voting and equal education by U.S. Supreme Court decisions. What industrial and agricultural education there was merely kept the mass of African Americans in the cotton fields in a condition that approached slavery, or more correctly, peonage, and was so expensive compared to a liberal arts education as to be self-limiting to a half dozen really adequate programs and colleges. For most African Americans nationwide, separate but equal had become separate but unequal.

The Niagara Movement soon found that many philanthropists were willing to contribute to Washington's programs, but few would back DuBois's notions. Their protests had drawn attention, however, and by 1909, as the Niagara Movement wound down, its members decided to organize a permanent civil rights group with broader appeal. Infuriated by a two-day race riot in Springfield, Illinois (the theme: Lincoln freed you, we'll show you where you belong), three individuals—a white social worker, Mary Ovington, a New York Jewish activist, Henry Moscovitz, and a muckraking journalist, William Walling—asked Oswald Garrison Villard, the grandson of famous abolitionist William Lloyd Garrison, to issue a document known as "The Call."

Signed by 60 notable American reformers of both sexes and races, including DuBois, Jane Addams of Hull House in Chicago, muckraking journalist Ray Stannard Baker, and anti-lynching crusader Ida Wells Barnett, the Call was issued on Lincoln's birthday in 1909 and resulted in the National Negro Conference meeting in New York City. This group agreed to and did organize the National Association for the Advancement of Colored People (NAACP), chartered in May 1910 and dedicated to equal civil, educational, and voting rights for African Americans. It placed Dr. DuBois in charge of editing its journal, *Crisis*, which was to challenge successfully Washington's Tuskegee Machine for the right to lead African Americans in the twentieth century. Emphasizing legal action through the courts (one of their foremost lawyers was the late Thurgood Marshall, later Associate Justice of the Supreme Court, and only recently retired), the NAACP was and still is in the forefront of the fight to guarantee equal social, educational, and political rights for African Americans.

Women Demand the Vote

Most men know well the anguish, pain, and immobilizing effect of a stiff blow to the groin. Well, women marching down Pennsylvania Avenue during the late years of President

Woodrow Wilson's administration (1913–1921) learned the immediate debilitating effects of a full fist blow to the breast administered by street thugs challenging their public assertion of the women's right to vote. Long before common press terms like activist or confrontation were common, British and American women demonstrated to gain attention for their causes. Properly dressed middle-class women in London would quietly march; then suddenly, at a prearranged signal, they would smash all the glass in sight and set fire to trash receptacles.

On this side of the Atlantic, the cause reached its peak during World War I with women asking why it was so desirable for President Wilson to fight a war for democracy in Europe when women could not even vote in the United States. Women were arrested in several instances and imprisoned. When they refused to eat, they were force-fed at a danger to their health, with metal-hinged contraptions used to hold open their mouths. Certainly Wilson did not want to be held responsible for further injury or indignity, so he released them by presidential order. It was all a sad spectacle.

Regardless of the methods used or means by which male minds were changed by the war's end, women gained the right to vote in 1919 with the Nineteenth Amendment. A contributing factor was revealed by a British war study that indicated that it took six people working in war-related industry at home to support each soldier in uniform. Now, if the majority of men were off fighting the enemy in the field, many of those six people working at home ultimately must have been women. When the laurels for victory were won, it was hard to leave out the critical efforts behind the lines performed by women. In return for the recognition they received, the women showed their "appreciation" by voting out the Democrats who had dragged their feet during the Wilson administration by voting largely for the Republican candidate, Warren G. Harding.

Pancho Villa's Ride-By Shooting

During the desert heat of the summer of 1916, the United States sent the largest expeditionary force to leave the nation's borders

162   THE AMERICAN EMPIRE

since the Spanish American War (approximately 12,000 men and a reconnaissance airplane or two) on a chase around northern Mexico, all to capture one Francisco "Pancho" Villa. On 16 March of that year, Villa had sent a raiding party of his troops into Columbus, New Mexico, killing 10 American citizens and 14 cavalrymen from the local military post.

Villa was born and raised in Mexico's Durango state, where he learned early on to live by his wits. He became a guerrilla fighter in the lengthy revolutionary struggle that followed the death of General Porfirio Díaz. Escaping from his imprisonment by General Victoriano Huerta in 1912, he fled to El Paso, where he gathered up a band of followers and became a regional power in the struggles connected with the Mexican Revolution in Chihuahua State. Not offered what he viewed as proper influence in these developments—and resisted by General Venuistiano Carranza, whom the United States had recognized recently as the legitimate *líder* of Mexico—Villa sought to embarrass Carranza by attacking Columbus, where American authorities had seized and held some equipment and stores in transit to Villas's legions. The attackers narrowly missed the Southern Pacific's crack passenger train, the Sunset Limited, in the process.

Villa's raid made him by far the best known Mexican north of the border, especially after he successfully avoided American vengeance in the form of U.S. General John J. Pershing's pursuing punitive expedition. After fighting several small skirmishes and a pitched battle with Carranza's regular army at Carrizal, Pershing withdrew. (Conforming to public opinion, *el presidente* had changed his mind about the *gringo* invasion he had reluctantly approved a few months earlier.) Villa, for his part, though once reduced to three followers, survived the many bouts and crises of his nation's tumultuous struggles, made peace with his political enemies, and retired as a general with full pay. However, grudges died hard south of the border. In 1923 he was assassinated by long-time enemies in Parral, Chihuahua.

One small footnote to the Villa raid: In the middle of downtown Tucson, Arizona, at August 20 Park, which marks the founding of the original community by Lieutenant Colonel

Don Hugo O'Connor (an Irishman in the service of Spain), stands a statue of a Mexican cowboy on a rearing horse with the following inscription at its base:

"In Friendship"
This Equestrian Statue of the Mexican
General Francisco Villa
1877–1923
presented by
President Jóse López-Portillo
Republic of Mexico
to the State of Arizona
June 30, 1981

One cannot help but wonder what the dead Americans at Columbus, New Mexico, would say if they could come back and see this. As for Pancho Villa, surely he would dismiss the whole matter with a smiling *no le hace* (it's not important), laugh, and motion for the mariachi band to begin playing his rousing, boisterous theme song, "La Cucaracha," which relates the exploits of a marijuana-seeking cockroach.

Perhaps it is no worse than the Jean A. Houdon statue of George Washington that has dominated the Virginia state capitol building since 1796—and the yard of the British National Gallery at Trafalgar Square since 1932. The British copy was sent across the sea during the bicentennial of Washington's birth, complete with two tons of good, noble Virginia earth used for keeping the feet of Washington's proud image from standing on British ground. Politics do indeed make for strange bedfellows.

CHAPTER VIII

World War I and the Interwar Years

A Very Big War

A few statistics quickly offer convincing proof of the size and hence the potential for casualties in the conflict that, until 1939, history books and newspapers would call the Great War. During the 1914–1918 period, Germany, Austria-Hungary, Turkey, and Bulgaria would place in uniform no less than 22 million combatants, the Allied and Associated powers some 42 million. More souls would die on European battlefields between 1900 and 1925 than in all the lapsed time since William the Conqueror defeated the Earl Harold at Hastings in 1066. So much for the twentieth-century demigod, progress.

Ironically, the largest expeditionary force ever sent beyond U.S. borders prior to the Great War was the 12,000 men led by General John J. Pershing, nicknamed Black Jack because of his lengthy prior service with African-American troops. Not until after two and a half years of submarine losses and the provocation of the famous Zimmermann telegram did the United States declare war on the Central Powers in April 1917, thus becoming an Associated Power.

Well prior to the entry of the United States in the war, American officials and citizens had been reasonably well saturated with the newly expanded technique of wartime propaganda, of which the well-embellished atrocity became a crucial part. The aim was to curry favor to the cause; this was easier for the British than the Germans because they held the English language in common with Americans. England also had cut the trans-Atlantic cable to German-held parts of the continent, a move deemed necessary because there was much sympathy for the German cause among Americans of German, Irish, and Jewish descent. For example, victory celebrations were held in New York City's Central Park for Central Powers successes. Even the famous American writer H. L. Mencken of Baltimore went to the Eastern Front to report on German advances and victories there, which were many.

The British Empire countered German victories with well-conceived propaganda, recognizing the great size and ethnic variety of the United States. They used different approaches to reach the safely isolated residents of Topeka, Kansas, and the relatively exposed dwellers of Boston, who feared possible U-boat attack. For American Catholics there was the tale of two priests that Germans hanged from twin bell towers in Belgium; each victim was of nearly equal weight so they could toll the bells indefinitely as they hanged. The ringing of the bells was a warning to Belgians to behave, while it provided malicious entertainment to the invaders. Along with posters of a German jackboot crushing out European civilization with a "Halt the Hun" inscription, Americans heard that the kaiser intended to conquer North America and place his capital in the middle of it, a notion that was lent veracity by the Zimmermann telegram. Although this story was intended to move the stoic Kansans and Nebraskans, one muses that the kaiser might have felt quite at home in the vast German settlements of the Great Plains, and the settlers with him.

Understanding the need to reach all Americans more effectively, the British eventually even hired a U.S. citizen to create, scrutinize, and edit various press releases aimed at the Yanks. After the United States entered the war, there appeared more homegrown propaganda, including Liberty Bonds, the notion of the war to end all wars, liberty cabbage (formerly known as sauerkraut), and the unfortunate removal of German language study from hundreds of schools, colleges, and churches. Under pressure from other Americans, many U.S. citizens of German descent even changed the spellings of their names to a more agreeable Anglo form (for example, Karl became Carl, Krankheit became Cronkite). The famous American author, John Steinbeck, who both witnessed and suffered the persecution dealt out to those of German ethnic background, wrote in *East of Eden* about those whose only crime was to be conspicuous in their ethnicity by name or accent. The novel later became an Elia Kazan film, well known for the scene in which German American merchants had their shops painted yellow.

World War I: The More Things Change, the More They Remain the Same

Until we had a second one, our First World War was always referred to simply as the Great War. Because it occurred after more than four decades of intense scientific, industrial, and population growth, in terms of explosive power it just had to be a dandy. As a result, the war tested the wits of both the bitter and well-meaning individuals who directed this concentrated destruction for four years. Individuals and governments did things they would not have ordinarily done, believing themselves in a life-or-death struggle for the so-called civilized world. Decisions came to affect whole populations of Europe, their Asian and African colonies, Japan and the United States. Consider the following:

1. Of all the nations that entered the Great War, only Britain and the United States did not possess mandatory universal military service, whereby all males must participate in two or more years of military training and be enrolled in a complicated reserve system. The demands and pressures of battlefield losses forced the British to adopt conscription in 1916, and the United States initiated the practice as a matter of course when it joined the fray in 1917. It was the first draft in the United States since the Civil War. Times had changed, not only in the size and scope of war, but morally, in terms of values, attitudes, and the temperament of those touched by the crisis. Initially the British and then the Americans faced the fact that some citizens of serious conscience refused to serve as riflemen. A new draft classification with appropriate terminology was born—conscientious objector. Most of these persons, however, served in

some alternate capacity of a nonviolent nature, often in the medical field.

2. The entry of the United States into the conflict brought with it the need to finance the war effort. Within 17 days of the war declaration, Congress provided the Liberty Loan Act, authorizing a $5 billion increase in the national debt. Liberty Bonds were sold at most public gatherings, and movie stars like Douglas Fairbanks and Mary Pickford hawked bonds at gigantic rallies in Times Square and on Wall Street. Overseas in Germany a patriotic citizen could support the war by purchasing an iron nail and driving it into a wooden statue of the renowned Field Marshal Paul von Hindenburg.

3. One of the great quotes of the era came from the lips of an American staff officer, an aide to General John J. Pershing, who, upon landing in France, stated, "Lafayette, we are here." More than thanking the French for their support in our revolution, it showed the optimism that the Americans brought to the Allied war effort. By 1918 this translated into American soldiers being the only ones who still possessed the fortitude to go over the top and recklessly attack the enemy. By then, the Allies were too war-weary (and had recently suffered a disastrous troop mutiny), and the Germans had just shot their bolt in a final offensive stopped at the gates of Paris (Belleau Wood and Chateau Thierry) by sharpshooting Yankee riflemen.

   Did the United States have a genuine war hero who typified the noblest qualities of the reluctant yet talented citizen soldier in the Great War? Yes, indeed. The most decorated American hero of World War I was unassuming Alvin Cullum York of Pall Mall, Tennessee. His talents with the rifle came from hunting with an old muzzle loader, yet at first he asked to be excused from conscription because of his religious beliefs. York had second thoughts, however, and joined the 328th Infantry of the 82d Division (the All Americans), a move that eventually cost several dozen German soldiers their lives.

   York was made corporal and in the Battle of the Meuse-Argonne in October 1918, the uncomplicated Tennessee farmer destroyed an entire German machine gun battalion, single-handedly killing 25 and capturing 132. Reporting to his commander, prisoners in tow, the officer said, "Well, York, I hear that you have captured the whole damned German Army." The embarrassed, soft-spoken York responded with a grin, "Nossir,

I only have one hundred and thirty two." The Allied Supreme Commander, French Field Marshal Ferdinand Foch, called York's act "the greatest thing accomplished by any private soldier of all of the armies in Europe." York was promoted to sergeant and received no less than 50 decorations, including the French Croix de Guerre and the American Congressional Medal of Honor. His home state awarded him a farm after the war. When a film of the exploit was made, Sergeant York gave his proceeds to a religious institute and a home for the physically infirm.

4. For the American history student there are several films on the Great War:

(a) *All Quiet on the Western Front* (1930) is a black-and-white treatment of a young German student who experiences the brutal destruction of war. Based on a semiautobiographical novel by Erich Maria Remarque, the film starred Lew Ayres. The role so moved the actor that he became a pacifist and refused to participate in World War II, for which he was blacklisted by Hollywood producers. A later television version appeared starring Richard Thomas and Ernest Borgnine.

(b) *Paths of Glory* (1957) concentrates on the lowest point of French defense and subsequent mutiny on the Western Front in 1917. Kirk Douglas stars as a French line soldier in an army commanded by a weasel-like Adolphe Menjou. Arbitrary executions of soldiers, one from each rank, result.

(c) *A Farewell to Arms* (1932), an Ernest Hemingway classic offered in film, concerns an American ambulance driver in the Italian army and is semiautobiographical. Convalescing from a wound suffered in the great Italian defeat at Caporetto, the American decides to flee with his English nurse to the solitude of Switzerland.

(d) *Gallipoli* (1981), based on the ill-fated British-Australian expedition against the German-supported Turks, concentrates on the misery of the common soldiers trapped against the sea in their original landing spots. For his part in this plan, Winston Churchill lost his political position, and his career was placed in limbo for some time.

(e) *Reds* (1981) looks at the conduct of American intellectuals and professionals who were faced with the demands of war and the challenges presented to their values when the Bolshevik

Revolution changed their outlook. This long but well-done film concentrates on the life of John Reed, the only American buried in the Kremlin.

(f) *Sergeant York* (1941), starring Gary Cooper as the Tennessee farmer who became the war's most-decorated hero, is a must. Some viewers will find the parallels between the reluctant York and Private Will Stockdale of the later *No Time for Sergeants* (1958), as portrayed by Andy Griffith, uncanny.

(g) *The Guns of August* (1964) is a quasi-documentary approach to the outbreak of World War I based on Barbara Tuchman's incomparable history of the same title. It captures well the transformation of the conflict from a romantic conquest to a brutal holocaust. It is interesting to note that the beginning of the twentieth century is usually marked by the outbreak of the Great War with the assassination of the Austrian Archduke Franz Ferdinand at Sarajevo, in the province of Bosnia, and the seemingly never-ending clash of Roman Catholic, Orthodox, and Muslim cultures in the southern Slavic lands that became Yugoslavia. Eighty years later, the world faces the same cultural clash as it approaches the end of the twentieth century—in the same area, at the same city.

John Barleycorn: Strong Drink in the U.S.A.

On 16 January 1920 the Eighteenth Amendment to the U.S. Constitution went into effect. It banned the manufacture, sale, or transport of any intoxicating fluid that contained more than 0.5 percent alcohol. On that same day, prominent evangelist Billy Sunday preached to a crowd of 10,000 in Norfolk, Virginia, over a coffin that supposedly contained the remains of John Barleycorn, the caricature of the demon, booze.

Within two years common observation substantiated the existence of large-scale illegal importation of liquor at key points such as Detroit, Miami, and Seattle. There was also an increase in arrests for public drunkenness, an expanded use of hip flasks, the rise of poorly concealed undercover drinking parlors called speakeasies (where customers were often greeted with a boisterous "Howdy, sucker!"), and greater drinking on the part of women. American English soon enjoyed the use of the new term, *bootlegging*, and citizens who profited from the illicit trade, like one Alphonse Capone, became millionaires. Organized crime never had experienced such a benefit (with the possible exception of the modern drug trade), nor had bureaucrats and law enforcement personnel who accepted bribes to look the other way. Those who preferred to keep their drinking private brewed their own, and the era of bathtub gin was born.

All of this provides the student with an instructive lesson on both human nature and the role of government and law in society—a teaching already propounded by the English philosopher John Stuart Mill half a century earlier: One violates the principles of utility if one passes or attempts to enforce a law that is either contrary to the habits and customs of the people in general or violates the essential rights of privacy. In more common application, why worry about the purchase of six boxes of grapes, which might indicate an illegal still for someone's dinner wine, when there are bigger, more vicious problems facing society as a whole?

The Aerial Bombardment of Tulsa

On 31 May 1921 a 36-block section of Tulsa, Oklahoma, was burned to the ground in one of the most vicious race riots in U.S. history—the culmination of two years of post-World War I race riots that had affected localities as varied as Minnesota, Nebraska, Illinois, and Pennsylvania, as well as at least 60 sites in the American South. As explained by Scott Ellsworth in his book, *Death in a Promised Land* (1982), the riot grew out of the increasing success by blacks in economic competition during the World War I era. As large numbers of blacks moved north out of the Deep South, fleeing the deadening peonage of agriculture for the economic vibrancy of industrialized cities, white hostility in the upper South and North began to grow. Of all the places of opportunity, nothing compared with what blacks achieved in Tulsa. There, the African-American section of Greenwood saw such a spectacular increase of land ownership, the creations of industries, jobs, housing, and especially financial wealth, that it caused Tulsa to be nicknamed the Negro's Wall Street. Efforts by "respectable" whites to buy out this perceived black success story and save the city's reputation as a "nigger town" were rebuffed.

By the 1920s the racial situation in Tulsa was at a breaking point, merely needing some incident to set it off. It occurred on 30 May 1921, when a white woman emerged from a downtown elevator screaming that a black rider on the same car had tried to rape her. The accused, one Dick Rowland, was immediately arrested and charged, despite his remonstrance that he had only accidentally stepped on the accuser's foot. As if to confirm his story the whole matter was dropped and he was released a few days later. It was already too late.

The incident was quickly exaggerated by rumors and nasty newspaper headlines—allegedly the local newspaper called on whites to attack the "cancer" of Greenwood and wipe it off the map, but mysteriously no copies of the edition are extant. In any case the white community was at last determined to put an end to "uppity" black behavior in Tulsa, and proceeded to do just that. The area was cordoned off and torched. Soon the 36 blocks were ablaze, according to black witnesses, assisted by the aerial bombing of Greenwood by a biplane carrying homemade dynamite bombs. When trapped blacks fled one building, the mob shot them down and threw the bodies back into the fire. The official death count was 36, but others claimed that ten times that many had died.

Blacks were determined to build Greenwood back to its former glory. Unfortunately, they learned that the city government, shocked at the easily burned structures that predominated in Tulsa, had passed a new stricter fire ordinance for the safety of the community. Naturally all existing structures were exempted from the new law, but new ones, like those going up in Greenwood, had to face complicated, expensive building and licensing regulations enforced by a hostile, white, city bureaucracy. Meanwhile, white businessmen let the African Americans know that they would buy up the whole area as proposed before, cheaper now that it had been ruined by fire, of course, but nonetheless, at a fair price. That ultimately broke the rebuilding attempt. The demoralized blacks finally gave in, as eager white land developers played them off against each other. Eventually Greenwood was rebuilt as an industrial park, and the black community was put in its place for decades to come.

America's Negro Presidents and Others: The Burning Question of Race

Has the United States had a president who was of black descent? African-American journalist and historian Joel Augustus Rogers thinks so, and his pamphlet, *The Negro Presidents According to What White People Said They Were* (1965), written the year before his death, sets forth this controversial thesis as a sort of capstone of his life's work.

Born in Negril, Jamaica, Rogers came to the United States in 1906 and was made a naturalized citizen in 1917. A lifelong journalist, he traveled widely, was the one newspaperman who covered the Italo-Ethiopian war during the 1930s from Emperor Haile Selassie's side, and was a member of the Paris Society for Anthropology. He wrote for several prominent black newspapers, authored the series "Your History" (sort of a "Ripley's Believe It or Not" of black history), and published 15 books and essays on Africans and their descendants in world and American history. Most of these books were so challenging to the standard historical treatment of blacks that he was forced to publish them himself through a company run by his wife. They at times seemed to lack incontrovertible proof (the Confederate General Thomas J. "Stonewall" Jackson is confused with President Andrew Jackson, for example) and were often too emotional and too subjective, especially in the eyes of established white historians and publishers.

Perhaps the most thorough endeavor of his publishing career was his three-volume *Sex and Race*, released in the early 1940s. It is from this work that the following ten notions were popularized:

1. Ludwig van Beethoven was possibly of black descent, coming

from the Moorish soldiers of the Spanish army who mingled
with the white population of Flanders

2. Johann Wolfgang von Goethe and Franz Josef Hayden were
probably of similar parentage, their black descendants being
the Africans who accompanied Turkish armies into southeastern and central Europe

3. Winston Churchill's grandmother was not one-fourth American Indian but (as alleged by James Joyce) a quadroon

4. George Washington fathered a black son

5. Thomas Jefferson had two black daughters, later sold after his
death to "fancy houses" in New Orleans (one of the girls
committed suicide rather than submit to prostitution)

6. Alexander Hamilton, the first secretary of the Treasury, was a
black man from Nevis in the British West Indies, whose wool-
haired, dark skinned portraits, once revealing, have since been
caucasianized (and Rogers compares two of them to prove his
point)

7. Ancient Egypt was a primarily black nation and civilization

8. Marie-Theresa, the wife of Louis XIV, bore a black daughter

9. Charlotte Sophia, the consort to George III, was black, along
with a picture as proof

10. Jews in general and Jesus Christ in particular were of Negro
origins

Such ideas are allegedly gaining credence with renewed
vigor among certain elements of black scholarship today.

The presidents who supposedly had black ancestors begin
with Thomas Jefferson. Using a half-baked accusation from the
so-called Johnnycake Papers, which paints the scion of
Monticello as the "half-nigger . . . son of a half-breed Indian
squaw, by a Virginia mulatto father," Rogers does admit that
the specific details are hard to find. Similarly, he relies much
on rumor and political attack in the case of Andrew Jackson,
his second president with alleged black ancestry. He stresses
that Jackson's father was long dead by the time Andrew was
born (a fact denied by Jackson's stellar biographer, Robert V.
Remini, who has him dying shortly before the boy's birth), and

that the family lived on a plantation staffed by Negro slaves with whom his mother cohabited. Remini points out that Andrew's mother helped out the lady of the spread (who was a semi-invalid and a close friend), and that his brother was so dark as to be sold as a slave. There are also conflicting claims that Andrew Jackson was born in North Carolina, South Carolina, on the high seas, or in Ireland, too, although the president himself claimed South Carolina as his birthplace.

Rogers is more loquacious in the cause of Abraham Lincoln, this third candidate as black man in the presidency. While Jefferson and Jackson rate a mere paragraph, Lincoln's story is five times longer. Again it is the rail-splitter's mother giving birth to an illegitimate son, one whose hair was "more Negroid than Caucasian," according to Rogers, who quotes Lincoln's confidant, law partner, and biographer, William Herndon, that Lincoln had "very dark skin." Herndon went on to explain that the president had "something about his origin, he never cared to dwell on." "Was it his race?" wonders Rogers.

The black historian also inserts a few paragraphs about Vice President Hannibal Hamlin, attacked in the press even more than Lincoln as a mulatto. "He has black blood in him," stormed South Carolina secession fire-eater, Robert Barnwell Rhett. "The Northern people . . . design to place over the South a man who has Negro blood." In a stinging bit of sarcasm, Rhett offered to buy "the boy, Hannibal" from Lincoln, if the price were reasonable. Rogers also refers to a statement he attributes to General Benjamin Butler, who was raising black regiments for the Union Army in occupied Louisiana, that the men would be mulattos about the complexion of Vice President Hamlin. (Rogers in another place made the same attribution to Butler with a reference to Daniel Webster, known as Black Dan due to his dark facial features).

Returning to Lincoln, Rogers reveals his most damning evidence. For the premier of its movie, *Abe Lincoln in Illinois*, in 1940, RKO Studios held a nationwide look-alike contest with a prize offered for the man who most resembled Lincoln. The judges picked Thomas Bomar from the thousands of pictures submitted. In person he was even more the spittin' image of

Old Abe. Just before the premier, however, the moguls discovered that Bomar was black. Rather than the planned gala presentation, the studio awarded Bomar the prize and let him sit in the front row seat of honor, but kept the whole matter as quiet as possible.

Rogers's fourth candidate as one of country's black presidents was Warren G. Harding. Here he seems to have more than the usual innuendo to go on, relying on sworn affidavits; a broadside distributed shortly before his election through the federal mails (which then-President Woodrow Wilson ordered destroyed) and then by hand; and a book by William Estabrook Chancellor, *Warren G. Harding, President of the United States,* which evidently was destroyed so thoroughly by the Department of Justice that only three copies are extant. Rogers accuses Harding of having a mulatto father and a black grandfather. Evidently the evidence made an impression on Rogers, because he used the transposition of pictures of Harding and his black ancestor as the cover illustrations for the whole pamphlet. Rogers also has materials that assert that Harding was known for his black antecedents long before his successful run for the presidency, and that Harding often referred to himself as colored to attract local black voters. He refused to deny stories of his black forebearers. "How should I know," he said with a malicious vagueness. "One of my ancestors might have jumped the fence."

According to Rogers, one other president's relatives also jumped the fence, but he declines to name him, saying only that portraits (Rogers relies heavily on the subjective analysis of paintings and photographs in all cases) show the man's mother to possess Negroid physiognomy and that pictures of the man in question reveal the same. The public service program "Tony Brown's Journal" labeled him well-known, but one other black commentator said that this possibility was nothing but a smear.

Rogers concludes his study by stating that some presidents could be seen as white by some and black by others, which "shows how ridiculous is this burning question of race." The subject might best be left alone with that, his wisest comment of all, the crux of his whole study.

Biology Teacher on Trial, but Not for Dissecting Frogs

Charles Darwin's thesis on biological evolution continued to produce academic and social controversy throughout the last decades of the nineteenth century. It received special attention as a result of the militant fundamentalism that arose after the appearance of a series of pamphlets (*The Fundamentals*) published in 1910. By the early 1920s several states moved to prohibit inclusion of the thesis in public school texts and instruction. Three-time presidential candidate William Jennings Bryan had become a national spokesman for the antievolution cause, and a Tennessee governor in 1925 signed a popularly supported bill prohibiting teaching of evolution in public schools and colleges. While the governor, interested in other legislative support for school programs, willingly signed the bill with the assumption it might never need be applied, the American Civil Liberties Union reasoned differently.

On 13 July 1925, biology teacher John T. Scopes of Dayton went on trial in the most famous test case to date. By the date of the trial the small Southern town of Dayton was overburdened with a carnival crowd and atmosphere, which featured reporters from across the country, the curious, professional evangelists, outspoken atheists, novelty salesmen, and hustlers of every stripe. One of the country's better-known trial lawyers and confessed agnostic, Clarence Darrow, defended Scopes. When the judge refused to admit scientific testimony, Darrow called upon Bryan as an expert in biblical interpretation. Bryan faced entrapment in support of several Bible stories not supported by historical fact, such as Jonah and the whale and Joshua causing the sun to stand still. The result was worldwide publicity for Dayton, Tennessee.

The only real legal issue before the court was whether Scopes had violated state law by teaching about Darwin in the classroom. No one could deny that. Scopes was properly found guilty, an appellate court waived his $100 fine, and the case was dropped. Ironically, Bryan, who had described the trial to the press as a "duel to the death," died suddenly a few days after the trial, a victim of a heart condition aggravated by heat and fatigue. The entire episode has gone down in American history as the monkey trial, aping the popular conception of Darwin's alleged idea that man had descended from the primates.

Duke University in 1925: America's Wealthiest College

Having already changed its name from Trinity to Duke as a result of earlier generosity by its benefactor, the modest Durham, North Carolina, college received in 1924 a $6 million trust fund to give the state "preachers, teachers, lawyers, chemists, engineers, and doctors." A year later, upon the death of James Buchanan "Buck" Duke, the gift rose to $25 million, making it the nation's wealthiest institution of higher learning at that time.

Just after the Civil War, Buck's father, Washington Duke, began a tobacco enterprise on 50 cents. By 1872 he had expanded to the factory stage and, utilizing the business knowledge and advertising skills of his son, he saw his empire expand rapidly. By 1890 Buck had brought most of the competition under his control with so much success, particularly in new machine-rolled cigarettes like Lucky Strikes, that in 1911 the U.S. Supreme Court ordered a breakup of the monopoly exercised by Duke's American Tobacco Company.

One particular advertising promotion of the 1920s resulted in a corporate and legal struggle with the sugar industry. Buck Duke wanted to expand the taste for cigarettes among women, who generally were nonsmokers. Using the catch-phrase, "Reach for a Lucky instead of a sweet," which occurred to him when he observed a heavy woman eating bon bons at a bus stop, Duke tied dieting and smoking in an extraordinary way. His advertising proved effective—tobacco use by women did in fact increase—while the confection industry gained nothing from its legal efforts.

Never one to wait on others, by the time of his death Duke

had already amassed a second fortune in the development of hydroelectric power throughout the southeastern states.

That Silent Cal, Calvin Coolidge

Calvin Coolidge earned a reputation for being a man of few words and simple tastes. Teddy Roosevelt's daughter Alice, wife of Senator Longworth and until the 1950s a prominent Washington, D.C., hostess, raconteur, wit, and no slouch of a ripsnorter in her own day, referred to him as having been "weaned on a pickle." The most legendary story about his verbal reserve has Coolidge seated at a banquet next to a prominent lady who says, "President Coolidge, someone bet me that I would not be able to get you to say three words," to which Silent Cal cryptically answered, "You lose."

To many Americans Coolidge always resembled a New England Protestant pastor, so it was a bemused public that observed a press photo of him on the campaign trail out West wearing a full-feathered headdress of a Native American chieftain with his business suit and vest. Humorist and popular wit Will Rogers wired him immediately: "Politics make strange *red*-fellows." When campaigning in 1924 Coolidge was asked for a photo by a friendly congressman who explained, "I only have one taken when you were Lieutenant Governor [of Massachusetts]." Coolidge simply responded, "I don't see what you want another for, I'm using the same face."

Some of the Nation's Most Notorious

1. On 31 May 1924, in a murder case that was noted for decades as both an example and a frame of reference, two brilliant students and sons of millionaires, Nathan Leopold and Richard Loeb, confessed to the strangling of the latter's cousin, Bobby Franks, and placing his remains in a culvert near the Illinois border. They concocted a phony ransom note, but it was the rented auto records and Leopold's accidentally leaving his eyeglasses at the murder scene that provided the evidence

necessary for conviction. The case spawned a fictionalized book, *Compulsion*, and a movie version that featured the talents of such Hollywood notables as Dean Stockwell, Bradford Dillman, E. G. Marshall, and Orson Welles.

2. The kidnapping of Charles A. Lindbergh, Jr., from his crib in New Jersey had unique ramifications (both public and legal) in American history. The boy's father, Charles Lindbergh, was world famous for the first solo flight across the Atlantic in an era much impressed with the growth of aviation; thus the whole nation had followed the developments on radio and in the newspapers. Eventually one Bruno Hauptmann was arrested and, on evidence of a ladder used in the crime, convicted and executed. All this occurred in 1934–1935, but any child of ten in 1945 would have known of the event. Federal legislation after the incident made the transportation of a kidnap victim across state lines a capital offense.

3. Even more well known than the romanticized activities of Bonnie Parker and Clyde Barrow was the 1930s career of John Dillinger, whose antics included much-publicized bank robberies, shoot-outs with law officers, arrests, and escapes—including one from Indiana State Prison using a pistol carved from a bar of soap and blackened with shoe polish. Ultimately, with the aid of tips, federal agents led by the FBI's Melvin Purvis narrowed down Dillinger's location to northside Chicago. Despite disguise, the notorious gangster was cornered when he chose to watch a Clark Gable gangster movie at Chicago's Biograph Theater. The final tip-off was his date, a lady wearing red. Dillinger was shot down after his departure from the theater, an episode that has been the finale in several television productions and three films that document his violent career.

St. Valentine's Day: A Massacre Instead of Flowers

On 14 February 1929 in a garage at 2122 North Clark Street, headquarters of the George "Bugs" Moran gang of northside Chicago, seven men were forced against a wall and riddled with bullets from two tommyguns. This was the ultimate gangland rub-out, an event that shocked even a booze-swilling public and bribe-taking bureaucracy. The assassins were Al Capone's gang members dressed as Chicago policemen, and their main target, Bugs Moran, had escaped. He had been late that day and noticed the raid's beginning. He slipped into a local coffeehouse and missed the execution Capone had arranged for him and his cohorts.

While Moran reacted with the phrase "only Capone kills like that," the response of Prohibition director Frederick Silloway to reporters reveals to the modern audience exactly how much corruption permeated the Chicago law enforcement establishment. His inaccurate view, which must have tickled Capone, was:

> The murderers were not gangsters. They were Chicago policemen. I believe the killing was the aftermath to the hijacking of 500 cases of whiskey belonging to the Moran gang by five policemen six weeks ago on Indianapolis Boulevard. I expect to have the names of these five policemen in a short time. It is my theory that in trying to recover the liquor the Moran gang threatened to expose the policemen and the massacre was to prevent the exposure.

Ballistic experts soon demonstrated that the fatal bullets did not come from Chicago police weapons. Even later, experts found the killing weapons in the home of Fred Burke, a professional killer, who was well known for having done jobs for the Capone organization.

Tidbits: Presidential Wives (Hoover, Roosevelt, and Truman)

In 1930 First Lady Lou Henry Hoover entertained the wives of several congressmen at an afternoon tea. Included was Mrs. Oscar DePriest, wife of a black congressman from Chicago. Southern segregationists immediately accused the first lady of defiling the White House. A Mobile, Alabama, newspaper referred to the "arrogant insult" and went on to claim that social mixing was acceptable to neither race, that although African Americans were entitled to their own separate social life, race intermingling at teas or other official functions was quite inadvisable. Other major newspapers from large cities, however, defended and praised the first lady's conduct, reminding readers that Hoover was president of all the people, and describing the action as putting into practice the brotherhood of man. As if to emphasize this point of view, President Hoover, who had been raised a Quaker, free from the standard racial prejudice of his day, put an end to the matter by backing up his wife and inviting a black professor from Tuskegee College for lunch at the White House the following week.

In 1939 Anna Eleanor Roosevelt attended the Southern Conference on Human Welfare in Birmingham, Alabama. She entered an auditorium that was segregated by race according to local law and custom. She expressed her disapproval of the seating arrangements by moving her chair into the middle of the center separating aisle, creating quite a buzz in the proceedings. A short time later back in Washington, D.C., the Daughters of the American Revolution refused to permit the renowned diva, Marian Anderson, to perform in Constitution Hall, the lone structure in the capital large enough for such an esteemed event. The first lady promptly resigned from that patriotic organization, and with the aid of Interior Secretary Harold Ickes arranged a splendid Marian Anderson outdoor concert on the steps of a most appropriate landmark, the Lincoln Memorial. Needless to say, the aftermath brought forth both grand praise and condemnation from a wide variety of quarters.

Most historians agree that Bess Truman was in the general sense a quiet, reserved lady, who sought no special attention or glamour from the role of first lady. All would agree she had considerable influence on the president and that he shared with her the decisions he had to make. In addition, she always did her best to keep a rein on his abrupt outbursts of profanity. During the 1948 election campaign, Congresswoman Clare Booth Luce referred to Mrs. Truman as an "ersatz first lady." When Truman confounded all the polls and experts by winning in November, Mrs. Truman's joy was expressed in the triumphant question: "I wonder if Clare Booth Luce will think I am real now?"

While playing host to presidents of leading women's garden and floral clubs from around the country, Bess Truman hosted a luncheon for the ladies at the White House. As a special treat, she arranged for the president to make a brief appearance so all could tell the folks back home they had seen him. The president complimented the organization's national leader on her lovely, healthy flowers, adding, "You must use a very high quality of manure." The slightly flustered lady politely responded, "Mr. President, we refer to that as fertilizer," at which time Bess chimed in: "Leave him alone, it has taken years for me to get him to say manure."

The Kingfish Show

The voice on the phone would say, "This is the Kingfish." In 1930 in Louisiana no further identification was needed—the governor was on the line, and all who were smart listened. Perhaps no one had such an enduring effect on the twentieth-century Southern political scene as Huey Pierce Long of Louisiana, who took his nickname from a character of the then-popular radio parody, "Amos 'n' Andy," which mimicked black life in the United States. Long, something of a Southern demagogue, was loosely portrayed by actor Broderick Crawford (who won the best actor Oscar for his efforts) as Willie Stark in the film *All the King's Men*, based on Robert Penn Warren's 1940s best-selling novel of the same name.

Criticized as a proto-Nazi by Southern opponents who understood and feared the challenge he presented to the old order, and considered a buffoon by Northern intellectuals who did not understand the peculiar challenges he faced as a Southern reformer, Long was in fact a consummate power artist, a political realist attacking unique problems. At a time when Southern politicians ignored their region's acute economic misery in favor of the romance of the bygone Confederacy, Long wanted to face the real social and economic problems confronting his state, section, and nation. He did it by ignoring traditional racial antipathies and conquering the problem that has done in almost every Southern politician since the beginning of the nation—how to change the system by walking a narrow path between the extremes.

In his successful drive to achieve that goal he became even more extreme and outrageous than his opponents, and it bothered Huey that it had to be so. "They say they don't like my methods," he declaimed. "Well I don't like them either...I'd much rather go up before a legislature and say 'now this is a good law; it's for the benefit of the people, and I'd like for you to vote for it in the interest of the public welfare.' Only I know laws ain't made that way. You've got to fight fire with fire.... I would do it some other way if there was time or if it wasn't necessary to do it this way."

Long's big problem was not having more than 18 votes in the legislature when he became governor, and he needed more than a simple majority. Because of quirks in the Louisiana constitution, he needed to pass many of his measures as constitutional amendments, requiring a two-thirds vote. Long encountered many reverses in his attempt to create a loyal legislature, but he did it. In the process he became the first Southern reform politician since the Civil War who did not have to compromise his goals with the opposition. Long was crass, determined, and tough. He did what had to be done by blackmail, intimidation, going over the heads of local politicians directly to the people, and lubricating the squeaking wheels of government in the traditional fashion. "They didn't all come for free," said one crony, aptly. Or as Huey said of one politician, "I bought and paid for him like you would a load of potatoes."

Long went into each parish (county) and set up his own men in power. He had complete statewide appointive powers that allowed him the direct control of all patronage. Interestingly, Long had read his history—the Radical Republicans had controlled the state in the same manner during Reconstruction. He appointed committees to run each parish under the old adage, divide and rule. Each appointee made regular political contributions to the Long machine. Special funds were set aside to cover up shortages if someone got too friendly with state appropriations. Those who received appointments submitted signed, undated letters of resignation to ensure their loyalty. There would be only one Kingfish in Louisiana, and his name was Huey Long. Long was a master at the task, making sure everyone got a piece of the pie, be they loyalists, opponents, white, or black. Therein lay his secret: Every Man a King and Share Our Wealth were not merely flashy slogans—they were reality to Long.

His uniqueness as a Southern white politician lay in that he did not exclude African Americans from his formula. He refused to get sidetracked by the race issue, the boogeyman of Southern politics that Long knew was a false topic. "You can't help the poor white without helping Negroes," he said, adding, "but that's all right." Long wanted to "treat them the same as anybody else; give them the opportunity to make a living, . . . and to get an education." He did it in a manner that appears very offensive in today's allegedly more sophisticated society, but it worked at a time when African Americans got nothing anywhere else. For example, Long obtained health care for blacks by explaining to opposing whites, "You wouldn't want a colored woman watching over your children if she had pyorrhea, would you?" As Huey sagely concluded, "They see the point."

When black leaders approached him and complained that properly educated blacks could not get jobs in the massive state charity hospital system, Long reacted as only he could: rudely but effectively. He called a press conference and announced that a tour of the New Orleans Charity Hospital had revealed that pure, innocent white women nurses were waiting on colored men, an abomination in the eyes of right-thinking Southerners. Long promised to put an end to it by hiring African-American doctors and nurses to handle this situation. The whole state right down to the last bigot bought it, too.

This incident is portrayed in the recent Hollywood movie *Blaze* as happening during the regime of Huey's brother Earl in that late 1950s. It is historically inaccurate, but true as to its effect and as a portrayal of a Long in action. Huey never really integrated blacks into the voting process, but Earl did; and before the civil rights revolution of the 1960s Louisiana had a black electoral participation of 13% of all voters—not perfect but better than most. Indeed Earl Long maintained that he did more for segregation than all the loudmouthed bigots the state could produce. He did it by turning everyone to bread and butter economic issues, just like brother Huey, and just like his nephew, Russell, Huey's son and recently retired U.S. senator. Huey had set the family style. When the Imperial Wizard of the Ku Klux Klan threatened to campaign against the allegedly pro-Negro Long, Huey, in the words of his greatest biographer, T. Harry Williams, "issued a public statement reflecting unmistakably on the Imperial Wizard's ancestry and pledging that he would never set foot in Louisiana." That was the end of that.

The Kingfish Show was written, casted, acted, and directed by one man—Huey Long. He was no buffoon—he was a middle-class, college-educated political genius who understood his state and its problems and knew how to solve them. His opponents did everything they could to smear his name and compromise him—seemingly an easy task, as Long had an array of human appetites and frailties and often did and said funny things. He was so involved in politics he rarely had time for any distraction. This often led to embarrassing excesses. Once, for example, the opposition press cameras caught him coming out of a New Orleans whorehouse on the arm of the madam. Pictures of the event made the next editions all over the state, but Huey, knowing that New Orleans had its own reputation of sin that could beat anything he could do, casually shrugged the incident off: "What else are you going to do in New Orleans?"

He also struck back: "If you put [my opponents] into a room with a polecat," Long opined, "the polecat would walk out." He castigated his opponents with derogatory nicknames that often stuck for a lifetime: Kinky Howard, Liverwurst Nicholson, Shinola Phelps, Turkeyhead Walmsley, Feather Duster Ransdell, Whistle Britches Rightor, Sack of Potatoes Bennett, and Prince Franklin D. Roosevelt. When *The New York Times* printed his colorful speeches but opposed him in its editorial column, Long confronted a reporter and asked why. "We have this foolish idea that the news column should be honest," came the reply. "Goddamn it!" exploded an exasperated Huey, "I wouldn't run a newspaper that way if I owned one!"

Long got away with it because he delivered and he understood his constituents. He could literally feel his way through a speech until he found a theme the crowd wanted to hear ("Watch me vaudeville 'em," he would say as he rose to speak, never carrying any notes), and then he hit that point hard and called it a day. From member of the Public Service Commission, to governor, to U.S. senator, with side-trips leading the Louisiana State University band down the football field as it played the fight song he helped write, Long seemed to move inexorably forward. Felled by an assassin's bullet (or was it a ricochet from the fusillade fired by his body guards in response?), he never reached his final goal: president of the United States. He was what biographer Williams calls a mass leader. Huey, as usual, was more direct: "Oh, hell," he once immodestly analyzed himself, "say I'm *sui generis* and let it go at that!"

Events from Grandpa's Youth, 1931

Since the stock market crash in 1929, world trade and production had declined by a whopping 60 percent by 1931, hitting the near bottom of the famous Great Depression. This resulted not only in many growling, empty stomachs, but in plenty of psychological shock. Among historical developments of that year that affected grandparents of today's youth were the following:

1. While nearly ten million people across Western Europe went quietly without jobs, a similar situation in the United States produced regular demonstrations in the streets.

2. A new film called *Dracula* went into production, presenting in the title role a virtually unknown actor named Bela Lugosi. Since he was of Hungarian origin, an area that included the mysterious Transylvania, the public anticipated an authentic

vampire thriller. The film was based on English author Bram
Stoker's very loose interpretation of ancient Slavic legends.

3. Knute Rockne, famous player and then coach ("win one for the
Gipper") of the Notre Dame University football team died in a
Kansas plane crash. He had made the Catholic university at
South Bend, Indiana, a sensational football power, winning 29
of 31 games during his tenure, capped off by a win in the 1925
Rose Bowl.

4. The world's tallest building up to that time, the Empire State,
opened on 1 May, rising 1,245 feet above Fifth Avenue with its
102 floors. President Herbert Hoover was present for opening
ceremonies. King Kong was only a few years behind him.

5. Native Oklahoman and nationally known humorist Will Rogers
declined to accept an honorary degree of Doctor of Humanity
and Letters from Oklahoma City University. His response was,
"What are you trying to do, make a joke out of a college
degree?"

6. Two notorious public enemies, the gangsters "Scarface" Al
Capone and Arthur "Dutch Schultz" Flegenheimer, were convicted on federal charges: Schultz for multiple violations of the
prohibition laws and Capone for income tax evasion.

7. Boris Karloff turned in a superb film performance as the chill-
ing Frankenstein monster, a role to be repeated by him and
many others for years to come.

Vice Presidents: Insignificant?

At the 1932 Democratic Convention in Chicago, Franklin D.
Roosevelt won the nomination on the fourth ballot when House
Speaker John Nance Garner, winner of the important California primary, agreed to release his delegates. "Cactus Jack"
Garner's reward was the vice presidency, an office he later
pronounced "not worth a pitcher of warm spit." Though many
have said that the earthy Texan originally employed a more
indelicate word referring to another type of human excretion,
it is true that he relished chewing tobacco.

Throughout U.S. history, the names of most vice presidents

have been lost save when the death of a president catapulted them to the grandest office in the land. Few remember that Teddy Roosevelt's VP was Charles Fairbanks of Indiana, or that Woodrow Wilson's second-term vice president was Thomas Marshall, best known for having uttered that classic bit of American political wisdom: "What this nations needs is a good five-cent cigar." In contrast are the strong presidency of Harry Truman (FDR's successor), the active role of Richard Nixon (Ike's VP), and the presidential candidacies of both Hubert Humphrey and Walter Mondale after serving as vice presidents to LBJ and Jimmy Carter respectively; these have altered Garner's earlier visceral perception of the office. No one was more aware of this change than Vice President Dan Quayle, who suffered continual barbs from the media, the public, and the pundits who questioned his overall capability as the number two man to George Bush. Moreover, George Bush's vice president opponent in the 1984 election was Geraldine Ferraro, the first woman to run for so high a political post for a major political party. Americans would be well advised to pay close attention to the choices for the vice presidency in the future—a lesson William J. Clinton took to heart in his choice of Al Gore for vice president, a man who can fully act as copresident.

CHAPTER IX

World War II

Captain Elliot Roosevelt, the President's Son

By late 1940 most politically informed Americans, and most certainly the ranks of GIs that mushroomed to 12 million during World War II, were familiar with the refrain, "I'm Elliot and I wanna be a captain." It all started when the president's son, Texas businessman Elliot Roosevelt, volunteered for service in 1940 and was commissioned a captain and placed in charge of acquisition and use of radio equipment. The storm was stimulated in part by the fact that Elliot was ineligible for the current draft because of age and poor eyesight. No doubt the quick rank provided fuel for critics. Republican presidential contender Wendell Willkie soon made reference to overnight captains, and within a short time there were campaign buttons that read, "I want to be a captain, too." This was followed by a Want To Be A Captain, Too club and a song of the same title. Elliot felt compelled to submit his resignation, which his commander promptly rejected, declaring that "his services are needed." Indeed, everyone's services were needed, posthaste. France had already fallen to Hitler, Italy was actively in the war, and Pearl Harbor was only weeks away.

The Deaths of Big Al and the Enforcer

We have been taught by sensation-seeking headlines to think death comes to leaders of organized crime in the form of intricately planned hits prompted by gang rivalry for reasons of greed. Much of this is bolstered by film and television presentations, such as *The Godfather* and *The Untouchables*. On occasion, however, the end of big-name criminals occurs in a most pathetic fashion. Take the examples of Al Capone and his lieutenant, Frank Nitti.

Capone died in 1947 from complications arising from the advanced stages of syphilis. He had contracted the disease during his earlier career running whorehouses and, owing to his near-hysterical fear of being stuck by needles, it grew largely untreated. By the time of his release from prison in 1939 the disease had attacked his brain; his retirement was one in which he seesawed between partial lucidity and mental inertia. One report indicates that a member of the gang in Chicago went to visit him while he was still in prison, only to return and report that "Big Al is nuttier than a fruitcake."

Nitti, originally a barber who fenced stolen merchandise on the side, rose to be one of Capone's top underlings, no doubt through his nefarious talents. These earned him the ominous nickname, the Enforcer. The popular film, *The Untouchables*, has him flying backward off the top of a Chicago building and smashing through the roof of a parked sedan many floors below to his death. In truth, it was otherwise. In 1943 Capone mob leader Paul Ricca, who with several others faced indictments for extortion against the film industry, decided to reach a plea bargain by offering up a fall guy. Nitti was picked by the mob to cop a guilty plea and serve time for the mob's position and continuance.

By this time (March 1943) Nitti's former leader, Al Capone, was too mentally deficient to help out his one-time loyal Enforcer. Having already served an 18-month sentence some years before, Nitti was emotionally shocked that his pals chose him to take another dive, but he knew that to refuse would mean certain death. The day after the crucial decision-making meeting, Nitti walked along one of the many railroad tracks that ring and pass through the great city of Chicago, mulling over his predicament. Suddenly he pulled a pistol from his pocket and blew his own brains out, ending an era in American crime.

The Magic Defeat at Pearl Harbor

In 1948 historian Charles Beard posited that President Franklin D. Roosevelt, through an embargo on critical war materials, set up the Japanese by goading them into attacking an outdated fleet of battleships, bringing the United States into World War II on the side of the Allies over the opposition of the basically isolationist American public. According to Beard, FDR had the navy send the critical aircraft carriers out to safety at sea along with their fast cruiser and destroyer escorts, and let the Japanese modernize the U.S. fleet with its infamous bombing run on battleship row along Ford Island. Angered by this sneak attack, Congress declared war and Americans went to battle, united as never before in our country's history.

Ever since, historians and the public have wanted to know what the government knew, and if this knowledge reached Lieutenant General Walter Short and Vice Admiral Husband E. Kimmel, the commanders in Hawaii who were sacked for their alleged negligence. Consider the following:

1. During the Herbert Hoover administration, Secretary of State Henry L. Stimson, later FDR's bipartisan secretary of war, had rebuffed attempts to solve Japanese diplomatic ciphers with the stuffy retort, "Gentlemen do not read each other's mail." Nonetheless, by 1937 U.S. code breakers had solved the Japanese diplomatic code and could read the other gentlemen's mail with impunity. The Japanese, however, responded with the complicated new Purple code, one that relied on a complex machine cipher. The problem was turned over to Colonel William Friedman of army intelligence. By a determined personal effort that lasted 19 months and cost him a physical and mental breakdown in the end, Friedman brilliantly (without ever once seeing any of Purple's components) constructed Magic, his own version of the Purple machine, putting American code breakers back in business as of September 1940.

Hearing of the surprise attack on Pearl, Friedman, at home on leave, muttered, "But they knew!"

2. In San Francisco, a navy listening post tracked Japanese movements across the Pacific toward Pearl with uncanny accuracy and sent the news to Washington. The radio operator on a merchant ship out of San Francisco confirmed this when the ship docked in Honolulu on December 6.

3. Like the Americans, the British also had intelligence from their own code efforts. Through the Australians they had even been able to read much of JN-25 since 1939. They knew when the Japanese fleet was at sea and roughly where it was going. How much Winston Churchill passed on to Roosevelt is uncertain, but FDR had already promised that when war came, the major American effort would be against the Nazis first. Churchill's admission that he slept the "sleep of the saved" the night of the American declaration of war can be read in many ways.

4. The Dutch, whose empire included the East Indies (Indonesia today), also passed information along to Washington, including the fact that the Japanese fleet was at sea and headed toward Hawaii. However, General George Marshall, army chief of staff, angrily asked the American military attaché to Djakarta, "Do you expect me to believe this stuff?" and ordered him to stop sending further messages with a curt, "We're not interested." Departmental maps plotted the Japanese fleet near Hawaii anyway.

5. From an arrested German spy and British double agent, no less, J. Edgar Hoover knew the Japanese wanted regular information on Pearl. The German chargé in Washington also passed along a warning to Colonel "Wild Bill" Donovan (later head of the Office of Strategic Services, predecessor to the Central Intelligence Agency) that the Japanese would attack Pearl Harbor, turning down a million-dollar bribe in the process. Why, no one knows.

6. Secretary of State Cordell Hull called in his journalist friend, Joe Leib, the week before the attack and told him the Japanese would strike Pearl Harbor on December 7. Hull said he wanted to cover his reputation in the investigations that would ensue. Leib put the story on the United Press International wire but only one paper picked it up. Lieutenant Commander Joseph

Rochefort, who was in charge of listening to Japanese fleet radio traffic and who had been completely fooled by its volume to think the fleet was elsewhere, read the story and dismissed it. Rochefort's thinking was like many informed military men of the day—since the Japanese lacked the necessary resources and industrial strength to win an all-out war against the United States, why start one? Rochefort was not alone in his opinion. FDR in a cabinet meeting argued with Secretary of the Navy Frank Knox that the Japanese were heading south to the Dutch East Indies, where they could secure the tin, oil, and rubber needed to run the Japanese war machine. Is this why Rochefort believed what he did?

7. On the morning of 7 December, an army assistant to General Marshall called in another officer to witness the fact that he could not reach the chief of staff because he was out riding his horse. The message to Marshall was that the Japanese were going to attack Pearl Harbor that day. Hours later Marshall sent the information to the Hawaiian Islands via deferred precedence (the regular form of Western Union telegrams), which the delivery boy in Hawaii delivered too late: he had been hiding from the falling bombs in a ditch.

Having received none of this information, General Short and Admiral Kimmel nonetheless became the scapegoats for the acts of others in the know. Was it a conspiracy? Was there so much information that the important material was lost in a sea of meaningless messages? Did the Americans react to information too rationally, arrogantly expecting the Japanese to act as they thought they should? Historians are coming to believe more and more like Charles Beard. Their conclusion is that FDR, Secretary Stimson, Secretary Knox, General Marshall, and Colonel Donovan, with the assistance of Prime Minister Churchill and the rich, powerful, westernized Soong family of China (whose English-speaking daughter, Mei-ling, was the popular Madame Chiang Kai-shek), conspired to maneuver the United States into World War II over the isolationist sentiments of the average citizen by creating a shooting incident with the Japanese. The result was Pearl Harbor at sunrise, 7 December 1941. It is truly a day that will live in infamy, but for more reasons than President Roosevelt dared admit.

Thirty Seconds over Oregon and the Bat Bomb

Everyone has probably at least heard of Colonel Jimmy Doolittle's B-25 bomber raid over Japan on 18 April 1942, launched from the decks of the carrier USS *Hornet* in revenge for the losses and embarrassment of Pearl Harbor. The event was popularized in Captain Ted Lawson's famous account, *Thirty Seconds over Tokyo*, which later was made into a movie. The Japanese government was greatly incensed at the raiders' success—not in destroying any real target that threatened the war effort, but in the loss of face it represented. They planed an immediate reaction.

Having just suffered losses at the battles of the Coral Sea and Midway, which crippled the Combined Fleet's air arm, the Japanese resorted to subterfuge. On 29 September 1942, as recounted in historian Bert Webber's book, *Silent Siege II*, Japanese submarine I-25 surfaced off Cape Blanco, Oregon. Specially modified, the submarine carried a single-engine float plane in a hangar on the deck. Piloted by Chief Flying Officer Nobuo Fujita, with Petty Officer Second Class Shoji Okuda as observer, the plan was to drop two 170-pound incendiary bombs into the heavy forest, creating a fire storm that would cause panic along the Pacific coast. The pair flew 50 miles inland and dropped the bombs, which exploded like clockwork. Unfortunately, however, the weather did not cooperate and incipient rain and fog extinguished the flames before any major damage was done. Three weeks later they tried again with the same result. Twenty years later local citizens invited Fujita to come and help commemorate the incident. He did so with good humor and graciously left behind his family's 400-year-old samurai sword as a memento.

Before anyone condemns Fujita's mission as harebrained, consider the American's planned *coup de grace* against the Japanese homeland, Project X-Ray—the dreaded bat bomb. As suggested to President Franklin D. Roosevelt by Dr. Lytle S. Adams, the scheme involved training bats to carrying miniature incendiary devices to ignite various Japanese cities, known to be built largely of wood and paper. Adams recruited a research staff that included such misfits as a brilliant Harvard scientist, an argumentative biologist, a cowboy movie star, a Texas guano collector, a Maine lobster man, an ex-mobster, and a hard-driving enlisted man known as Top Sarge.

Historian Jack Couffer relates in his story, *Bat Bomb: World War II's Other Secret Weapon*, how the "scientists" raided caves in the American Southwest for bat recruits in absolute secrecy. Then they attached the incendiaries and loosed the horde of bombers to see if the experiment would work. It did! The bats burned down an entire airfield. Unfortunately it was an active American field. The plan was achievable, but uncontrollable. In addition, the Army Air Corps was not about to allow its bombing efforts to be shown up by whimsical flying mice, and the plan never came to fruition. The end result was the massive B-29 incendiary bombings in 1945—a concept just as deadly but with results infinitely more predictable.

In the Big One, Doughboy Simply Becomes GI

From the experience of the Mexican War (1848), the American infantry inherited a new term, *doughboy*. It began as a condescending derision, but by World War I (1917) it had graduated into a term of affection. Climatic conditions marked by sparse precipitation in south Texas and northern Mexico produced marching conditions that often left infantrymen liberally coated, mustaches and eyebrows included, with the beige powder of dust churned up during a long day's march. Conditions in New Mexico Territory (the current states of Arizona and New Mexico) were so bad that units often marched abreast in line of battle rather in the long column of fours, the normal marching order, to avoid the rising dust. Enjoying the partial benefits of a mount, the cavalry derisively referred to the footsloggers as doughs or doughboys, as though the infantrymen were bakers fresh from their labor with flour. The infantry's fine combat record in World War I, however, caused the term to become a badge of honor referring to the heroic rank and file, comparable to the French *poilu*—our Sergeant Yorks, our saviors of Europe, indeed, of all Western civilization, our men over there, across the Atlantic in the bloody trenches of France.

World War II, apart from all the propaganda techniques designed to produce mass support of the war effort, was too mechanized to save and preserve the special, identifiable image of the dusty, marching doughboy. In that war American infantry moved by truck whenever possible. Even the cavalry was reduced to riding to battle in armored personnel vehicles and tanks. In his book *Wartime*, noted literary analyst Paul Fussell, himself a participant in this greatest of all wars, points directly to how the average soldier was reduced to the simple, impersonal GI. Everything associated with the military service became "strictly GI "—be it regulation haircuts, an officer who was a stickler for obeying orders, or merely the task of cleaning the barracks floor. GI was allegedly an abbreviation for either general issue or government issue, but in reality it stood for galvanized iron and was stenciled on garbage cans by supply clerks.

With more than 16 million Yanks in uniform spread across the globe, and all of the conditions of international human/materiel management, one could not find that single or representative soldier when identity was left to the public relations officers and headline manipulators. It ultimately led to the only form of pride left to be recognized, the anonymity of the man in uniform. The future offered wide use for the marketability of GI Joe, as a glance in any modern toy store display will reveal.

Slang: The Idioms of a Soldier's Life

Literary specialist Paul Fussell has focused much attention on the common soldier's language and usage under the conditions of war, a circumstance that produces fear, boredom, injury, and disease. In his World War II study, *Wartime*, he examines the latter under the general title, "Chickenshit," the third syllable of which was raised to near sainthood by Norman Mailer in his *Naked and the Dead*. While it was the misery of World War I that elevated the ultimate four-letter word, *fuck*, into general exclamatory and adjectival usage, the scope of World War II generated enough slang to fill a mini-sized dictionary of soldier talk, as some of the following examples more politely illustrate:

1. Diarrhea has been common enough to soldiers for centuries, though not often mentioned. The French tell us that Louis IX (St. Louis) died of *le peste* in 1270 near Tunis on the Eighth Crusade; his malady was probably dysentery. The American Civil War fairly enshrined such intestinal plagues with the quaint, descriptive terms such as the *Tennessee Trots* and the *Virginia Quickstep*. British and Australian soldiers on the Turkish coast during the ill-fated Gallipoli landings of World War I did not complain of fear as much as they cursed their general bodily filth, claiming they "could not stop shitting." Ironically, the later World War II medical adjective used to describe such upsets was gastro-intestinal, which led to common soldiers referring to stomach maladies as the *GIs*—the same name they used for themselves. Sooner or later fungus ailments became "crotch rot" and discharge from the service for the same was a "ruptured duck."

2. While the World War I miracle wound that sent you home without amputation or disfigurement was called a "blighty," showing the British influence among the newly arriving Americans, the same in World War II became labeled a "Hollywood wound," demonstrating the overall American influence among the Allied side.

3. Disgust with the army's repetitious paper forms was quickly converted into slang for toilet paper, *bum*. Now commonly used to refer to one's posterior, it was a short version of the more formal *bum fodder*.

4. To be placed on report was to wind up on the "shit list." One who ate everything in sight was a "chow hound." A hospital orderly became a "bedpan commando" and radios became "walkie talkies." Well known today is the term *jeep*, which derives from the vehicle's first official designation, G.P., for General Purpose. Also common is the word *bazooka* for the 2.36-inch rocket launcher. It received its name from its similarity to a homemade tubular musical instrument invented and used by popular Ozarks entertainer and comedian Bob Burns.

In all of the foregoing, has it crossed the mind of the reader that most vets of the Vietnamese experience never refer to that country as anything but "Nam"?

Rationing in Wartime

The popular war song "Yes, We Have No Bananas" carried concrete meaning well beyond modest humor during the war years, when a gigantic, bureaucratic regulatory apparatus supervised the rationing and consignment of materials and products. The list came to include many basic items used by the American public—gasoline, meat, butter, sugar, and rubber tires. Only a handful of doctors and auto dealers could afford to drive the scant number of 1942 cars produced prior to Pearl Harbor, but the silk needed for parachutes and other military needs created long lines at hosiery counters, even with the advent of nylon.

A youth born after 1938 most likely believed by 1946 that such desired candy bars as Baby Ruth, Three Musketeers, Snickers, and Milkyway, or chewing gum like Juicy Fruit, Spearmint, and Dentyne, were new products. They weren't; they just hadn't been available. Not until 1945 did Double Bubble bubble gum reappear, to be doled out for months by the grocer at two per customer. All of the regulations left butchers, grocers, service station operators, and department store clerks collecting, tabulating, and accounting for millions of stamps and coupons. Autos sported window stickers ranging from A through D to which gasoline stamps were inseparably tied. Allotments were geared to need and/or significance of employment or function as judged by government regulatory agents. Thus a single-car family at close proximity to their employment received an A sticker, while a farmer with trucks, tractors, and other equipment might obtain a C or D sticker. By 1943 rationing had even led to the elimination of ice cream flavors, and sometimes the genuine item altogether. Millions of youth made do with synthetically flavored orange and pineapple sherbet.

Wartime also brought the first widespread use of something called oleomargarine. In its most economical form it came as a large, malleable, lard-colored lump. By placing it in a plastic bag, along with accompanying food coloring in the shade of reddish rust, and then squishing with the hands for several minutes, one could gain the desired butter color. It became a dietetic mainstay for millions. Even one of Bill Maulden's famous cartoon clips depicted two Soviet soldiers with pocket Russian-English dictionary in hand staring in puzzlement at a box of margarine with the conspicuous but untranslatable label, NUCOA.

Corruption: The Bridesmaid of War and Soldiers

In the fifteenth century, French martyr Joan of Arc, noting the bands of prostitutes that followed the army and the foul language of soldiers, attempted to clean up the situation. The results of her efforts were short-lived, it seems, for demographic historians searching sixteenth-century archives for developments can easily pinpoint the locations of venereal disease epidemics by the movements or locations of European armies. Centuries later, returning Yanks from the Great War also brought home "gifts" from *la belle France.* One of the crucial areas of friction between the army's General Joseph W. Stillwell and air force Colonel Claire L. Chennault (of Flying Tigers fame) arose over corruption and black-marketing, of which Chinese bordellos formed a key feature in the China-Burma-India theater of World War II. Stillwell saw all this as intolerable. Chennault, the ever-practical, open-minded Louisianan, preferred to acquiesce (let's be nice about this) when American troops chose to enjoy what their Chinese counterparts took for granted as normal rest and recreation in a time and place that boasted mainly of long hours, pestilence, shortage of supply, and life-threatening danger. In light of the more serious problems the American war effort faced in the area, many U.S. airmen were perplexed at the quarrel between their two head officers, as was historian Barbara Tuchman, Stillwell's prize-winning biographer. No wonder observers called the acerbic general Vinegar Joe.

Stillwell never saw Vietnam, which raised opportunities of military corruption and sin to a new high. If U.S. government statistics are correct, at the war's height, 555,000 U.S. troops

were encumbered in Southeast Asia, of which no more than
55,000 saw combat duty at any one time. Add to this an
excessively large concentration of supplies, the ennui of duty
away from the front, and the sociologically damaging efferves-
cence of readily available drugs, the problems of wartime vice,
graft, and corruption pretty well got out of hand. Only in the
recent Desert Storm operation in the Persian Gulf did such
afflictions not produce flagrancy and notoriety, thanks to the
isolation of American troops from the population as a whole,
the empty desert, and a strict Muslim moral code. The inci-
dence of fraternization among male and female soldiers, voluntary or otherwise, is only beginning to be explored fully.
Saint Joan and Vinegar Joe might not have approved, but
Chennault of the Flying Tigers would have understood. As the
French say, "The more things change, the more they remain the
same."

Women at War, Mostly on the Home Front

For nearly half a century prior to 1940 the relative quantity of
women in the workplace had changed by only a fraction. After
Pearl Harbor, the developments of change were so radical as to
affect the United States forever. Nearly 200,000 participated in
the Women's Army Corps (WACS), the navy's Volunteer Service (WAVES), and the Coast Guard (WAFS) during the war.
By the war's end in 1945, more than six million women were
active in wartime production. One popular wartime film featured an actress whose role as Rosie the Riveter became a
household phrase. Many of the multi-storied factory structures where women worked during the war, like Kellogg's in
Battle Creek, Michigan, had several upper floors with covered
windows. Here, under the cover of normal production, special
war materiel was manufactured under tight security.

Wartime and Song

The impact of wartime conditions, especially monotony,

loneliness, and separation from loved ones, exhibits itself in a variety of fashions, and one of the most common is sentimental songs. Anyone over 50 years of age knows why composer George M. Cohan received congressional and presidential recognition for spirited writing and performance of patriotic tunes from the Great War experience. The impact of war offers its creative provocation in the mind of the songwriter, where it spreads by the written music sheet and the voice of many singers to millions of listeners. It would be safe to claim that by 1945 the voice of Bing Crosby had been heard by more humans than that of any other person on earth, even if "White Christmas" were his only offering.

World War II occurred during the all-important age of radio. American youth were quick to associate with the songs that directly recalled military life, valor, or danger—"This Is the Army Mr. Green," "Praise the Lord and Pass the Ammunition," and "Coming in on a Wing and a Prayer." More subtle and lingering in their impact were songs about separation from loved ones or dreams of those left behind (which for Americans, in contrast to other allies, meant left behind in *obvious security*).

Resonant in the ears of all at home or abroad were the many tunes that pointed to the doldrums of war. Among them: (1) "I've Got a Gal in Kalamazoo," words that immediately invoke memories of a city to the Michigan soldier but are also relevant to the soldier who hailed from Casper, Wyoming, sitting in a mud-filled foxhole in rain-drenched Italy; (2) "Don't Get around Much More," which is especially difficult to do when one's fingers are freezing to his M-1 rifle stock near Bastogne on Christmas 1944; (3) "You'd Be So Nice To Come Home To," which needs no explanation; (4) "Don't Sit under the Apple Tree with Anyone Else but Me" proved most appropriate for the GI from rural or small town America; (5) "When I Go to Sleep, I Never Count Sheep, I Dream All the Dreams about Linda," relevant to millions with the swap of a name; and (6) "There's Going To Be a Hot Time in the Town of Berlin, When the Yanks Go Marching In," never a hit classic, but in which Frank Sinatra poignantly pointed out the goal of the whole war effort in Europe.

Promotion of Wartime Morale

To an American rural or small town resident during World War II, news on the progress of the conflict came via radio, newspapers (often days late, depending on how far from the source of publication one lived), and the popular Movietone news segments at local theaters. The most famous personage of the war was stoic British Prime Minister Winston S. Churchill. His two-fingered V sign for victory caught on during and after the war with expanded and varied applications until it actually came to mean peace to antiwar activists during the Vietnam conflict.

During World War II, front lawns of urban residential homes were torn up and tilled into victory gardens. Towns of but 400 residents became centers of victory piles of scrap metal that often reached three stories in height. The United Service Organizations (USO), comprised of the Young Men's Christian Association, the Young Women's Christian Association, the National Catholic Community Service, the National Jewish Welfare Board, the Salvation Army, and the National Traveller's Aid Association, held social gatherings for men in uniform much like Farm Bureau picnics, all under the banner of victory, with of course victory women and girls serving food and drink and providing dancing partners. Eventually the V met the eye several times a day—on soap, taxi cabs, stamps, cigarettes, cosmetics, and in backdrops of store window displays. Even Frogie of the "Our Gang" comedies entered the post office under the victory banner to purchase his 10-cent stamps, which would ultimately add up to the $18.75 needed for a $25 dollar war bond.

Lord Haw Haw and Tokyo Rose

Born in Brooklyn in 1906, William Joyce left his impression on the twentieth century during World War II. Born of an English mother and an Irish American father, he went to Britain in 1921, graduated with honors from London University, and became a part of the budding English Fascist movement. In

1939, just before the outbreak of war, he travelled to Germany. There he became Joseph Goebbels' chief radio propagandist against England. He was quite popular in Britain, not because he was believed, but because his supercilious, sinister voice appealed to the British sense of humor; hence his moniker, Lord Haw Haw. At the end of the war British authorities arrested him and he was tried for treason. Joyce claimed that he was an American citizen by birth and the British court had no jurisdiction. The English, however, pointed to his British passport and tried, convicted, and hanged him in 1946, despite Joyce's appeal to the House of Lords, which has ultimate jurisdiction as the highest appeals court in all of England.

In the Pacific, allied troops were entertained and propagandized by a variety of female radio broadcasters, at least a dozen of whom spoke in English. The most popular one was Iva Ikuko Toguri D'Aquino, an American of Japanese parentage who was better known as Tokyo Rose. Although her programs were designed to upset Allied troops in the field with disturbing references to conditions at home, she also played the best nostalgia and dance music in the Pacific, guaranteeing her a wide audience. Arrested and convicted of treason in 1949, despite pleas that she was trapped in Japan by the war and forced to broadcast by Japanese authorities, she spent six years in prison and was fined $10,000. Released in 1956, Tokyo Rose campaigned for a full presidential pardon, which was granted by President Gerald R. Ford on 19 January 1977, his last day in office.

Dumb Bombs, Guns, Blunders, and Fear

Literary critic and analyst Paul Fussell provides historians with one of the most intriguing and valuable studies of the literature and ironies of World War I with his *The Great War in Modern Memory*. In World War II he too received his Greetings from the President of the United States, as did millions of others. Thus in his *Wartime* (Oxford University Press, 1989), he writes of World War II's well-propagandized air war from firsthand experience as well as from scholarship. This includes events that remind us of the ironies of the earlier 1914–1918 struggle:

1. While the massive U.S. B-17 Flying Fortress four-engine bomber was advertised as defensively secure at an altitude of seven miles, no less than 22,000 ended as crumpled metal on the ground of Europe and Asia along with 110,000 dead crewmen. The film *Memphis Belle* is an enhanced treatment of the air war's first plane and crew to ever complete the almost impossible assignment of 25 missions before rotating homeward.

2. In late 1941 a typical British Royal Air Force (RAF) command mission suffered the poor rate of one bomber in ten actually finding its way to within five miles of its target. In early German Luftwaffe raids on London, of the 500 tons of bombs dropped, only 30 tons actually hit the city. German bombers on a 1940 mission to Dijon, France, mistakenly hit Freiburg, Germany, killing 57 of their own citizens and causing massive destruction of the city. Even as late as D-Day in 1944, rather than softening up German beach defenses near the landing points, some 480 U.S. B-24 Liberator bombers mistakenly destroyed French farms well inland from the battle.

3. Testimony from the Nuremberg Trials reveals that "incredibly large numbers of cases on the Allied side of mistaken identification were throughout the war the curse of the American and British navies. . . . " Fear and often stark panic caused ground to ground, ground to air, air to ground, air to air, and ship to ship errors in target acquisition. For example, a Canadian bomber pilot reported that "jittery army gunners always cut loose at you, despite the fact we were flying to the south, and there were 800 of us." One of the most glaring errors came in the 1943 invasion of Sicily when, despite previous alerts that friendly transports and gliders would fly over, Allied ground batteries blasted away shouting, "German attack! Fire!" Before it was over 23 U.S. planes with 229 men of the American 82d Airborne Division had met disaster from friendly fire. Hereafter, Allied airborne troop carriers were marked by three wide white stripes around both wings and the tail section just ahead of the horizontal stabilizer to assist proper identification. These World War II incidents should help explain, or at least put into perspective, similar and better-publicized occurrences during the Vietnam conflict, which was so scattered as to have no well-defined lines of defense (much like the Indian wars in the

American West), and the Desert Storm attack in Iraq and Kuwait, which moved so rapidly and caused such confusion in target acquisition that one-fourth of all American casualties were from friendly fire. Of course few of these incidents were revealed until after the fighting formally ended.

4. The greatest cover-up of World War II unfolded in late April 1944 off the beaches of Slapton Sands on the British south coast of Devonshire near Dartmouth. Intended as a realistic rehearsal for D-Day, Operation Tiger as initiated by Convoy T-4 involved the removal of civilians as well as the participation of thousands of men and 200 ships of all sizes, all supported by air attacks, the laying and clearing of mines, and the use of live ammunition. Quite by accident, nine German E-Boats came upon the fleet in the dark and torpedoed and shot up three Allied troop-carrying LST's (Landing Ship, Tank), causing an estimated 749 American deaths (to this day no one knows for sure) mostly from drowning and hypothermia as they abandoned ship. (E-boat was short for enemy boat, called *schnellboote* or fast boat by the Germans. These motorized craft, about 100 feet long, were armed with torpedoes and various combinations of light automatic guns, much like the American PT boat.)

   The dead were placed in a mass grave, the wounded quarantined in hospitals and, along with the survivors, threatened with courts-martial if they talked. The American commander of the exercise, Rear Admiral Don P. Moon, eventually committed suicide over the debacle, the only high ranking U.S. officer to so die during the whole war. Families back home received the usual killed in action telegrams, with no further explanation. Oddly enough, the U.S. 4th Infantry Division received fewer casualties landing on Utah Beach in Normandy than it did in the practice exercise at Slapton Sands. The debacle only became public 44 years after the actual event with the 3 May 1984 airing of "The Tragic Secret of Slapton Sands" on ABC's "20/20" news program. This was followed by the publication of Nigel Lewis' book, *Exercise Tiger: The Dramatic True Story of a Hidden Tragedy of World War II* (New York: Prentice Hall Press, 1990).

5. Over 400 British and American bombers wound up in neutral Sweden or Switzerland, where their crews were interned for the duration of the war, living in comparative luxury, while their comrades continued to fly missions that had 50 percent

losses. The great fear among the Allied command was that these flights were intentional attempts to avoid flying, caused by what the British labeled LMF—lack of moral fiber. Americans launched an official Pentagon investigation into their side of the matter, much to the disgust of the commander of the United States Army Air Force (USAAF), General Carl Spaatz, who defended his crews' performance. At one point, long-range fighter escort pilots of Tactical Air Command were briefed to inspect such peel-off flights over German targets; the hint (never formally expressed) was to shoot down any suspicious bomber. The fighter pilots, however, unable to tell if a crew was intentionally abandoning the war or really in trouble, refused to act. The problem ended in late 1944 with the defeat of the German Interceptor command and a better Allied survival rate. After the war, the overwhelming majority of internment flights allegedly proved to be the result of lack of gas or damage that would have caused a crash and death or imprisonment before the safety of English airbases could be reached. Needless to say, German propagandists, aware of Allied Command's fears, had a field day with the vagaries of the situation while it lasted.

Normandy Beach: The Deadly Walk

There is a classic photo taken from within an infantry landing craft of American troops wading waist deep towards the sands of the bloody Omaha beachhead on 6 June 1944. The viewer can easily see that all soldiers, if not cut down by enemy fire, would walk in the water for the length of a football field, and then, before reaching the relative safety of the bluffs that tower over the landing area, run the length of three more football fields over sand through heavy German defensive fire. A communications officer who followed the same path 48 hours later reported that upon reaching the beach his feet never touched the sand—he was walking over the bodies and abandoned equipment of the dead.

Today a visitor to the Normandy beaches finds the tide and sands essentially the same. The bluffs are now covered with a massive cemetery with its manicured lawns and row upon row of crosses and stars of David, all carrying the name, rank, and state of origin of the 3,000 fallen Americans. Strolling the memorial structure and grounds leaves one with the feeling of having entered a great outdoor temple, much like touring the inner ramparts of a historic cathedral like Chartres or Notre Dame.

A few miles away lies the small, ancient city of Bayeux, where a small museum next to William the Conqueror's monastery houses the Bayeux Tapestry, one of France's greatest historical art treasures. The detailed tapestry depicts William's famous invasion of England in 1066, a successful move in the opposite direction of the later D-Day invasion.

The First Battle of the Philippine Sea, 19 June 1944: The Marianas Turkey Shoot

In order to gain land bases close enough to the Japanese mainland to launch B-29 raids, the United States landed army and marine divisions on Saipan in the middle of June 1944. The Japanese responded with their plan A Go, which called for a cooperative counterattack by land-based aircraft from the other Mariana islands backed up by carrier-based aircraft launched from a fleet steaming from the Philippine islands. Unfortunately for the Japanese, by this stage of the war, experienced pilots were a rarity because of earlier losses. The result was a one-sided battle that the gleeful American carrier pilots of Task Force 58 named the Marianas Turkey Shoot and historians have labeled the First Battle of the Philippine Sea, fought 19–20 June 1944. (The Battle of Leyte Gulf, 23–26 October 1944, is the Second Battle of the Philippine Sea.)

The Japanese decided to launch their planes from nine carriers at a great distance from their American targets. As their naval aircraft had a greater range than the American planes, their surface fleet could not be counterattacked. The Japanese pilots would bomb TF 58's 15 carriers and other miscellaneous surface craft and land on the Marianas, refuel, and make a second raid on the way back to their carriers. However, they failed to consider three major factors—American radar fighter direction, superb American fighter pilot training, and the superior qualities of the U.S. Navy's heavily armed and armored F6F Gruman Hellcat fighter.

Directed by radar operators, the Americans put up fighter groups over a six-hour period at midday, shooting down 243 of 300 attacking Japanese aircraft. By contrast, the American naval pilots lost only 31 planes, hence the name Turkey Shoot. The next day, the American fleet sent out scouts who located the Japanese surface flotilla late that afternoon, still waiting for news of the battle. Risking all, as he would have to retrieve the returning planes after dark (a stunt never before done by most American pilots), Vice Admiral Marc Mitscher launched an immediate bombing attack that cost the Japanese a half dozen capital ships and 65 more planes. Despite the fact that Mitschner turned on all of the fleet's lights to assist the pilots' nighttime landing (taking a chance that no enemy planes or submarines were lurking nearby waiting for such an opportunity) the Americans lost 20 planes in the attack and 80 more in ditchings at sea or crash landings, nearly half of the attacking force. This American victory was the last classic carrier-versus-carrier air battle in the Pacific war.

Battle of the Bulge: Translating "Nuts!"

Following the near-destruction of the German armies in France at Falaise Gap and the liberation of Paris in the summer of 1944, Allied armies swept relentlessly across France and threatened the German homeland guarded by the Siegfried Line. A very real threat to the Allies' drive was an internal squabble between British Field Marshall Bernard Montgomery and American Lt. Gen. George Patton over who would get enough of the Allies' limited supply of gasoline to be the first to Berlin and the glory such a coup represented. As usual, overall Allied commander General Dwight D. Eisenhower skillfully maneuvered between the extremes, satisfying neither Montgomery nor Patton and allowing Hitler's generals time to replenish and rearm for the battle for Germany.

By December, fueled by the combined Allied quartermaster

truck companies called the Red Ball Express (many of which were staffed by African-American soldiers), the first battles for the Reich occurred around the city of Aachen. Hitler decided to attempt to set back the Allies' schedule by an attack through the Ardennes Forest in southern Belgium, the same tactic that defeated the French in 1940. This ferocious lunge into a weakly held sector of the American line has been dubbed the Battle of the Bulge, from the westward-pointing geographic bubble it made in the Allied lines. Backed by the largest concentration of tanks available, the Germans thrust west and north toward Antwerp in an effort to split the Americans off from the British and take the Allies' best supply port, Antwerp. The confused fighting resulted in the largest mass surrender of American troops in U.S. history in the mountains of the Schnee Eifel. It also left large numbers of U.S. soldiers cut off and isolated behind German lines, soldiers who refused to surrender after hearing news of the massacre of a hundred capitulated Americans at Malmédy, Belgium.

Since many of these surrounded outposts held vital road junctions, the Germans sent in negotiation teams hoping to gain these areas on the cheap from the bedraggled Americans. The most important of these junctions was the town of Bastogne, Belgium, commanded by Brig. Gen. Anthony C. McAuliffe of the U.S. 101st Airborne Division. McAuliffe faced a heavy decision. Greatly outnumbered, his men were surrounded and short on ammunition and other supplies. Relief was promised but no one knew if or when it would arrive. McAuliffe's response to the diplomatic German request to save lives and surrender was just one word, "Nuts!" His men received the German attack and managed to hold on in one of the greatest defensive battles in American military history. The road junction that was denied the Germans slowed their advance and was instrumental in the crushing of the Bulge that followed.

On American television in 1957, CBS newsman Walter Cronkite interviewed the German general who sent McAuliffe the surrender ultimatum, asking him the particulars of the incident. Speaking English with a heavy German accent, the aging and retired General of Panzer Troops Heinrich von Lüttwitz confirmed that he and his staff officers had no idea of how to translate McAuliffe's response. They checked their best dictionaries and used their best translators, but could not arrive at a meaning that did not include food. Score one for colloquialism in the American English idiom.

The Unromantic War

While World War I put to rest forever the concept of a romantic war, especially when mankind performed a 1919 audit of human and material costs, World War II left no doubt that war was serious business. As Paul Fussell points out in his volume, *Wartime*, what was unthinkable for those who endured the former war became acceptable for those experiencing the latter. Japanese soldiers and sailors tended not to surrender and engaged in suicidal assaults with no hope of victory. Hostages were taken and publicly hanged. Jews, Gypsies, and other minorities were incarcerated in concentration camps and worked to death or summarily gassed. The United States dropped the first nuclear weapons on Hiroshima and Nagasaki. British literary personages Leonard and Virginia Woolf determined to commit suicide should German troops successfully invade England, and they acquired poison in preparation for the deed. It would have been unthinkable during the First World War for a mother like Magda Goebbels to methodically poison her six children, and then very calmly join her husband in joint suicide in the Führer's bunker beneath embattled Berlin. Of even greater weight in contrasting the two world wars is the startling fact that American-born author Kurt Vonnegut, who was a prisoner of war during the Allied firebombing of Dresden in 1945, witnessed that the results of the ensuing fire storm took more lives than did either of the atom bombs dropped on Japan. He could not bring himself to report his observations in the printed word until 25 years later in his novel, *Slaughterhouse Five*.

CHAPTER X

The Cold War and the Modern Era

Fast Food for the Cold War

Between June 1948 and September 1949 American and British armed forces delivered 2,323,738 tons of food, fuel, machinery, and supplies to the area of West Berlin at a cost of $224 million. This gigantic airlift was labeled Operation Vittles. The success and appeal of it all brought forth a film called *The Big Lift*, starring Paul Douglas and Montgomery Clift.

The reason for such a monumental airlift arose from the Allied treaty arrangements for the occupation of Germany, which divided the defeated nation into a free American-British-French-dominated western section and a Soviet-controlled eastern section. The German capital, Berlin, lay within the Soviet sector, but was itself divided into zones held by each of the four conquering powers, with guaranteed land and air access routes for the Western powers. Unwilling to cooperate on any German reunification that might threaten communist control, the Soviets attempted to use pressure tactics to force the Western powers out of their zones in West Berlin. Because the Russians boasted 40 army divisions to less than a dozen for the West, they instituted a land blockade that isolated West Berlin by cutting off all access to Berlin by rail, highway, or canal.

Faced with this impasse, U.S. President Harry Truman reacted in his usual, immediate, direct fashion. Reasoning that the West's air power was superior in quantity and technology to that of the Soviets, Truman gathered up every transport plane available and flew needed supplies over the blocking Soviet army. Soviet Premier Joseph Stalin did not challenge the flights, probably not believing that the Allied aircraft could succeed in supplying the three million citizens of West Berlin any more than the once-mighty Luftwaffe could have saved the vast German army at Stalingrad. He failed to consider American air traffic control technology, pilot skill, and expert machine maintenance. Combined with a Western embargo on all goods from the Soviet bloc, the Allied airlift broke the Russian blockade and enabled the citizens of West Berlin to hold on and defeat the Soviet intimidation of their city.

Post-War: A Rich, Fat America

Most of the major industrial nations of the world—England, France, Germany, Japan, Russia—had been physically devastated by the war, which left American producers and manufacturers with a near-monopoly on trade in consumer goods as well as new trends in automation in the workplace. Thus for the years 1950 to 1970, specific facts about resources, production, and supply help explain the era:

1. By 1970 the United States, with only 6 percent of the world's population, produced and also consumed two-thirds of the world's goods.

2. The return of 15 million soldiers to private life helped generate the post-war baby boom. Between 1945 and 1960 the U.S. population grew by nearly 40 million. In terms of production and consumer goods, this had quite an impact in diapers, baby food, medicines, schools, teachers, and housing.

3. The most popular new home appliance was the television set, which led to TV dinners and the TV tray, all of which changed habits involving card-playing, reading, visiting, or going to the movies.

4. In 1955 *Life* magazine described shoppers filling a "$15 million grocery store, picking from thousands of items on the high-piled shelves until their carts became cornucopias filled with

an abundance that no other country in the world had ever known." What a broad contrast with conditions we can now observe on television, such as starvation in the Sudan in the 1980s and the wretched conditions in Somalia since 1989.

5. By the late 1950s the cash available to teenagers had risen from $2 to about $12 or more a week in just a few years. Just what does one suppose that meant in terms of radios, phonographs, records, and clothes? Elvis Presley's financial advisors did not need to guess.

How tame this situation seems in an age in which we assume nearly everyone can afford a portable tape player, a video tape recorder, or a compact disc player to replace the old tape systems. Will one ever dial a number again, walk to change a TV channel, or not know who telephoned while they were away?

Teenager Money and the 1950s

On the subject of a morose person who is unable to assuage his down feelings through religious confession or starting a revolution, a line from the Arthur Miller play, *The Price*, suggests: "Today you're unhappy? Can't figure it out? What is the Salvation? Go shopping!"

There is much truth in these words for the period of American history that boasted unlimited transistor radios, Hula Hoops, 37-cent phonograph records, *Seventeen* magazine, and all the pop movies oriented to teenagers. Contrary to the conditions of earlier younger generations, be it time, location, or available currency, one market observer indicated that "the teenager's income runs $10 to $15 a week as opposed to $1 to $2 fifteen years ago [a war, with rationing in between]." By the 1950s the United States had generated a tremendous market for radios, phonographs, record albums, jewelry, and stylish clothes—styles that changed often, too, with a sort of planned obsolescence.

The American student of the 1990s should understand that the foregoing conditions were enjoyed in the United States while Europeans still walked through the rubble of bombings and Asians sought to move forward in an area that had witnessed the only true test of the atomic bomb. The term *Third World* had not yet been invented.

Havin' Wheels

All sociologists and economists of the modern United States concede the overwhelming impact of the automobile, an effect so broad and varied that accurate measurement is rendered impossible. It is inextricably woven with topics as varied as trucking, the World War II jeep, and the significance of Middle East oil and OPEC. Indeed, one cannot imagine a solid treatment of the Roaring Twenties without healthy reference to the automobile. From the romantic liaison in the proverbial back seat, to birth in the automobile on the way to the maternity hospital, to a lifetime participation in carpools, to a funeral motorcade escorted by motorcycle police, Americans literally can claim to be begotten, born, living, and buried on wheels.

Although the first motorcar had been manufactured for sale in 1895, it was the founding of the Ford Motor Company in 1903 that thoroughly revolutionized production and availability. A pioneer in the assembly line technique (typified by Ford's alleged statement, "You can have any color you want so long as it's black") and taylorization (making the most efficient use of each worker's time and motion on the line), Ford introduced the then-unheard-of notion that if a manufacturer paid his employees well they would become his chief customers, too. Most reliable and practical, the Ford Model T (everywhere affectionately referred to as the Tin Lizzie) came out in 1908 at a price of $850, a price that would drop to $290 by 1924. In 1920 there were eight million cars of various makes registered, and by 1929, more than 23 million. The result fit hand in glove with oil gushers in Texas and Oklahoma and stimulated production of steel, glass, rubber, and textiles. Autos also motivated the growth of suburbs and real estate developments. Sociologists agree that the auto has provided the most liberating influence ever presented to American youth.

The First Platinum Record Album

Most know that the gold record is awarded for the sale of a million records with one recording per side, and that today it is platinum for the sale of a million record albums with several hit songs on each side. With both the expansion of pop music and the increased buying power of youth during the 1950s, coupled with the advent of the 45 rpm recordings (selling for a while at about 37 cents), record sales expanded each year. Albums with several offerings per side began to boom as well. By the mid-1950s an album for the first time sold well over the treasured million mark, a historical landmark. Whose album was it? It was not a recording of country, gospel, blues, rock 'n' roll, classical, swing, movie theme, or novelty—it was Harry Belafonte's *Calypso* album that garnered the majestic first. It is just possible that because it was not a collection narrowed to a particular taste, it seemed to impress all as pleasing and refreshing—thus its ability to conquer the one million sales goal.

1957—Sputnik, *Shock, and Humor*

The Soviet Union's launching of an outer-space satellite called *Sputnik* (Little Vagabond) created shock and near disbelief in a normally complacent United States in the late 1950s. How could they possibly do that? While we talked of the quality of dishwashers, new effective deodorants, hi-fi sets, and the largesse of goods for the American consumer economy, the Russians could not even supply their citizens with adequate amounts of food, shoes, stockings, or windshield wipers. How could it be?

The U.S. launching three months later of *Explorer I* did not quiet the American outcry for renewed scientific efforts. During 1958 Congress had appropriated more defense funds for intercontinental ballistic missiles (ICBMs) and the North Atlantic Treaty Organization (NATO) than President Eisenhower requested, and went on to establish the National Aeronautics and Space Administration (NASA) and enact the National Defense Education Act, creating grants for students taking math, science, and foreign languages.

A humorous sidelight, typical of Americans, evolved from the early Soviet space successes. Because *Sputnik II* carried a dog named Lajka (Barker) for the observation of the effects of space travel on living creatures, one heard frequent references to Muttnik. The inevitable pun soon followed—the Soviets planned a future flight to include several cows, went the story, which of course would be known as the herd shot around the world.

By the early 1960s the so-called space gap between the U.S. and the U.S.S.R. had been closed, but not before the Russians sent up the first cosmonaut to orbit the earth in the person of Major Yuri Gagarin, followed shortly thereafter by the first woman in space, Valentina Tereshkova, and orbits of the moon with their Luna series of unmanned satellites. Then following up on President Kennedy's promise of a man on the moon by the end of the decade, Americans sent up their own manned rockets (the first to orbit the earth being flown by current Ohio Democratic U.S. senator, Marine Major John Glenn), culminating in the moon landing of Neil A. Armstrong and Lt. Col. Edwin E. "Buzz" Aldrin on 20 July 1969.

Fight Communism or Support Racism: Choose Your Cold War

As the United States and the Soviet Union squared off in the international political sphere in a contest commonly referred to as the Cold War, Americans faced another struggle on the domestic level, a civil rights cold war often referred to by historians as the Second Reconstruction. Although historians and participants alike have not often seen the link between the domestic and foreign aspects of these two political tournaments, they were more interrelated than most suppose. It is the old theme of dividing the attention of a nation's agencies, talent, and power between internal and external problems—a struggle successful nations from the beginning of recorded history instinctively try to avoid in the never-ending fight for survival. It was brought forward again in the 1992 political campaign where President George Bush, glowing in the success of the end of the Soviet Union, the collapse of the Berlin Wall, the freedom of Eastern Europe, and the Arabian Gulf War, was accused of neglecting important domestic issues, such as the nation's economy.

A major problem in approaching civil rights in the twentieth century is the limitations of the lineal, chronological approach. The movement is compressed into a decade beginning with the 1950s, which obscures the fact that the domestic struggle for human rights is one of centuries. This tends to conceal the effort of thousands of ordinary, oppressed people to come to terms with the dictates of society and the quiet challenges they met throughout their lives that culminated in the public movement historians note most. Often a cursory treatment strips the movement of its militancy and deeper meaning.

One way to overcome these limitations is to approach the civil rights struggle in an analytical or thematic format. As pointed out in the American Historical Association's newsletter, *Perspectives,* popular themes include the following: the centrality of local activism (the role of self-improvement cooperatives and churches) and its white opposition (the role of the Ku Klux Klan, the private education movement, and the White Citizens' Councils); the roles of gender (black women have traditionally lead in many efforts), class (black barbers and ministers have had pivotal roles in community activities), and age; the tensions and disagreements between local and national organizations (for instance, support of the nomination of Clarence Thomas to the United States Supreme Court by many local branches of the NAACP while the national group opposed him); the role of the media in the public perception of the movement; and the interaction between the federal government and the movement.

This last theme leads directly into the role of the Cold War in

the Second Reconstruction. The Cold War reveals two seemingly contradictory aspects of the government's approach to
the civil rights struggle. As pointed out in Mary L. Dudziak's
seminal article in the November 1988 *Stanford Law Review*
(based on earlier work by Derrick Bell), on the one side was the
intervention of the Department of Justice and the Department
of State in the pivotal case of *Brown v. Board of Education* as
amici curiae for the plaintiff, while on the other side was the
role of the Federal Bureau of Investigation as devil's advocate
in its surveillance of the various civil rights organizations as
subversive entities. Why was this so?

   As the Cold War advanced, American officials became painfully aware that the nation's stance toward its own nonwhite
minorities was costing it much of the advantage democratic
institutions should have had in the world struggle with communism. The Russians wasted no time publicizing numerous
racial difficulties in the United States (most of which were
confirmed by the American press on the 6 o'clock news), and
Third World nations notified the U.S. State Department of this
dichotomy in America's international reputation. With the
Soviets' atom and hydrogen bombs, their launching of the first
successful spacecraft, their sending up the first cosmonauts,
and their military advances in Korea (and later Vietnam), they
seemed on the verge of pushing the United States and its
Western allies into defeat. The United States had to at least
look invulnerable on the human rights issue, the very place the
Russians were most vulnerable, themselves, as the Helsinki
Accords demonstrated in the 1980s. The domestic racial
struggle, however, prevented the United States from exploit-
ing this advantage fully. Hence the governmental intervention
on behalf of the integrationists during both the Truman and
Eisenhower administrations, a bipartisan tradition continued
in various civil rights measures passed by succeeding administrations to date.

   At the same time, the African-American challenge to the
status quo was seen by some as a traitorous dividing of the
country's united effort to win the Cold War. Southern white
leaders referred to the government's support of desegregation
as communist propaganda and lambasted the content of Swed-

ish sociologist Gunnar Myrdal's *American Dilemma,* upon which much of the federal stance allegedly was based. J. Edgar Hoover had his FBI blacklist members of civil rights organizations, and he instituted counterintelligence activities against them, which included illegally taping phone calls, sending anonymous, threatening, and obscene materials through the mail, and even outright extortion, broadly using the fullest interpretation of post-Civil War constitutional law to defend his actions as an assault against communist sympathizers or fellow travelers. He plead states' rights, however, when asked to intervene on behalf of civil rights workers in the South. In so doing, according to historian Kenneth O'Reilly, Director Hoover demonstrated the fundamental contradiction of the Cold War era— "the United States' presentation of itself to Third World peoples as freedom's hope while consigning its own nonwhite peoples to an unequal status."

This is not to deny the importance of outright idealism or the fantastic commitment of civil rights workers to their goal of equal rights. It does, however, raise a very germane question in this day of the decline of communism worldwide, represented by the disintegration of the Soviet state: what will be the impact of the Cold War's collapse on the government's future role in the Second Reconstruction? Ironically enough, as the Cold War ends, the United States approaches the anniversary of the repeal of the Enforcement Acts and the Supreme Court decision *Plessy v. Ferguson,* events that signified the end of the first Reconstruction 100 years ago.

What Are Race Records?

By the early 1950s the immense new popularity of black rhythm and blues among white audiences created a marketing dilemma for major record producers. Much of black music had been segregated from major markets by the companies' practice of distributing them under subsidiary labels that weren't available in standard music stores. One of the producer responses to the new demand resulted in what came to be known as the race record. The tactic was still to exclude the black artist from the open market by covering the original rendition from the segregated market with a white artist's version on the major label. Thus, with minor lyric changes, Bill Haley and the Comets recorded the classic Joe Turner "Shake, Rattle, and Roll," Peggy Lee did Little Willie John's "Fever," and more than one artist, the most famous being Elvis Presley, recorded Willie Mae Thornton's "Hound Dog."

The change in some lyrics is of special interest, since there appears to have been a practice smacking of mild censorship seeking to render the cover version more acceptable to the nationwide (white) audience of television's "Ed Sullivan Show" as opposed to the more select patrons of Harlem's Apollo Theater. For example, the double entendre found in the black version of "Work with Me, Annie," accompanied by sounds of would-be passion (and a follow up record, "Annie had a baby, cain't work no more"), became in the cover version "Dance with Me, Henry." These record business antics resulted in personal tragedy for original artists on subsidiary labels. It was a sad commentary on American racial mores when LaVern Baker observed her "Tweedle Dee" played on a few black radio stations, while Georgia Gibbs saw her version become a million-seller backed by powerhouse white radio networks.

It took a great deal of time to break this sad situation created by big company policies that responded to perceived racial stereotypes. The work of Nat "King" Cole, Nancy Wilson, Ella Fitzgerald, Aretha Franklin, Ray Charles, Lena Horne, Sarah Vaughn, Pearl Bailey, and Sammy Davis, Jr., led the way—so much so that Charles became the spokesman for Pepsi Cola's new generation while Fitzgerald could show off her wide voice range and ask Americans, "Is it real or is it Memorex?"

Rock 'n' Roll: Music Trend or Code Name for Sex?

In 1951 Cleveland radio disc jockey Alan Freed, observing a record-buying shift away from Perry Como, Frank Sinatra, and Patti Page toward rhythm and blues artists like the Dominoes,

Johnny Ace, and the Clovers, changed the name of his program
from "Record Rendezvous" to "Moon Dog Rock 'n' Roll House
Party." The soon-to-be-widespread popularity of the term *rock
'n' roll* for what was essentially black rhythm and blues must
have sent laughter throughout the black community across the
nation. After all, for decades that term used in song was a code
word for the most intimate aspects of lovemaking among black
entertainers. So when Billy Ward with the Dominoes says,
"Rock me, roll me, all night long, I'm a sixty minute man," he
ain't referrin' to dancin', man.

Disneyland Forbidden to Khrushchev

During the Cold War, journalists measured relationships between the United States and the Soviet Union in meteorologi-
cal terms such as *hot, cold, thaw,* and so forth. After what was
described in the press as a tranquil meeting between Premier
Nikita Khrushchev and President Dwight D. Eisenhower at the
executive retreat at Maryland's Camp David (named after
Eisenhower's grandson), the Soviet head of government journeyed to the American West and finally reached Hollywood,
where he was feted on a movie set. What a place for the number
one representative of the Workers' Paradise, smack dab in the
center of bourgeoisie decadence! Tranquillity turned quickly
to hostility, however, when Russia's chief was informed that
he would not be allowed to visit his first choice of unreality,
Disneyland. "What is it?" he shouted. "Do you have rocket
launching pads there? Is there an epidemic of cholera or something? Or have gangsters taken hold of the place who can
destroy me?"

In truth, the most important figure in the Los Angeles area
was Mayor Norris Poulson, and he had concluded that security
forces were inadequate to protect Khrushchev at so large a
place as Disneyland, especially given the premier's populist
penchant for moving into crowds to touch the flesh with
American voters. In a nuclear age with its continued friction
and confrontation, how could Mayor Poulson risk Khrushchev's
injury or assassination, which might result in the war to end all

wars and everything else? So the mayor stuck to his guns and refused the Disneyland visit request, leaving the head of the Soviet bloc to fuss, fume, and throw temper tantrums, and finally satisfy himself with the ultimate in childishness—the vandalism of the train provided for his entourage.

Frisbees and Hula Hoops: A Craze

Starting in business after World War II, the Wham-O Company moved on from slingshots to what we know as the popular Frisbee. So simple, so useful, so adaptable to outdoor fun, it was a score for a young firm and required little in high technological production. Its management informed of the popularity of a large wooden hoop in Australia, the Wham-O Company soon went into similar production, making a hoop out of colored plastic and marketing the item as the Hula Hoop. Despite being copied by competing firms, in all the sales within a year were in the tens of millions. One interesting ramification appeared in several nations: people enjoying the Hula Hoop so much that heart problems developed, spinal discs went ajar, and respiratory excess was experienced. Yet in Japan, lines of customers stretched for blocks to purchase them, and even Prime Minister Nobusuke Kishi received one as a gift for his 62d birthday.

The Sore Feet of Rosa Parks

On a chilly day in December 1955, Mrs. Rosa Parks, a quiet African-American lady, was arrested in Montgomery, Alabama, for refusing to relinquish her seat on a city bus to a white male. She had not intended to make a scene, but her feet hurt from a day's work, and she was not about to stand for the ride to her stop. The next night at the Dexter Street Baptist Church, with Pastor Martin Luther King presiding, the congregation voted to launch a boycott of the bus system and all public services. Rosa Parks's tired feet and Pastor King's supporting congregation had by their simple act of defiance begun a far-reaching change in U.S. racial history—the modern civil rights revolution. The Second Reconstruction had begun.

Nearly 40 years later, Rosa Parks still lives in Montgomery. King fell to an assassin's bullet in 1967, but his name has become a household word for reform in the post-Vietnam United States. Is it not possible that the hit movie *Ghandi* owed some of its success to our awareness of his influence on King? How few of the great names of the twentieth century, names like Churchill, both Roosevelts, Wilson, DeGaulle, Hitler, Stalin, and Lenin, owe their fame to the nonviolent approach. King stands with a small group (including Mohandas Ghandi, Albert Schweitzer, and Alexsandr Solzhenitsyn) that influenced the world for the better by trying a different approach: the denial of violence for reason and using the written and spoken word to reach solutions to the world's problems.

Satchmo Says Ike Has No Guts

"No guts." That is the phrase popular jazz great Louis Armstrong employed to describe inaction on the part of the executive branch of government well after the landmark decision outlawing segregation on racial grounds. Following the 1954 *Brown v. Board of Education* ruling, massive resistance to school integration continued in the South. Then, in 1957, Governor Orville Faubus of Arkansas sent National Guard troops into Little Rock ostensibly to prevent violence, but they did it by halting black enrollment, too. When Faubus refused to back down, President Eisenhower sent in the 101st Airborne Division with orders to carry out the effect of the Brown decision. Satchmo, the man of music, quickly shifted to another tune and immediately praised Ike's show of determination at Little Rock.

It would be an interesting, challenging, and educational exercise for an American student to visualize the following situation and imagine how he or she would respond: You have just arrived in a European country as an American exchange student two days after Eisenhower's move on Little Rock. At the dinner table that first evening, your host family, bubbling with interest in the United States, asks why bayonet-wielding airborne soldiers are necessary for the fall session to commence at Little Rock's Central High. Remember, on the other side of the Atlantic, we all are Yanks. It represents a relevant topic for discussion then and now.

For Car Lovers: The Edsel Bomb of 1957

In part as a reaction to the success of General Motors with Buick, Oldsmobile, and Pontiac, and for want of typical American inventive initiative, the Ford Motor Company sunk a quarter of a million dollars into the production of an experimental, medium-priced auto, which was eventually marketed in 1957 as the Edsel, named after Henry Ford II's father. Secrecy at Ford rivaled that of the D-Day invasion in France, and production and promotion involved no less than 800 executives, 15,000 workers, and a host of expensive advertisers.

The model featured advance style in grill and rear end design, push-button operational controls, and a competitive middle-range price. However, the Edsel moved into auto showrooms during an economic recession that affected the auto industry especially hard. The auto became the immediate brunt of jokes for comedians and the cause for tears for its dealers. Looking back from the perspective of the 1990s, one is likely to compare it roughly to the more recent Yugo disaster. The first Edsels on the market lacked quality. Brakes failed, push buttons did not function, oil pans fell off, trunks and hoods could not be opened, and doors could not be closed. The list of malfunctions seemed to go on forever, and would-be buyers turned away in droves. Only the future would prove the Edsel's greatest value—as a collectors' item.

JFK—The Tarnished Martyr

Few political figures in U.S. history have received anything close to the degree of image-building enjoyed by John Fitzgerald Kennedy. Through the combined and well-orchestrated efforts of a string-pulling father, well-placed media friends, some underworld support, and an influential church, his reputation bordered on the marvel of a public relations creativity seminar. Facts surrounding the rise of Kennedy's political fortunes should be of special interest to students of mass media impact in the 1960s:

1. The original account of Kennedy and PT-109 (which ultimately became a film of that name) presented a valiant hero, while later revelations exposed the fact that he and his crew were asleep in a combat zone when a Japanese destroyer rammed them. Father Joe used his enormous influence to make sure John was decorated by a high-ranking naval officer.

2. Father Joe arranged for the original heroic, but inaccurate, version of the PT-109 event to be published in *Reader's Digest* precisely at the time son John ran for the House of Representatives, making certain every registered voter in the district received a copy.

3. The publication of JFK's first book, *Why England Slept*, was arranged by close family friend and journalist Arthur Krock, who then himself reviewed it favorably in *The New York Times*.

4. Kennedy's second book was largely a collaboration by a group of scholars headed by later speech writer Theodore Sorenson. For this volume, *Profiles in Courage*, Kennedy won a Pulitzer Prize.

5. Recent scholars have exposed a host of boosts in media coverage to enhance the Kennedy image, and also uncovered clandestine financial resources from Hollywood stars and the entertainment world. Most shocking has been the revelation of Kennedy's numerous sexual liaisons inside and outside of the White House.

The Bullet Silences Humor

The presence of John F. Kennedy as president of the United States furnished the opportunity for one Vaughn Meador to earn a most prosperous living, at least for a short time. Somewhat a look-alike of the president, with hair so thick the part was lost, he possessed the voice and a verbal delivery cadence that mimicked the thick Kennedy Bostonian accent to a tee. Joining with other performers, who took on the roles of JFK's wife, Jackie, and other members of the White House family, his albums became best sellers and millions tuned in the "Ed Sullivan Show" to view him on television. Then on 22 November 1963, after less than three years in office, Kennedy fell to an assassin's bullet as he rode in a motorcade through Dealy Plaza in Dallas. The American public heard Vaughn Meador no more.

Spring of 1968 brought astounding news from Kennedy's successor, Lyndon B. Johnson, that he would not seek a second term. Robert F. Kennedy, brother of the late president and his attorney general, was now a senator from the state of New York and a strong contender for the Democratic party's presidential nomination. Like his brother, Bobby employed a similar speech pattern and accent. Thus, another humor group offered a Meador-like parody of the new Kennedy, based on the pop rock song "Wild Thing," by the Trogs. A Bobby-sounding voice was heard to narrate the piece, even asking wife Ethel to keep the kids out of the studio (he had a large family) and then suggesting that younger brother Teddy (the current senator from Massachusetts) "lighten up a bit on the ocarina," a popular, simple wind instrument that accompanied the mimicry with its overwhelming flute-like tones. Then, after 8 June 1968, the public heard the humorous rendition no more, for just two months after the tragic murder of African-American leader Martin Luther King, Robert Kennedy, too, was cut down by a bullet in the kitchen area of a Los Angeles hotel after delivering a thank-you speech for his victory in the crucial California Democratic party primary. Once again in American politics of the 1960s, brutality had squelched the laughter.

The Beatles and America

A common trivia question asks: When was the first time Americans saw the Beatles on television? Most answer that it was on the "Ed Sullivan Show" during the Fab Four's first tour of the

United States. However, they actually were seen first on the old "Tonight Show" with Jack Paar, whose custom it was to tape his show two weeks a year from London, where the Beatles played a guest spot long before their popularity was assured on this side of the Atlantic. In 1963, while the Beatles were being mobbed by London fans in near riot proportions and their songs "She Loves Me," "I Wanna Hold Your Hand," and "Standing There" were big hits in the United States, the top-selling British group at that time in this country was in fact the Dave Clark Five.

One of the more serious controversial developments surrounding the Beatles' popularity here did not directly involve aspects or opinions of their music. It arose when the first pope (Paul VI) ever to visit the United States held a 1965 mass in Yankee Stadium (home of the Mets baseball team) for more than 67,000 communicants. Later, as a part of a U.S. tour, the Beatles played in Shea Stadium to an even larger crowd. In a post-concert interview, alerted to the statistics by a reporter, John Lennon made an unfortunate offhand remark that the group was more popular than Jesus Christ. Although he later apologized for the crack, a reaction swept religious areas of the country. Few reactions topped Birmingham, Alabama, which went so far as to have a public bonfire for Beatles' records, tapes, and other memorabilia in a vain attempt to preserve youthful public morality.

LBJ versus AUH₂O in 1964

The 1964 Republican candidate for president of the United States was Arizona Senator Barry M. Goldwater, whose bumper stickers read AUH_2O the scientific symbols for gold (Au) and water (H_2O). Much that he had to say before and during the campaign, where he faced Democratic President Lyndon B. Johnson, made it easy for press and critics (and his supporters claimed them to be one and the same) to portray the desert challenger as a warmonger. It was the middle of the Cold War, both the space race and the Vietnam War were heating up, and it was too much to expect that the Democrats could hold back on the vigorous Goldwater candidacy. They needed to make him an extremist, and his caustic rhetoric made the job relatively easy. The most memorable attack on the senator came in a television advertisement that pictured a cute little three-year-old girl picking flowers in a meadow that gave way to a mushroom cloud rising in the background. Words seemed unnecessary.

Goldwater campaign workers hoped to counter with a short film called *Choice*. The choice was between an acceptable, pastoral United States and the lurid world of the big cities: topless joints, pornographic bookstores, delinquent youths, and riots in black ghettos. Playing upon accurate news reports of LBJ cruising around his expansive Texas ranch sucking on a beer, the final scene portrayed a beer can being tossed from a large Lincoln sedan, obviously Johnson littering the country in more ways than one. After viewing the piece, Goldwater forbade its use and angrily described it as a racist film. It was noble and just conduct for the senator, but its use probably would not have helped or hindered his cause to any significant degree.

Love at Woodstock, Hate at Altamont

Few events appealed more as a rallying point to the love and hippie culture of the late 1960s and early 1970s than outdoor rock music concerts, especially those featuring artists whose songs delivered an appealing message. The largest of these concerts was the Woodstock Music Festival in August 1969, where more than 400,000 spectators gathered for three days at a 600-acre farm near Bethel, New York. Musicians, much revered by the throng and (to judge from their record sales) by millions more Americans, included Joan Baez; Jimi Hendrix; Crosby, Stills, Nash, and Young; Santana; Richie Havens; Country Joe and the Fish; and a host of others. Over the three days, pleasing music and free love engulfed the rural event, as did cheap marijuana and other chemical substances. One journalist, after comments on the exuberant nude swimming in the local lake, added that the country had never "seen a society so free of repression."

Just four months later, the promoters of the successful New York counterculture event attempted to stage a repeat event in southern California at Altamont, just south of San Bernardino. This time a less-than-love-oriented criminal element was present. The Rolling Stones enlisted Hell's Angels motorcycle gang members to provide security for their show there. While Mick Jagger performed "Sympathy for the Devil" on stage, some of the white motorcyclists, armed with baseball bats and cut-off pool cues, proceeded to beat to death a black spectator in front of the stage. Three other crowd members died that night in various fights. From that moment on the innocent, would-be flower child essence of the counterculture began to wilt. It eventually died in a fashion not unlike the New Left did after its role in disrupting both the 1968 Democratic Convention and the judicial process that followed that violent episode.

This comparison and contrast might suggest to those who seek avenues for change what type of route might prove more successful.

Who in the World Is Ego Brown?

In the late 1980s a civilian voucher examiner for the U.S. Navy, Ego Brown, got tired of working for the government and decided to open a business of his own. As a youngster he had shined shoes for spending money, and he was convinced that a conveniently located shoeshine stand in the heart of the nation's capital would be profitable if run by an adult on the principles of an organized business. He quit his job, practiced shining shoes at a barbershop on the Howard University campus, and got ready to "spread the shine," as he put it. Dressed in a tuxedo and using his flamboyant personality to attract customers, Brown envisioned operating shoeshine stands on street corners throughout the District of Columbia. In a unique twist, he would hire the unemployed to staff his stands. A shower, clean clothes, a shave, and a little basic education in the Ego Brown Method, and the unemployed would have a real opportunity to pull themselves up by the bootstraps. Brown, then, envisioned cleaning up not only Washington's millions of scuffed shoes, but the unemployment problem as well, all at a tidy profit to himself, his employees, and the city. It worked so well that local social workers began referring likely job candidates to him.

Brown, however, neglected to consider the intransigence of the city administration. Citing a 1905 law preventing the existence of shoeshine stands on public streets, the city government of Mayor Marion Barry shut Brown down. Unlike so many entrepreneurs before him, Brown challenged the action in court. After all, how could it make sense that a service industry like his shoeshine stands could not legally exist on the public streets, while it was permissible for people to panhandle or run almost any other kind of economic activity there?

To Brown's surprise, however, traditional civil rights organizations refused to take up his case. They stood by the city administration and called the shoeshine business an undignified relic of past racism. Finally Brown interested the Institute of Justice and its vice president and director of litigation, Clint Bolick. Under legal advice from the Landmark Legal Foundation Center for Civil Rights, the case *Brown v. Barry* (1989) was heard by the District of Columbia federal court, which ruled the 1905 restriction illegal, permitting Ego Brown to continue in business. The case was prominently displayed in *Wall Street Journal, The New York Times,* and the *Washington Post.* Brown was the Person of the Week on "ABC-News," and a repentant District of Columbia government finally bowed to public opinion and common sense by declaring an Ego Brown Day in his honor.

Two important items emerged from the Ego Brown case. The first was the restrictive nature of licensing boards composed of members of a trade or industry that often apply regulations not so much to protect the public as to shield themselves from competition. Lawyer Bolick blames this problem on the slaughterhouse cases heard in 1873 by the U.S. Supreme Court. In his volume, *Unfinished Business: A Civil Rights Strategy for America's Third Century* (1990), Bolick asserts that the Supreme Court's 5–4 decision permitting New Orleans, Louisiana, to set up an economic monopoly on slaughtering, which put many independent butchers out of business in an alleged effort to protect the public good, subverted the privileges and immunities

clause of the Fourteenth Amendment and its implicit guarantee of economic opportunity, thereby hindering entrepreneurs
of lesser initial wealth trying to enter selected areas of economic endeavor.

Nowadays, maintains Bolick, such licensing and regulation
by professional boards has gone well beyond the public interest to excluding anyone who might be able to present established tradesmen with legitimate competition, as did Ego Brown
to the traditional barbershop shoeshine stand. Conveniently,
many of these efforts appeared as African Americans began to
migrate north to escape Southern white legal discrimination
against newly freed slaves who could successfully use their
plantation skills during the so-called Black Reconstruction
(1867–1877). The laws usually grandfathered in existing white
tradesmen, but the applied fees, zoning, regulations, and the
confusing bureaucratic red tape limited or negated the economic competition of arriving blacks. This not only guaranteed existing jobs but raised prices to the public through
limited production, enhancing industrial profits.

The second facet of the Ego Brown case concerns the direction of the modern civil rights movement. Again, Bolick, who
idolizes and quotes Thomas Paine, articulated this aspect both
in another book, *Changing Course: Civil Rights at the Crossroads*
(New Brunswick, NJ: Transaction, 1988), and on the weekly
black public affairs television program, "Tony Brown's [no
relation to Ego Brown] Journal." Bolick sees the modern civil
rights establishment, with its emphasis on entitlements, racial
set-asides, quotas, affirmative action, and redistribution of
wealth through the poisonous atmosphere of the regulation of
private behavior, preferential legislation, and double standards for blacks and whites, as increasingly out of contact with
the need of its constituency—namely, the creation of equal
economic opportunity.

Bolick believes that the litigation of cases such as Ego Brown's
will bring idealism back to the civil rights movement that
essentially disappeared with the murder of Martin Luther
King. He also thinks the results of the slaughterhouse cases
should be attacked as methodically as was school segregation
in the first half of the twentieth century. What he seeks is not

an assurance of equal *result*, as do most civil rights advocates, but the guarantee of an equal *chance* to participate in the promise that brought (and still brings) immigrants to this country, the inalienable right to live out one's life free of interference so long as one engages in peaceful, voluntary, mutual transactions with others.

A Trip to the World of Afrocentricity

Now in its third edition, Molefi Kete Asante's classic volume, *Afrocentricity*, named for a concept earlier referred to as negritude, is considered one of the more influential statements in modern Pan-African thought. Briefly stated, Afrocentricity holds that the importance of classical African civilizations is critical to understanding the place of African Americans in post-modern history, since the roots of all African people, regardless where they live now, go back to East Africa. He calls for a renunciation of "Negroness and western influences" as the key to the national recovery of American blacks. The comprehension of Afrocentric images, symbols, life-styles, manners, and historiography, says Asante, is as liberating to the black person as the truth of the Bible is to a born-again Christian.

Asante traces the roots of the current Afrocentric movement through many black scholars scattered through the diaspora of slavery into many other countries, cultures, and languages. Several African Americans figure in this story. The first is Booker T. Washington, whom Asante calls one of the most astute and courageous blacks who ever lived. Asante belittles the differences that traditional historians find between Washington and his archnemesis, W. E. B. DuBois, correctly pointing out that their goal was the same—the liberation of the African people. He sees Washington's alleged accommodationist stance, such as the famous Atlanta Exposition speech, as an elaborate sham, designed to allay the fears of his white audiences and to allow his work to continue with their economic support.

Washington's emphasis on mechanical arts and sciences had as its goal the economic independence of all blacks in the United States, but Asante criticizes him for not realizing that economic power could not produce freedom. This was the contribution of Marcus Garvey and his Universal Negro Improvement Association and African Communities League. He was truly a Pan-Africanist in thought. Although the press concentrated on his back to Africa movement, Garvey was more interested in inspiring blacks to respect themselves and inspire this same respect from others. His success in recruiting ten million blacks to contribute to the concept of Africa for the Africans, Asante says, attests to American blacks' memory of their African past, however distant that may be.

At the helm of black intellectual and political advancement stands W.E. Burghardt DuBois, according to Asante. Author of 2,377 articles and books on all aspects of African-American history and life, DuBois was not Afrocentric in his outlook until later in life, after he had been thoroughly disillusioned in his vain efforts to work within a Western intellectual framework. Emphasizing what he called the talented tenth as the advance of all black efforts, DuBois was unwilling to give ground to discrimination as Washington had done with his five fingers, one hand concept. He sought to fight segregation from an intellectual and legal perspective, says Asante, until he finally realized that the country lacked the moral character to fully integrate Africans into its society. DuBois blamed capitalism for this, and he turned toward socialism, then Marxism, to explain the nation's perceived faults. However, these ideologies DuBois found too limiting, too material, too restrictive of the role of the innovator, theoretician, inventor, and discoverer; ultimately, he moved on to Ghanaian citizenship and his African roots, but as with Washington, it was too little, too late to satisfy a nonetheless admiring Asante.

Unlike DuBois, Dr. Martin Luther King was able to appeal to the spirit of the times in the language and ideas of the common person. Although Asante credits King with redefining the limits of nonviolence and civil disobedience to achieve unheard-of legal and social changes in the United States, Asante finds fault with him in that he stood with one foot in the white camp and the other in the black world. Asante praises King as an instigator of an action philosophy that inspired millions and continued on after his death in the persons of his wife,

Jesse Jackson, Ralph D. Abernathy, Andrew Young, and others, but decries his lack of Afrocentrism—a fault he sees as stemming from King's early death.

Another figure who possessed more of an Afrocentric outlook than King, but still had many limitations in the eyes of Asante, was Elijah Muhammad, with his Nation of Islam. Asante sees Muhammad as liberating African Americans from the religion of the master and taking them back to a more African form of worship. Muhammad saw the white race as essentially evil, a thought that has since permeated the ideas of others, such as the Reverend Louis Farrakhan. According to Asante, Muhammad stressed that the white choice was not necessarily the right choice, but he still sought to convey his notions through Islam, which Asante sees as imposed upon the black past as much as Christianity and, hence, not truly Afrocentric. Like King, Muhammad had a compromising foot in an enemy camp, but he inspired others, the most known of whom, in the white world at least, was heavyweight boxer Muhammad Ali.

Elijah Muhammad's disciple, Malcolm X, became the standard-bearer for Asante's true challenge to Western influences among African Americans. He challenged what Afrocentrists see as the historical arrogance and political assertion of racial supremacy in the United States by asserting Pan-Africanism in historical, economic, and social ways. Malcolm X said the only true basis for discrimination in the United States was racial, based on skin color alone. He used an earlier analogy developed by actor Paul Robeson, calling blacks who had made it in white America to repudiate their privileged positions as house slaves and to rededicate themselves to the black community— the field slaves left behind, who worked hard and hated their white oppressors. Asante especially finds significant Malcolm X's statement that African Americans needed to use any means necessary to rid themselves of the baggage of slavery and self-doubt. By so doing, says Asante, he opened a thousand ways to fight for black liberation and stand up for individual rights, which inspired people such as Bobby Seale, Huey Newton and the Black Panthers, and Maulana Karenga with his systematic black nationalism.

While others fought the Afrocentric battle in the streets and courts, Maulana Karenga sought to reconstruct African-American life and history. In so doing he established a systematic ideology called Kawaida, based on the pillars of history (combining the spiritual and material and promoting heroes and heroines), mythology (to give purpose, identity, and direction), creative motif (African language forms, dress, behavior, and games), ethos (the collective personality of a people), social organization (called Njia, or the Way, essentially a ritual acceptance of oneself as African above all else), political organization (Pan-African meetings and consultations and a shared African awareness, often expressed by adopting an African name), and economic organization (generally some form of socialism).

So it goes in the world of the Afrocentrist, who studies Africa B.B.A.—before the beginning again, that is, before the 1619 importation of the first African indentures to Virginia—to understand what has happened to African Americans A.B.A.—after the beginning again, anything after 1619. (In this scheme, 1993 A.D. becomes 374 A.B.A.) According to one critic, the Western world has become a society whose culture was based on an Egyptian civilization created by blacks and stolen by Alexander the Great, who slipped it to his tutor Aristotle, who passed it off as white.

By emphasizing African culture in a form of self-segregation by subject matter, it is hoped that predominantly black schools of big city ghettos will produce proud, disciplined, achieving students. Not everyone agrees it will work. Newspaperman Paul Greenberg notes that the South once had such a bicultural educational system called racial segregation. While granting that the study of African culture might help reverse many old stereotypes, Greenberg wonders if current multiracial, multireligious, and multicultural American culture is too pervasive to be breached by a mere fad. After all, many European cultures are trying in vain to prevent Americanisms in music, language, clothing, and life-styles from taking over their countries. Greenberg also points out that African Americans are not Africans, but Americans, indelibly part of the Western tradition that, in the words of a group of historians critical of the

Afrocentric approach, "is the source of ideas of individual freedom and political democracy to which most of the world aspires." Arthur Schlesinger, Jr., one of those critics, calls Afrocentrism "history . . . as social and psychological therapy," and questions whether it really raises anyone's self-esteem or if it has any use in the real world. "If some Kleagle of the Ku Klux Klan wanted to devise an educational curriculum for the specific purpose of handicapping and disabling black Americans," he concludes, "he would not be likely to come up with anything more disabling than Afrocentrism."

The Real Sex, Lies, and Videotape: Scandal in Washington

One of the more pervasive themes dominating the seat of U.S. government in Washington, D.C., has been political scandal. There is nothing really unique about that—governments everywhere seem to attract shameful behavior. In the United States, however, the pace of high jinks at the taxpayers' expense seems to have accelerated since the assassination of President John F. Kennedy in 1963.

Many pundits trace this phenomenon to the politics of the 1960s: in her 1991 book, *Scandal: The Crisis of Mistrust in American Politics,* Suzanne Garment sees the beginnings of the present trend originating in the 1960 civil rights sit-ins at Greensboro, North Carolina, which questioned the openly segregated society of the South and the more subtly de facto separations of the North and West; Rachel Carson's *Silent Spring,* a 1962 environmental missive against her perceived fundamental flaws of modern society, particularly the overuse of agricultural pesticides; the Warren Commission's flawed report on the Kennedy murder at Dallas still haunts us today and has been the victim of numerous books, television documentaries, including Oliver Stone's sensational 1991 movie *JFK;* Ralph Nader's 1965 criticism of the American auto industry's open flaunting of easily applied safety measures appeared in *Unsafe at Any Speed;* and especially the American intervention in the Vietnam civil conflict, in which President Lyndon B. Johnson expanded Kennedy's initial commitment into a full-fledged war. Indeed the 1967 off-Broadway play, *MacBird,* accused Johnson of complicity in Kennedy's death to achieve his dirty warmongering deeds, a viewpoint that overlooks his well-meaning domestic agenda for the Great Society, which has come under more substantial criticism for better reasons in the 1980s.

The war's opponents, like all the other critics of American society, brought a new moral attack forward—the ills were not merely the result of badly conceived policy but of moral corruption of the foulest kind. Their criticisms were full of a previously absent self-righteousness and want of restraint. When one adds a lessening of political party control and protection of its members through a failing good ol' boy network and the increasing influence of an often-irresponsible, muckraking media seeking subscriptions or a greater number of viewers, the end product is a fundamental change in the way Americans look at politics.

Activities that were winked at in the past or actually hidden by the press, like President Franklin D. Roosevelt's secret taping of White House meetings or Kennedy's clandestine affairs with numerous women, became front-page, career-ending news, to the embarrassment of many. By the time of the 1972 presidential election, it had been revealed that the break-in at the offices of the Democratic National Committee was sponsored by advisors of President Richard Nixon who ran his reelection campaign, a group whose name, the Committee to Reelect the President, had the idiotic, spine-tingling acronym of CREEP. The ensuing investigation was covered up by the president, who had secretly taped implicating conversations and then "lost" 18 key minutes of the tape, and the incident ended with the first presidential resignation in American history. It also made the independent counsel a permanent addition in Washington investigations.

Author Garment estimates that over 400 high-level government officials have been skewered by the scandal sword. She wonders if the result of what she calls the "criminalization of politics" has been better government or mere scandalmongering for its own sake, pointing out that good husbands and fathers do not necessarily make capable politicians. Consider the following:

1. Texas promoter Billy Sol Estes was indicted, tried, and convicted for abusing governmental agricultural assistance programs, a process that he claimed was assisted by his political friends, Vice President Lyndon B. Johnson and Texas Senator Ralph Yarborough.

2. Bobby Baker, Senate Secretary to the Democratic majority and a close crony of Johnson and Oklahoma Democrat Senator Robert S. Kerr, used his influence to get a business acquaintance a lucrative vending machine contract with a defense plant. When Baker then tried to buy out the vending company, the former benefactor screamed to the press. Subsequent investigation revealed that Baker had skimmed $100,000 in Democratic campaign fund contributions for his own use.

3. Connecticut Democratic Senator Thomas Dodd, Sr., a man of impeccable credentials and lifelong government service, was censured by the Senate in 1967 for misappropriating campaign funds and double billing government and private contributors for senatorial junkets disguised as legitimate business. The information was leaked to columnists Drew Pearson and Jack Anderson by disaffected members and former members of Dodd's own staff. His defenders, led by Senator Russell Long of Louisiana, pointed out that half of the Senate could not survive similar investigation, but their defense was to no avail.

4. President Jimmy Carter's advisor, Bert Lance of the Office of Management and Budget, resigned under fire, accused of unsavory banking practices in obtaining loans back in Georgia. He beat the rap after a lengthy legal battle that lasted well into the 1980s. Carter White House Aid Hamilton Jordan (pronounced Jer'dan) was accused of drug abuse at a New York City nightclub as well as insensitive, sexist speech and actions toward various women. Jordan beat the criminal charges on cocaine use after an expensive trial that left him penniless. Carter's alcoholic brother, Billy, marketer of the briefly famous Billy Beer, was accused of not properly registering as an agent for the government of Libya, with whom he had alleged shady business dealings. The press named it Billygate (everything has been sensationalized as something-gate after the Watergate episode), and blew it way out of proportion. While nobody really cared much about the faults of Carter's people, Carter's

promise to never tell a lie while president led to a different standard of morality being applied to all of his people.

5. *Public Trust, Private Lust: Sex, Power, and Corruption on Capitol Hill* (1977), a book by Marion Clark and Rudy Maxa, expands the congressional trivia list endlessly, involving all parties, all states, and all sexual preferences. Some of the more publicized incidents include a drunken Wilbur Mills dancing in the middle of the night in a Washington pond with stripper Fanne Foxe; Wayne Hayes employing buxom, blond Elizabeth Ray as a typist but utilizing her other obvious qualities instead (this kind of activity was practically endless among numerous 1970s congressmen); drinking womanizer John Jenrette being trapped taking bribes from federal agents disguised as wealthy Arab businessmen in the so-called Abscam operation (his beautiful wife, Rita, now a Washington social commentator, did a spread for *Playboy* in which she bragged that they had made love on the Capitol steps); Daniel B. Crane having sexual activity with a female page, and Gary E. Studds doing likewise with a male page; Gus Savage sexually assaulting a female peace corps volunteer in Zaire (she was sent home a psychological wreck); Barney Frank having a homosexual dalliance with a lover who ran a call-boy service out of his home; and Donald "Buzz" Lukens having sex with an underaged girl.

6. Nothing has had such an unfortunate impact on one man's political career as the automobile death of Mary Jo Kopechne did for Massachusetts Senator Edward Kennedy, who was allegedly driving. Although it cost him the Democratic party's nomination for the presidency, his senatorial career has been notable and lengthy, supported heavily by women voters—at least until 1992 when his nephew's acquittal on a rape charge, growing out of an incident on Kennedy's Palm Beach estate, threatened to renew old criticisms of the senator's lack of responsibility in his personal actions. Likewise, when Colorado's Democratic presidential contender Gary Hart challenged the press to catch him if they could, *The Miami Herald* took up the dare and photographed him dallying with model Donna Rice on a boat in Bimini, wrecking his chance for the 1984 nomination. (Meanwhile Miss Rice fairly cleaned up in the publicity market as the spokeswoman for various products and lifestyles.) In a similar situation, however, 1992 Democrat presidential candidate Bill Clinton managed to survive charges

of an extramarital affair with Gennifer Flowers and gain the executive office.

7. When the Senate Judiciary Committee investigated African American Clarence Thomas for the U.S. Supreme Court seat vacated by the retiring Thurgood Marshall (the lawyer who had represented the NAACP in the 1954 *Brown v. Board of Education* case that led to nationwide school integration), Anita Hill, a law professor from the University of Oklahoma, came forward to reveal numerous allegations of sexual misconduct that had occurred years before when she had worked under Thomas in the Civil Rights Division of the Justice Department. For her trouble, Hill was castigated by the all-male panel, which shot her story full of holes and approved Thomas.

A year later polls indicated that Hill's story had gained a great deal of credibility among the public at large, which resulted in a wave of female candidates for public office, many of whom ran on the veracity of Anita Hill's story, and many of whom were elected. Indeed, Senator Arlen Spector of Pennsylvania just managed to be reelected against an opponent who based her campaign on his interrogation and exposé of Hill's testimony before the Senate. Also surviving his reelection effort (against another male) was Senator Bob Packwood, a Liberal Republican from Oregon who bluffed his way through allegations that he had made unwanted sexual advances against several female employees. Packwood, an avowed supporter of women's causes, denied everything. He attacked his accusers as "round-heeled bimbos," in the words of one commentator, but when nine other women stepped forward to back up the original accusation with tales of their own, he noncommittally apologized to anyone who may have felt wronged (which many commentators saw as an admission of guilt). Most recently he has claimed to have an alcohol problem.

Women's victories in the 1992 election—four in the Senate alone—and the changed perception of Anita Hill's story may force a rapid showdown. To keep the whole thing nonpartisan, Senator Daniel K. Inouye, a Democrat from Hawaii, may have to join Packwood at the bar of the Senate Ethics Committee, he having been accused of forcing himself on his lady hairdresser some time past. The World's Most Exclusive Boys Club (the U.S. Senate) may be emerging from what political commentator Sandy Grady (male) has called "a Capitol Hill plantation on which the overseers, almost 100 percent middle-aged white males, had a free run with their libidos and egos," and evolving toward a more politically correct twentieth-century institution, providing that these solons can stomach a dose of the medicine they routinely dish out to the nation at large. "You wonder when these guys had time to make a quorum call," is Grady's poignant conclusion.

Watergate: A New Synonym

Still in use today, the Watergate building along the Potomac River in Washington, D.C., has become synonymous with any conduct of a clandestine, illegal, or unethical character. In 1972 the edifice happened to house the headquarters of the Democratic National Committee (DNC), which was working to elect candidate George B. McGovern. In June paid agents of the Committee to Reelect the President burglarized the DNC office to seize documents allegedly useful to the Republican campaign. The specific content of these documents remains a mystery. Rumors have linked them to a list implicating persons in a prostitution ring (allegedly composed of high-placed Washington wives and secretaries of both parties) to papers supposedly relevant to the assassination of President John F. Kennedy, as well as a dozen lesser items in between.

The agents' simple act falls into the category of what is now called dirty tricks, but the ramifications became monumental and led to the first resignation of a president in the nation's history. The investigation ultimately revealed that top presidential advisors and the attorney general of the United States were involved. Then an accidental slip by one of those questioned revealed that Nixon, like many presidents before him, had secretly recorded White House conferences. From these tapes, although they were missing 18 critical minutes of recordings, came the most damaging evidence, the so-called smoking gun. Evidence showed that all, including the president, had lied after the fact to cover up their actions or the actions of their underlings. Thus the cover-up became the most notorious aspect of the break-in.

The suffix *-gate* is now added to many terms in order to

identify actions suspected of foul or unethical behavior. For instance, Irangate is the common name of the illegal 1980s arms deal involving Marine Lt. Col. Oliver North, Admiral Richard Poindexter, and others.

For Viewers of The Godfather *Saga*

The Godfather, a film that broke all records up to its time for gross earnings, was soon followed by successful sequels that covered more of Mario Puzo's original novel. How close was the film series to real life? Puzo meshed together roles and events from the history of organized crime with much literary license, but there is much truth to his fiction.

1. The film's Don Corleone was a composite of several mafiosi dons among many New York families. As the person with the most political and police connections, he was most like the real Joseph Costello, who appeared before the Kefauver Senate Committee during the mid-1950s. Corleone's clearing money for building the first true resort hotel in Las Vegas (The Flamingo) was taken from the life of Bugsy Siegal.

2. When we see singer Johnny Fontaine needing a career boost from the influence of Don Corleone, that would have been Willie Moretti (alias Moore), who was close to Frank Sinatra and did in fact chide him about loyalty to wife and family when news photos displayed him cavorting with Ava Gardner.

3. In the film, Moe Green is shot over differences arising from a resort hotel ownership. This is obviously related to the actual death of Siegal, the corporate founder of a hotel operation. Most likely, as is thought by police authorities, the construction/promotion funds came from Joseph Costello and mob banker Meyer Lansky.

4. For viewers of *The Godfather II*, the Hyman Roth role best fits the life of Meyer Lansky (with a few exceptions), a friend of Siegal and Lucky Luciano since the 1920s. Lansky had become the mob's chief money changer/launderer/investor/financier/ economic consultant by the 1940s. Yes, there were crucial meetings in Cuba on occasion that dealt with the Siegal/ Flamingo problem and much else. Lansky survived the mob to die of heart ailments, harassed only by the U.S. government.

5. Among the dons, the issue of drug-dealing was always one of disagreement. To be connected with it on the street level was a threat to their paid judicial and police protection. Most would participate only at the top, involving large profits and high-priced movements into the United States from external sources. Below that, they collected from street sellers for the privilege of operating in the areas of their criminal jurisdiction.

Some Firsts in the Twentieth Century

First among women: In 1916 Jeanette Rankin of Montana became the first elected woman to serve in Congress, and she had the unique distinction of being the only person to vote against American participation in both World Wars. Wyoming gave the United States the first woman elected as governor in Nellie T. Ross in 1925, the same year Miriam "Ma" Ferguson became governor of Texas. In 1933 Frances Perkins became the first woman in a cabinet post as secretary of labor, serving until 1945. In 1984 Geraldine Ferraro became the first woman to represent a major political party as Democratic vice presidential candidate. The first woman to run for the presidency, however, was a nineteenth-century ex-prostitute and con artist, Victoria Claflin Woodhull, who ran in 1872 representing a women's rights, reform, and free-love ticket. By 1992 much had changed: four women won election to the U.S. Senate, an all-time high. These included both senators from California—former U.S. Representative Barbara Boxer and ex-San Francisco Mayor Diane Feinstein—Washington State's Mom in Tennis Shoes, Patty Murray, and the first black woman elected U.S. senator, Carol Moseley Braun. They join Barbara Mikulski of Maryland and Nancy Kassebaum of Kansas, already serving. The first woman seated in the U.S. Senate was Rebecca Felton of Georgia in 1922, but she served for only two days before her male replacement showed up. It was Hattie Caraway of Arkansas who, in 1932, became the first female elected to a full term as U.S. senator.

In addition to Carol Moseley Braun, here are the other firsts among African Americans: Jackie Robinson, a multiple-sport varsity athlete at UCLA who signed with the Brooklyn Dodgers and joined the Montreal farm team, quickly advanced to the parent club and was named National League Most Valuable Player in 1949. Hattie McDaniel was the first to win an Oscar for her supporting role in *Gone with the Wind* in 1939. Edward Brooke of Massachusetts was the first to be popularly elected as a U.S. senator, but in 1870 Hiram Revels of Mississippi was elected by the state legislature under the old system as the first black ever to serve in the Senate. Joseph Hayne Rainey was the first of his race to be elected to the House of Representatives in 1870. In 1968 Arthur Ashe was the first African American to win the U.S. Open tennis title; he suffered a heart attack in the early 1980s and became inadvertently exposed to the AIDS virus during open-heart surgery. Arguably the best fighter of all time, Muhammad Ali was the first Black Muslim to win the heavyweight boxing title; the title was taken away for his religious pacifistic refusal to serve during the Vietnam War, but was later restored. In 1956 Harry Belafonte cut the first platinum (million-selling) album, *Calypso.* In 1968 Shirley Chisholm from Brooklyn's 12th District was the first black woman elected to Congress. In 1979 Patricia Harris was the first black woman to hold a cabinet position and the first secretary of Health and Human Services. Vanessa Williams in 1984 was the first black Miss America. Sidney Poitier won an Oscar for best actor for his role in *Lilies of the Field* in 1964, commenting, "It has been a long journey." He no doubt spoke for others.

Only if we move our attention back to the nineteenth century can we include the first Native American in major league baseball, Louis Soxalexis, of the Cleveland franchise, the team that became the Indians because of him. One of the best pitchers on the Philadelphia Athletics for nearly a decade was Native American Paul Bender. Three Native Americans have been elected to the U.S. Senate. The first was Charles Curtis of Kansas, elected in 1907 after a 14-year stint in the House of Representatives. He also served as Herbert Hoover's vice president. Oklahoma's Robert Owen was in the Senate from 1907 to 1925, and Colorado's Ben Nighthorse Campbell was elected to the Senate in 1992 after serving his state for six years in the House.

Theodore Roosevelt was the youngest person to serve as president, while John F. Kennedy was the youngest elected president. Teddy was also the first to fly in a plane, but Dwight D. Eisenhower was the first to possess a pilot's license. Jimmy Carter was the first president to have been born in a hospital. In 1974 Richard Nixon became the first president to resign from office, but his running mate, Spiro Agnew, was the second vice president to resign, preceded by John C. Calhoun during Andrew Jackson's first administration. Because of the resignations of Nixon and Agnew, Gerald Ford was the first president to take office without being elected as either president or vice president—Nixon had appointed him to fill Agnew's place, and he was confirmed by the Senate. Ronald Reagan was the first U.S. president to address the British Parliament.

A Cold War Poker Game

Imagine a poker game lasting 40 years that gets out of hand and rapidly escalates into a game with multiple rule changes, mutual spying to look at the opponent's hand, bluffing that is characterized by brinkmanship, and betting that finally reaches the multimillion dollar range. Then, with each player nervously aware of their hefty monetary investments, and international prestige on the line, one player scrutinizes his hand carefully and says, "I'll raise you $300 billion." The player across the table is stunned and begins to argue over the rules of the game—but the very heat and pressures of the already-condoned cheating of the past 40 years has shown that there are no rules.

This was the situation at Reykjavik, Iceland, on 13 October 1986. The player who made the raise was President Ronald Reagan of the United States. The one who angrily contested the rules was Premier Mikhail Gorbachev of the Soviet Union. The poker game was the Cold War.

Although the confrontation received but routine journalistic notice at the time, the realities magnified by unresolved differences at Reykjavik have in fact proven Reagan's raising of the stakes to be the most important event in the history of the Cold War, one that shook the very foundation of the Iron Curtain and brought it crumbling down in a few short years. Why did

Reagan's move prove crucial, causing so much change in U.S.-Soviet relations and costing the Soviet Union its control of its Eastern Bloc empire, epitomized in the fall of the Berlin Wall?

For decades the Soviet Union had followed a strategy propounded by its founder, V. I. Lenin, and characterized by the slogan, "guns for butter." It was a notion predicated upon the belief that the Soviet Union existed in a hostile, threatening, capitalistic world and needed to protect itself to guarantee the success of the 1917 Russian revolution and the future goals of worldwide socialistic revolution. The most conspicuous feature of Soviet strategy from the 1930s to the 1980s was a mismanaged domestic economy, the problems of which were compounded by excessive spending of wealth and resources on the military-industrial complex. The Soviet economy was not merely in shambles, but it faced the possibility of immediate collapse should any new burden be assumed. These realities hung heavy over the Cold War poker table at Reykjavik. The new bet by Reagan meant a fresh financial burden of $300 million, the estimated price tag for Star Wars, as the Strategic Defense Initiative was labeled by a sensation-seeking press. Gorbachev, who pondered the bet, represented a nation already faced with shortages in such basic items as bread, meat, shoes, fruits, and vegetables.

In terms of the poker game, Gorbachev had to put up or fold his hand. He did what had to be done: he tossed in his cards. The events that followed over the next two years saw the removal of the Berlin Wall and the collapse of the Iron Curtain, as military-bureaucratic regimes came down all over Eastern Europe. It even produced a reunited Germany. As a bonus for Americans, it resulted in cut-backs in our own spending for the promised Star Wars program.

Some Slices of Twentieth-Century Political Humor

1. As the end of World War I approached with victory for the Allied and Associated powers in sight, it was obvious that the

three most important figures to attend the post-war peace conclave would be France's George Clemenceau, Britain's David Lloyd-George, and Woodrow Wilson of the United States. The latter had earlier announced and published his highly idealistic Fourteen Points as the best set of guidelines for a secure and lasting future peace. Unfortunately, Wilson exuded the image of an evangelical Protestant with all the moral import of an ethics professor, who, as an American, lacked the experience of growing up across the border from a powerful, brutal enemy like Germany. Wilson's concept of fairness contrasted sharply with the attitude of French Premier Clemenceau, a firebrand, nationalist, vocal agnostic, and German-hating leader who was obsessed with his nation's security. When first alerted to Wilson's Fourteen Points, Clemenceau's immediate reaction was: "God Almighty only had ten!"

2. During the campaign of 1924 the Democrats fell victim to internal dissensions that rendered the chances of Calvin "Silent Cal" Coolidge and his Republicans most favorable in the coming elections. With this situation in mind, prominent American humorist Will Rogers offered this classic statement: "I am a member of no organized political party. I am a Democrat."

3. In his *Off the Record with FDR*, William Hassett has preserved the following story told by Roosevelt to a cabinet meeting during World War II: "An American Marine, ordered home from Guadalcanal, was disconsolate and downhearted because he hadn't killed a Jap. He stated his case to his superior officer, [who] said: 'Go up to that hill over there and shout: To hell with Emperor Hirohito! That will bring the Japs out of hiding.' The Marine did as he was bidden. Immediately a Jap soldier came out of the jungle, shouting: 'To hell with Roosevelt!' And of course, said the Marine: 'I could not kill a Republican.'"

4. The emergence of Israel as a new and independent Middle Eastern state in 1948 has never ceased to be the center of international contention, as we are reminded by recent Gulf War events. There are more citizens of Jewish extraction in the United States than in Israel, and President Harry Truman faced tremendous pressure to award recognition to the new state, despite great opposition from Arab states. When pressed by reporters as to why he acted as the first national leader to recognize Israel, Truman responded bluntly, "I don't have any Arab constituents."

5. In the 1948 campaign, where President Harry Truman's effort for reelection faced the drain of two Democrat splinter parties (Dixiecrats for J. Strom Thurmond and Progressives for Henry Wallace), Truman offered this: "Give 'em Hell!" Most political observers described Truman as doomed, but the president continued to run with energy and purpose. Republican opponent Thomas Dewey, in contrast, ran a restrained campaign, always appearing confident and presidential in dress, conduct, and demeanor. We all know the outcome, but a comment by prominent Washington hostess Alice Roosevelt Longworth (daughter of Theodore) about Dewey's defeat was a barometer of average American attitudes. She simply pointed out that the reserved Dewey, far from seeming presidential as he thought, instead presented the unfortunate public image of "looking like a groom on a wedding cake."

6. Since 1945 no firing of an important official has drawn more attention than celebrated war hero General Douglas MacArthur's removal as commander in chief over disagreements in policy and strategy in the Korean War. Truman biographer Merle Miller (*Plain Speaking*) asked the President about it, and received a typically direct Trumanesque explanation: "I fired him because he wouldn't respect the authority of the President. That's the answer to that. I didn't fire him because he was a dumb son of a bitch, although he was, but that's not against the law for generals. If it was, half to three-quarters of them would be in jail."

7. Lyndon Johnson and Gerald Ford both reached the pinnacle of U.S. politics, the presidency. During the evolution of their political careers Johnson became Senate majority leader, and Ford was House minority leader. On paper, Ford had the more impressive academic credentials as a University of Michigan undergraduate who played football and later went on to law school, while Johnson graduated from a small Texas state teacher's college. Once, after a particularly tough tussle over policy, an exasperated Johnson reportedly declared that "Gerry played too many games without his helmet."

8. The threat of danger from leftist demonstrators in Japan, which forced President Dwight Eisenhower to halt his intended visit and fly on to another Asian location, supplied comedian Mort Sahl with new material, all based on factual reporting. At the new location, reporters demanded to talk to the president.

Press Secretary James Hagerty told them no. Mort Sahl offers the following version of the situation:"Why can we not speak to the president?"Hagerty responded,"Because he is asleep."Reporters ask,"When will he be awake and prepared to talk?" Hagerty responds, "Don't ask me, I am not God," an answer that comedian Sahl suggested was "way out of proportion to the question." Then the sardonic Sahl added, "But he said it *like the position was open.*"

9. Richard Shenkman *(One-Night Stands with American History)* offers the following from an interview with reporter Steven Gerstel: Hawaii was a new state in 1958 and its first congressman was Daniel K. Inouye, a Hawaiian of Japanese descent who had lost an arm in World War II while serving with the famous all-Nisei 442nd Regimental Combat Team in France. Understanding that Texan Sam Rayburn was not only the Democratic Speaker of the House, but also one of the more powerful figures in Washington, the new congressman sought him out and introduced himself, providing full name and state of representation. Rayburn replied, "I know who you are. How many one-armed Japs do you think we have around here?"

10. This offering from highly respected New York Republican Senator Kenneth Keating was recorded by Leon Harris in his *Fine Art of Political Wit:* "Roosevelt proved a man could be president for life, Truman proved anybody could be president; Eisenhower proved you don't need to have a president."

11. In the aftermath of *Sputnik* and early reported successes in the Soviet space program, a common theme emphasized by John Kennedy and other Democrats in the 1960 presidential campaign was the so-called missile gap, that is, alleged Eisenhower administration failures that had left the United States two years behind the Soviets in the space race and nuclear and ballistic missile programs. Comedian Mort Sahl could not pass this one up: "They have plenty of spies, don't they? So why don't we let them steal our secrets and then they will be two years behind, too?"

12. When a reporter asked President Dwight D. Eisenhower during the 1960 campaign what important decision the Republican candidate, Vice President Richard M. Nixon, had participated in during their eight years together, Ike responded: "If you give me a week, I might think of one."

13. During the 1960 campaign for president, John F. Kennedy reported to the press that opponent Richard M. Nixon had referred to him in a speech as no more than "another Truman." Kennedy responded by saying that he considered that a compliment, and "I consider him another Dewey."

14. Of special ironic import is the following entry by Bennet Cerf in his *Laugh a Day:* In the midst of congressional debates over a revision of U.S. immigration laws, then Vice President Hubert H. Humphrey received some pointed advice from a Native American resident of a New Mexico reservation: "Be careful in revising those immigration laws of yours. We got careless with ours."

15. How important was the office of vice president as late as 1975? Nelson Rockefeller, appointed to that position by President Gerald Ford, with just four months in office, was asked just how the president planned to use him. Ford's response: "It depends on who dies," a dry reference to the tradition of vice presidents representing the United States at the funerals of heads of state overseas.

16. By far the most startling event of the vice presidential debates during the election campaign of 1988 developed when Dan Quayle chose to excuse reservations about his youth by reference to the age of President Kennedy. Debate opponent Lloyd Bentsen of Texas responded: "I knew John Kennedy, Senator, . . . and you're no John Kennedy." That response brought tremendous applause from the audience. Although a humbled Quayle lacked a rejoinder, any number of humorists, in light of Kennedy's risqué conduct while president, could have offered a recounter such as: "No, Senator, you're right, I'm not John Kennedy. I always sleep with my own wife." Then the press probably would have called him vicious, truth notwithstanding.

Index

Gone with the Wind (film), 246
Gorbachev, Mikhail, 247–248
Gore, Al, 189
Grady, Sandy, 242–243
Graham, Sylvester, 56–57
Graham crackers, 57
Grant, Ulysses S., 97, 98, 99
    A. E. Burnside and, 102–103, 104
    Benjamin Franklin Butler and, 110
    and diet of Confederate soldiers, 101
    at Petersburg, 102
Gray, Elbert, 130
Gray, Thomas R., 69
Great Britain
    conscription in, 167
    customs enforcement by, 17
    debtors from, 9
    Jay Treaty with, 33–34
    militia regulars from, 18–19
    in Operation Vittles, 213
    propaganda by, 165–166
    in Seven Years War, 11–12
    in War of 1812, 43
    wheat sales in, 131
Great Depression, 187
Great Plains
    Indian wars in, 115–119
    mountain men of, 60–64
The Great Train Robbery (film), 156
The Great War in Modern Memory, 205
Greeley, Horace, 56
Green Bay Packers, 155
Greenberg, Paul, 237–238
Greene, Nathaniel, 25
Greenhow, Rose O'Neal, 127
Greenwood (Tulsa community)
    racial tensions in, 171–173
Grey, Charles, 25
Griffith, Andy, 170
Gringo (label), 65
Guiteau, Charles, 133
The Guns of August (film), 170

Hagerty, James, 251
Haiti, 67
Haley, Bill, 222

Half-Breeds faction, 132–133, 134
Halleck, Henry W., 92, 98
Hamilton, Alexander, 29, 130
    Aaron Burr and, 34, 35
    ancestry of, 174
    Federalist Papers of, 30
    James Callender on, 41
    and Pennsylvania excise tax, 33
    on transportation financing, 49
    on U.S. currency, 36
Hamilton, Henry, 19, 20–21
Hamlin, Hannibal, 175
Hancock, John, 31
Hancock, Winfield Scott, 133
Hanna, Mark, 150
Harding, Warren G., 176
Harpers Ferry, Virginia, 78
Harris, Joel Chandler, 74
Harris, Leon, 251
Harris, Patricia, 246
Harrison, Carter, 4
Hart, Gary, 241
Harvey, William H., 144–145
Hassett, William, 249
Hauptmann, Bruno, 180
Hay, John, 147, 148
Hay-Pauncefote Treaty, 153
Hayden, Franz Josef, 174
Hayes, Lucy Webb (first lady), 58
Hayes, Mary Ludwig, 24
Hayes, Rutherford B., 58
Hayes, Wayne, 241
Haymarket Square Incident (1886), 125
Health food movement
    19th century, 56–57
    See also Disease
Hell's Angels, 230
Helsinki Accords, 220
Hemingway, Ernest, 169
Hemmings, Sally, 40, 41–42
Hennessey, David, 139, 140
Henry, John, 122–123
Henry, Patrick, 31
Henry VIII, King of England, 10
Henry Expedition
    veterans of, 61, 62, 63

The Godfather and (book and
  film), 244–245
  prohibition and, 171
*Our Penal Machinery and Its Vic-
  tims*, 125
Ovington, Mary, 160
Owen, Robert, 246

Paar, Jack, 229
Packwood, Bob, 242
Page, Patti, 222
Paiute tribe, 118–119
  See also Native Americans
Pakenham, Sir Edward, 43
Panic of 1837, 70
Parks, Rosa, 224–225
Paths of Glory (film), 169
Patterson, John, 25
Patton, George, 210
Paul VI, 229
Paxton Boys, 8
Peace of Paris (1783), 15
Pearl Harbor
  U.S. intelligence on, 193–195
Pearson, Drew, 240
Peffer, William Alfred, 141–142
Pendleton Civil Service Act (1883),
  133–134
Penn, William, 7, 8
Pennsylvania, 30, 31
  Quakers in, 7–8
  tax rebellion in, 33
Pennsylvania Gazette, 13
Perkins, Frances, 245
Pershing, John J., 162, 165
Persian Gulf war, 202, 207
Personal Liberty laws, 84
Perspectives (newsletter), 219
Philippines
  U.S. conquest of, 147–148
Pickford, Mary, 168
Pierce, Franklin, 86
Pinkerton, Allan *(pseud.* E. J.
  Allen), 126–128
Pinkerton National Detective
  Agency, 123–124, 127–128

Pipe smoking, 58
Placquemines Rebellion (1811), 68
Plain Speaking, 250
Plains. *See* Great Plains
Platt, Tom, 149–150
Plessy, Homer A., 113–114
Plessy v. Ferguson, 113-114, 221
Poindexter, Richard, 244
Poitier, Sidney, 246
*Political Parties Before the Constitu-
  tion*, 31
The Political Progress of Britain, 41
Politicos, 128
Polk, James K., 64
Pontiac's Rebellion, 14
Poor Richard's Almanack, 13
Populist movement
  Benjamin R. Tillman in, 137–139
  reforms of, 141–145
Porcupine quills
  significance of, 6–7
Potosí, Bolivia, 37
Poulson, Norris, 223–224
Poverty
  of 1890s, 141–142, 143
Powderly, Terence V., 125
President
  as title, 32
Presley, Elvis, 222
Preston, Thomas, 17–18
The Price, 215
Prigg v. Pennsylvania, 84
Prison reform, 55
Profiles in Courage, 227
Progressives party, 250
Prohibition, 170–171
Project X-Ray, 196–197
Propaganda
  World War I, 165–167
  World War II, 205, 208
The Prospect Before Us, 41
Protest marches
  of Populist movement, 142–143
  of women's movement, 160–161
  See also Civil rights
Provenzano brothers, 139